LEGENDARY LOCALS

OF

WAKE FOREST

NORTH CAROLINA

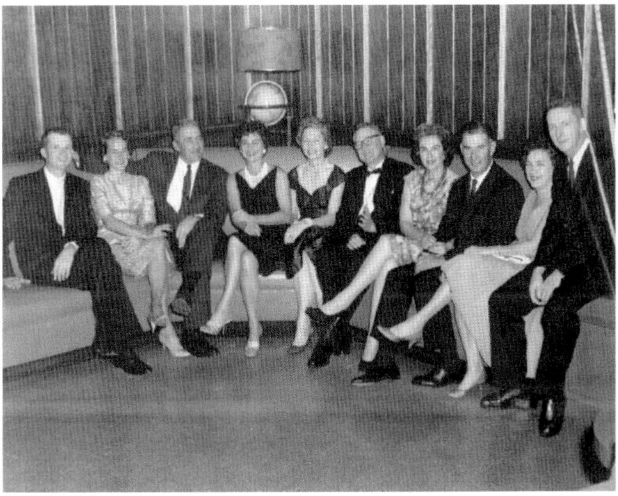

I0805798

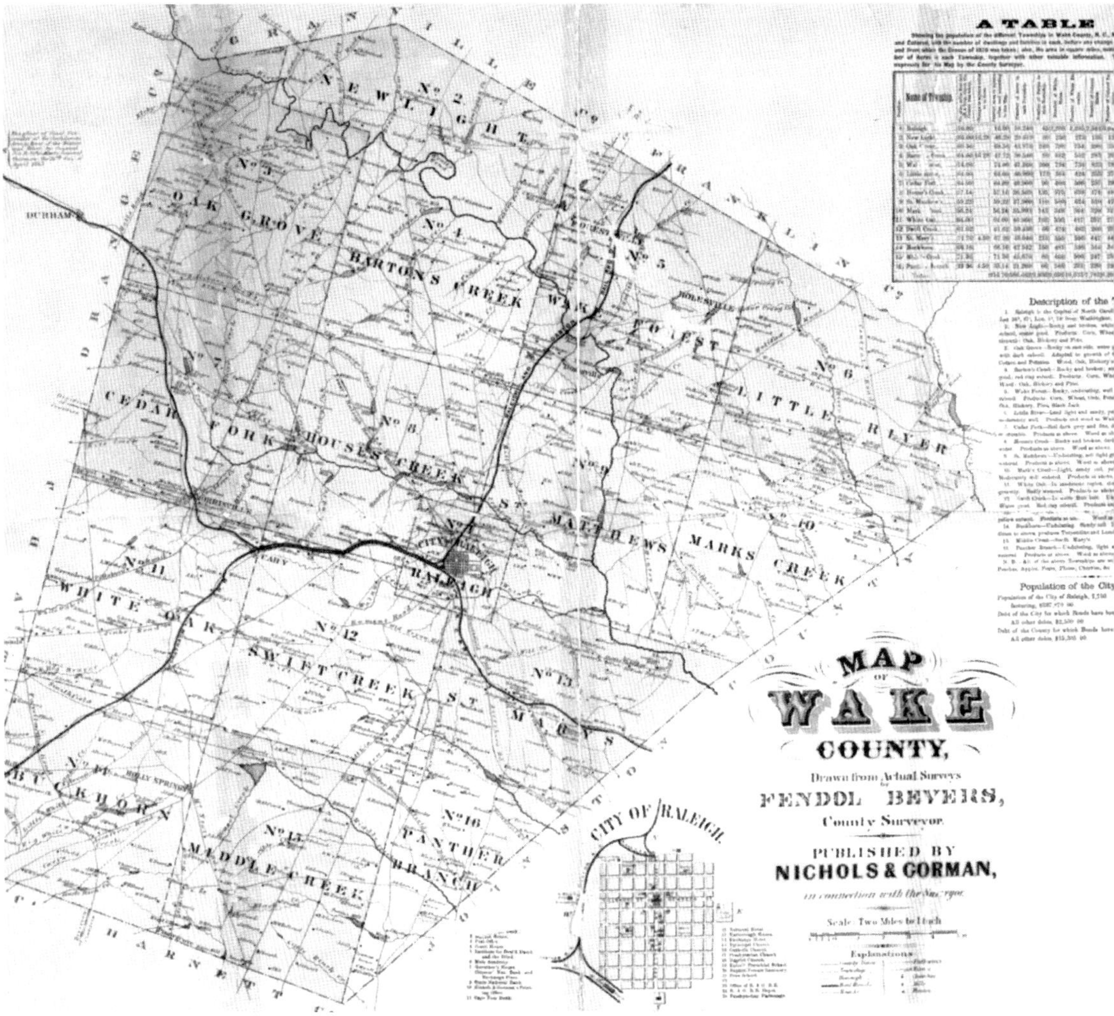

Map of Wake County Townships, 1878

By the time this map was drawn, Wake Forest College had already been in existence for more than four decades as one of the state's oldest institutions of higher education. Established only 45 years after the University of North Carolina, the college brought intellectuals, business owners, and students to the rural section of northern Wake County that first was known as "the Forest District." In 1874, the Raleigh & Gaston Railroad had agreed to move its depot from nearby Forestville. Improved transportation brought new opportunities in manufacturing and industry. Together, the town and college prospered. The ensuing boom of local culture and economy lasted well into the 20th century. (Courtesy of the State Archives of North Carolina.)

Page 1: The Glamorous Set

In the fabulous 1960s, these couples made up Wake Forest's most glamorous social set. Together they dined, danced, played golf, and established new standards of elegance and sophistication in the small Southern town. Seated from left to right are Nash and Janis Underwood, Wait and Jenny Brewer, Caddie and John Farish, Sue and Tommy Byrne, and Leila and Ben Aycock Sr. (Courtesy of Virginia Susan Rudd.)

LEGENDARY LOCALS

OF

WAKE FOREST

NORTH CAROLINA

DURWARD MATHENY AND JENNIFER SMART

LEGENDARY LOCALS

ISBN 978-1-4671-0180-6

Legendary Locals is an imprint of Arcadia Publishing
Charleston, South Carolina

Printed in the United States of America

Library of Congress Control Number: 2014941229

For all general information, please contact Arcadia Publishing:
Telephone 843-853-2070
Fax 843-853-0044
E-mail sales@arcadiapublishing.com
For customer service and orders:
Toll-Free 1-888-313-2665

Visit us on the Internet at www.arcadiapublishing.com

Dedication
Author royalties from the sale of this book directly support the Wake Forest Historical Museum.

On the Front Cover: Clockwise from top left:
Irene Mangum, Lib Greason, Irene Holding, Isabella Gill, and Nancy Harris, civic leaders (Courtesy of the Wake Forest Historical Museum, see page 86); Fr. Philip Tighe of St. Catherine of Siena Catholic Church (Courtesy of the Wake Forest Historical Museum, see page 67); Jenny Brewer, community volunteer (Courtesy of Virginia Susan Rudd; see page 31); Rose Lake and John Lyon, Wake Forest High School class of 1955 (Courtesy of Barbara Hollowell Lyon; see page 18); Mayor Vivian Jones (Courtesy of the Wake Forest Historical Museum, see page 38); Lincoln Robert Best, principal and leader of the DuBois School (Courtesy of Eric Best; see page 103); 1995 Wake Forest Citizen of the Year Virginia Olsen (Courtesy of the Wake Forest Historical Museum, see page 12).

On the Back Cover: From left to right:
The Mills family celebrating Christmas at their home on Faculty Avenue (Courtesy of John Garland Mills III; see page 116); Geraldine Hall-Taylor, seated, with family members outside their home in the East End (Courtesy of Geraldine Hall-Taylor; see page 89).

CONTENTS

ACKNOWLEDGMENTS

Wake Forest is fortunate to have an exceptionally long list of residents, past and present, who are charming, intelligent, accomplished, and unique. These wonderful people also have many devoted friends and fans—several of whom have suggested a series of sequels should follow this book. They are correct, of course. With so many worthy subjects, the decision to include a personality often came down to one simple question: Can we find a good photograph? As we combed through the collection of images held in the archives of the Wake Forest Historical Museum and began to receive old family photographs from those who have helped with this project, it became clear that Wake Forest is indeed home to many extraordinary people. We wish we could name all of them, but with limited space will only state we appreciate everyone who has worked to make this town such a spectacular place to live. In listing those who have contributed their time and talent to producing this book, special thanks go to Ed and Cathy Morris, Susan and Sherrill Brinkley, Dianne Laws, David Leone, the *Wake Weekly*, Beverly Whisnant, Geraldine Hall-Taylor, Suzanne Mills Erskine, Eric Best, Jessica Geter, and Jared Williard. We are indebted to Shirley Matheny for her patience, generosity, expertise in checking facts and spellings, and assistance with research. We would also like to acknowledge Wake Forest University (WFU) and the Town of Wake Forest; without their generous support, the museum could not continue to exist. We are grateful to the many volunteers, organizations, storytellers, and museum visitors who work with us to carry out the Wake Forest College Birthplace Society's mission to preserve and share the history of Wake Forest, town and college. Unless otherwise noted, all images appear courtesy of the Wake Forest Historical Museum.

INTRODUCTION

Even in its earliest incarnation, Wake Forest was able to naturally attract a citizenry accomplished in the fields of academics, religion, and the arts. This trend began with its first notable resident, Dr. Calvin Jones, a native of Sheffield, Massachusetts, who was educated as a physician in the Boston area and later moved to Raleigh, where he founded the North Carolina Medical Society, was a member of the general assembly, published the *Raleigh Star,* and served as a trustee at the University of North Carolina. His next stop was northern Wake County, an area he christened "Wake Forest" (a moniker he made from two existing names: "the Forest District" and "the Forest of Wake"), where he lived in the 1820s-era home now known as the historic Calvin Jones House.

By 1832, Jones was ready to move yet again, this time to Tennessee. His full plantation was 615 acres, and he searched for a buyer through newspaper advertisements, touting the quality of the citizenry: "The inhabitants, without I believe a single exception, are sober, moral, and thriving in their circumstances, and not a few are educated and intelligent." Influenced by local minister John Purefoy, Jones chose to accept a $2,000 offer from the North Carolina Baptist Convention, which intended to transform the farm into an institute of religious learning. Two years later, on February 3, 1834, the Wake Forest Manual Labor Institute opened. Its first class of 16 boys would perform farmwork in exchange for lessons, room, and board.

In these early days, cows wandered freely across the rolling hills of the school's modest campus, which was bordered by a split-rail fence and consisted only of the original house and outbuildings. The institute's first president, Samuel Wait, had come from New York to help create the North Carolina Baptist Convention and was one of only five college-trained Baptist ministers in the state. He was a visionary leader, and the manual labor was soon eliminated in favor of traditional tuition. Enrollment was growing, a brick campus was in the works, and the school was renamed Wake Forest College (WFC).

When the Raleigh & Gaston Railroad moved its depot from Forestville to Wake Forest in 1874, the small smattering of homes and businesses surrounding campus coalesced into a recognizable town with bright new economic opportunities. By 1907, the Royall Cotton Mill was operating at the north end of Faculty Avenue (now North Main Street), manufacturing cotton fabrics and providing hundreds of jobs. The working-class families in the small homes surrounding the factory established a thriving community of their own—a mill village complete with stores, churches, and a school.

The railroad also brought unprecedented prosperity to the business district around South White Street. This is where W.W. Holding and Company operated the warehouse (now known as the Cotton Company) from which they shipped enough raw cotton to become one of the largest suppliers in the southeast. Other successful homegrown businesses included Wake Forest Supply Company (later renamed Jones Hardware), Shorty's Famous Hot Dogs, Bolus Department Store, Wake Forest Federal Savings & Loan, Hollowell's Grocery, the College Book Store, and Oscar C. Smith's Shoe Shop, the only black-owned business in the white business district.

The town's other black-owned businesses were located in the East End, Wake Forest's historically African American neighborhood. For most of the 20th century, this was a network of interconnected families who together created a strong, industrious, and religious community. Two of the state's most notable African American educators—Allen Young of the Wake Forest Normal and Industrial School, and Lincoln Robert Best of the DuBois School—molded their academic institutions into such highly competitive environments that young black children from Wake Forest became trailblazers in professions previously limited to whites.

Finally, located on the northwestern outskirts of town, "the Harricane" was a vaguely defined area that took its name from a fierce 18th-century storm. Near this area is Crenshaw Hall, ancestral home of the Crenshaw family. But this section of Wake Forest is most closely associated with generations of the extended Keith, Ray, and Harrison families. As it is a tough and rocky area for crops, no description of the Harricane is complete without a reference to hardworking farmers, a deep loyalty to friends and neighbors, and a well-documented history of moonshine produced for economic reasons. The community had some members who supplemented their income by supplying illegal liquor to the broader Wake Forest community throughout the late 19th and 20th centuries.

Life in Wake Forest changed forever in 1956, when Wake Forest College moved to Winston-Salem. Financed by the R.J. Reynolds Foundation, the new campus would allow the school to grow, eventually becoming Wake Forest University. But the town residents, who had never known life without the college, grappled with grief and a pervasive sense of loss. Although the familiar brick buildings had already become home to the small groups of students who would populate the first classes of the campus's new owner, Southeastern Baptist Theological Seminary, it would be many years before the grounds and town would once again bustle and hum.

In the meantime, Wake Forest had to find new residents, a new economic engine, and a fresh identity. Over the next few years, the town's population continued to drop. Downtown movie theaters, restaurants, hotels, and department stores all shut their doors, never to open again. But by the late 1960s, a concerted effort to create new jobs began to pay off. The Schrader plant, maker of air-control equipment, and the Athey plant, builder of machines for moving heavy material, relocated to Wake Forest and sparked an economic upturn. It was what the town needed to survive, and by the time those plants permanently stopped production around the late 1990s, Wake Forest was well on its way to an exciting new life as one of the Triangle region's most highly regarded locations. The town that once was known for having a college, then became famous for losing its college, has returned to the spotlight in a dazzling third act—as a growing community dedicated to preserving the past, embracing the future, and cementing its reputation as one of America's most charming, original, and legendary towns.

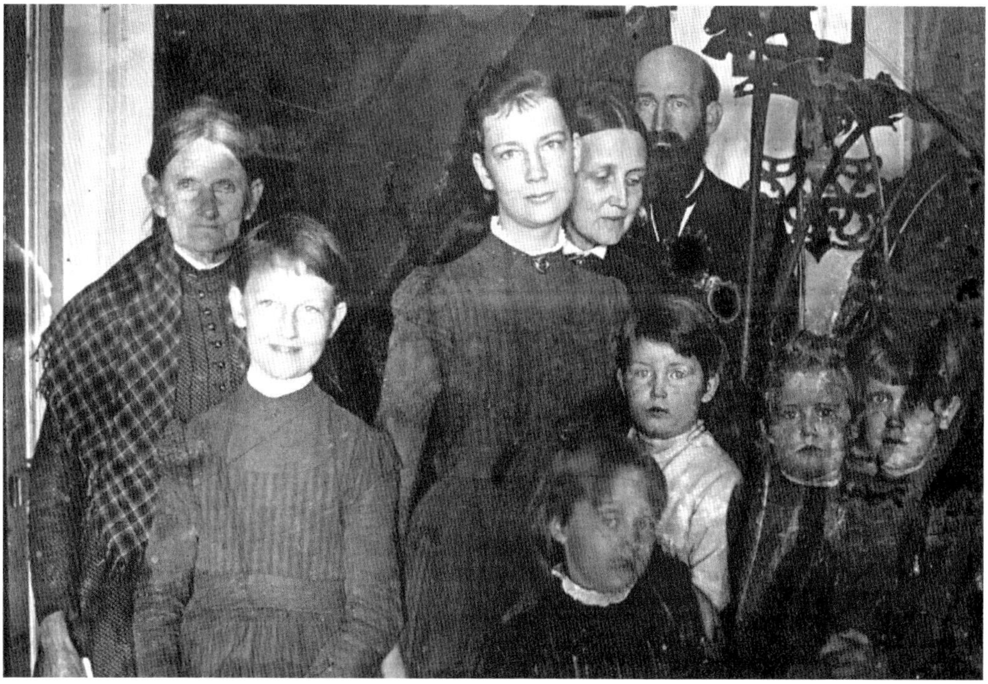

The Taylor Family

As Wake Forest College entered the 20th century, its students and faculty were fortunate to have Pres. Charles Taylor at the helm. It was an era of steady progress in education, industry, and agriculture. Even the environment got a boost. Teaming with "Doctor" Tom Jeffries to beautify the campus, Taylor sought to make the landscape resemble a nature park. Here, he is captured standing behind his wife and children in a rare family photograph.

CHAPTER ONE

The Children

Before there was a town of Wake Forest, there was Wake Forest Manual Labor Institute. The school, founded by North Carolina Baptist leaders, opened in 1834. Its first home was a modest, two-story farmhouse on a hill looking out over acres of farmland, and one of its first students was local child John Martin Crenshaw. Crenshaw, who hailed from a location west of town just short of the Harricane—in the area of present-day Crenshaw Hall—was just 12 years old when he enrolled at the institute. Students paid tuition by doing farmwork or contributing needed supplies. The school quickly grew; in its second year, Pres. Samuel Wait admitted approximately 70 students. By 1838, the manual-labor requirement was dropped, and the institute became Wake Forest College.

For much of Wake Forest's history, the sons and daughters of college professors, local business owners, mill employees, and laborers spent long, happy days learning, playing, and exploring; they climbed the campus magnolias, crept into Gore Gymnasium to run across the hardwood, and walked downtown for ice cream or a milkshake. These children were usually pleasant and respectful—and well aware that if they misbehaved, their parents would hear about it before they even got home.

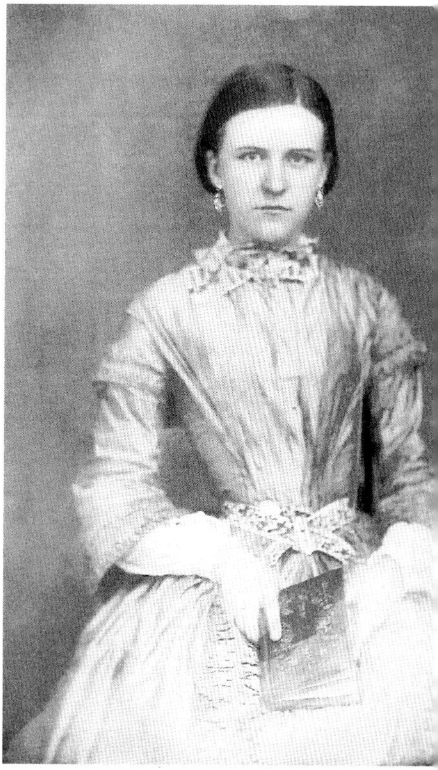

Araminta Purefoy

Young Araminta posed for this c. 1850 portrait while living in the Wake Forest area. She later married a grandson of John Purefoy, the leader who first encouraged the North Carolina Baptist Convention to purchase local property from Dr. Calvin Jones to establish a school for training ministers. Purefoy's daughter Emma Purefoy married William Louis Poteat (see page 58), the famed Wake Forest College professor and longtime president.

Simmons Family

The family of Wake Forest College professor William Gaston Simmons removed floorboards to hide supplies from marauding Yankee soldiers in the wake of General Lee's surrender at Appomattox Courthouse, Virginia, in April 1865. Nannie Elizabeth Simmons recalled her mother offering food to a "bummer," who then felt indebted and left without stealing. The women were courageous as Union forces took over the South. This house, once at the southeast corner of North Main Street, was torn down in the 1930s.

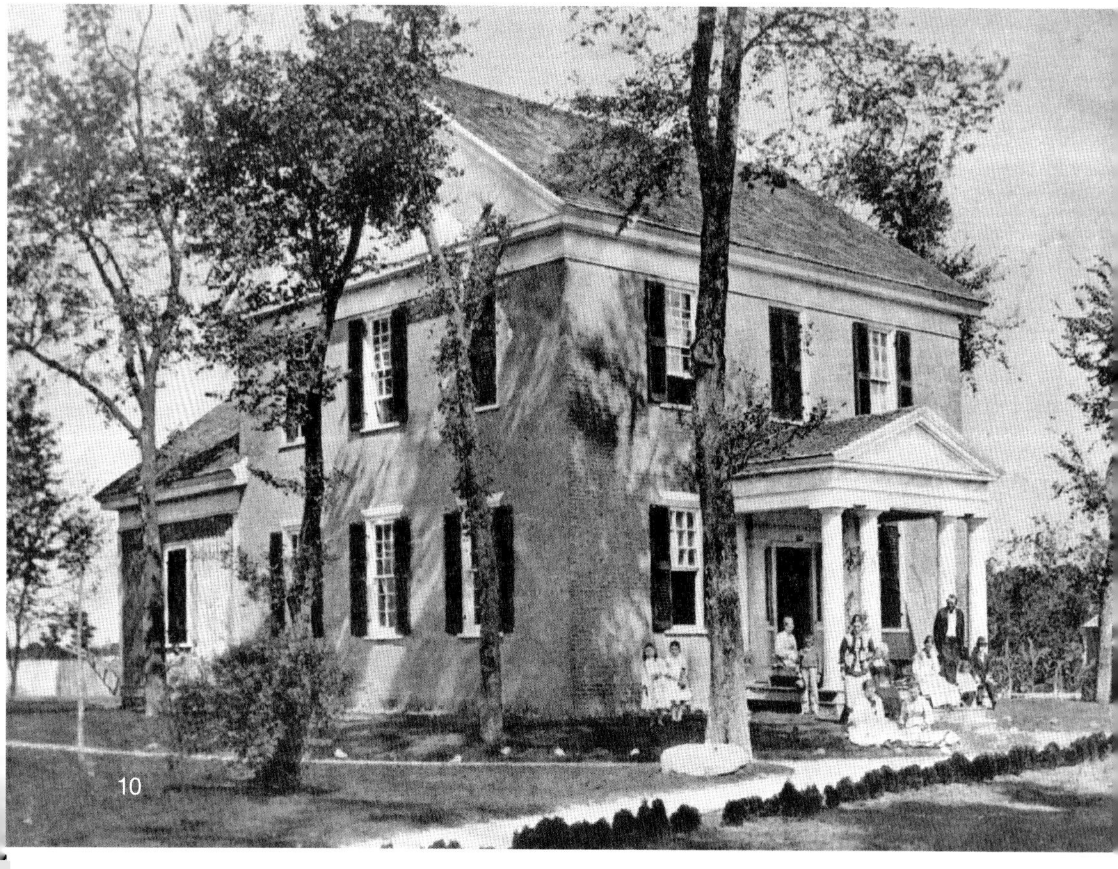

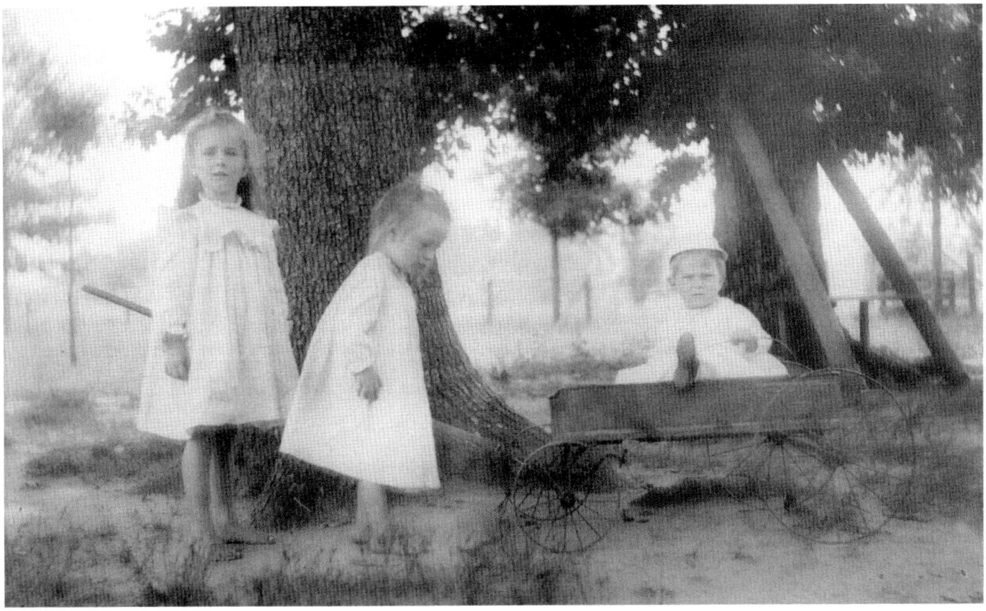

Children from Powell House, c. 1905
The museum received a windfall when Liz Ford, owner of the Powell-Ford House, donated a large steamer trunk filled with early-20th-century clothing and glass-plate slides. The artifacts date to the home's original owners, Susie Lanneau and William Royall Powell. The museum is working to identify these children, believed to have attended Susie's birthday party on Faculty Avenue in 1905.

Mill Village Children, c. 1950
Founded in 1899, the Royall Cotton Mill was soon one of the largest in the state. The village surrounding it included blocks of company-owned houses, a school, a commissary, and two churches. Theirs was a particularly close community, home to generations of children who recollect years spent playing in each other's houses and yards like one large extended family.

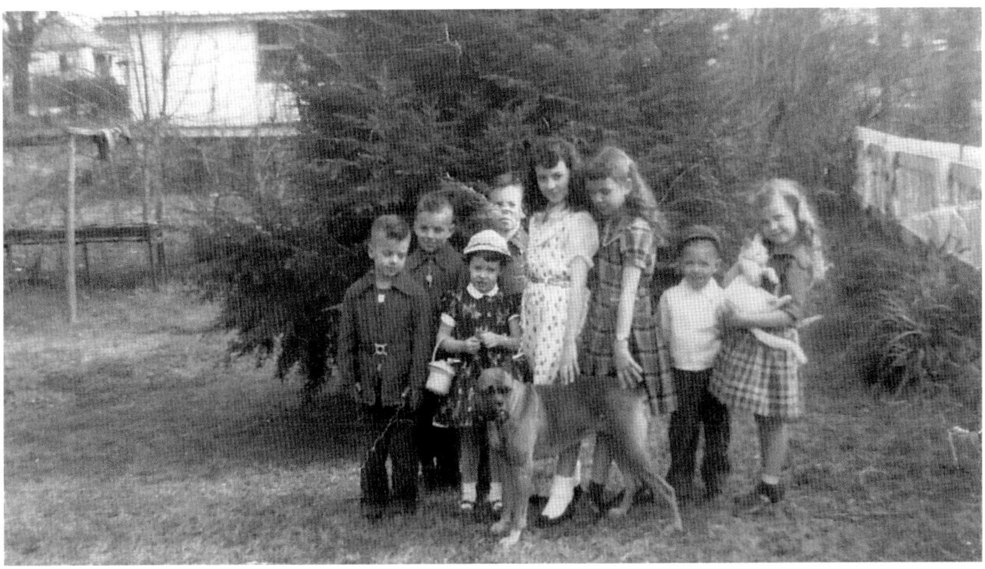

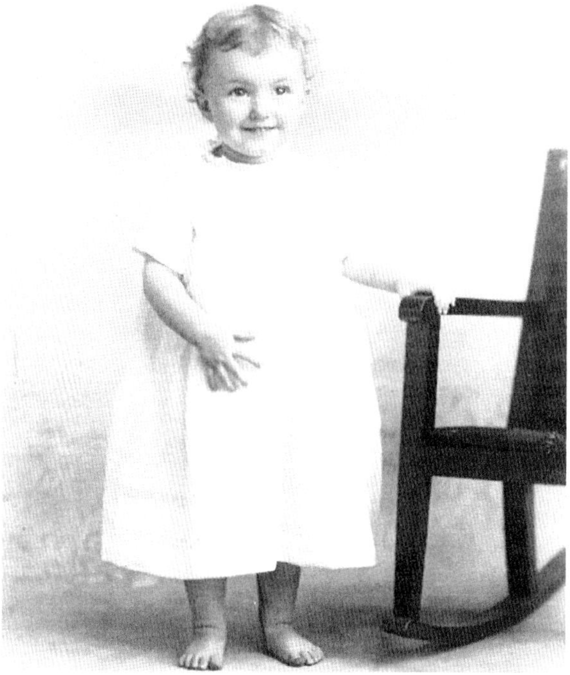

Virginia Olsen

Born in 1912, Virginia Olsen arrived in Wake Forest in 1964 when her husband took a job at the Schrader/Bellows metalworking factory. Olsen dove headlong into her new community and in 1995 was named Citizen of the Year. She made significant contributions as an employee of Ravenscroft School, an organizer of Meals on Wheels, and an active volunteer with the Episcopal Women's Organization. This c. 1914 photograph was displayed as part of 2013's Letters to Santa presentation at the 66th Annual Wake Forest Community Christmas Dinner.

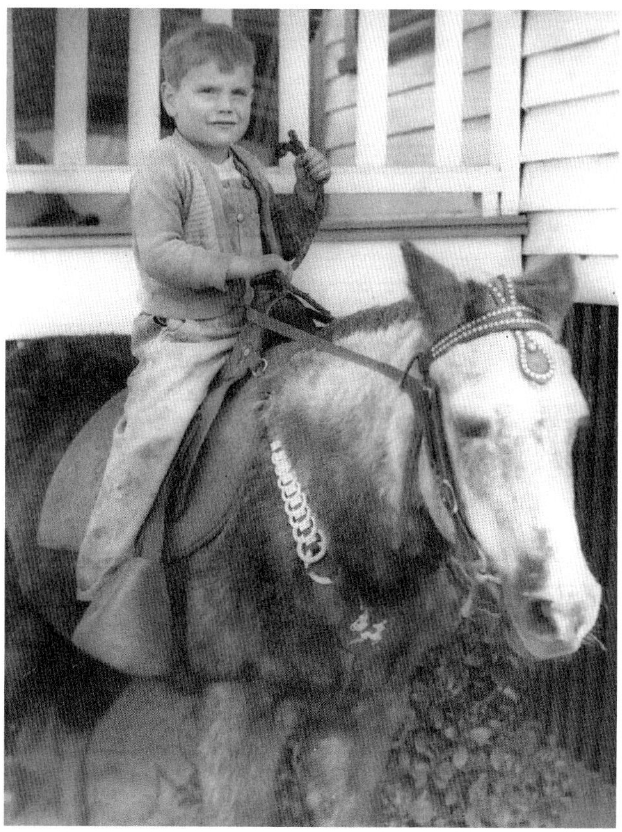

Ray Wall

In 1946, Ray Wall was growing up on Brick Street in the mill village, where his father ran a neighborhood store. Wall remembers afternoons of pickup football and kick the can played near the railroad tracks, and he told the *Wake Weekly* that train engineers sometimes tossed nickels or dimes to the kids from the passing locomotives. If they had to make a stop, they would visit his father's store for sardines, crackers, and Pepsi.

Harriet Bruce Dodd

In this photograph taken in January 1942, the newborn Harriet Bruce Dodd is dressed in a gown made in 1826 for her great-great-grandmother Ann Eliza Wait. The dress was made by Ann Eliza's mother, Sarah Merriam Wait, wife of Dr. Samuel Wait, the first president of Wake Forest College. The gown is now in the museum's collection.

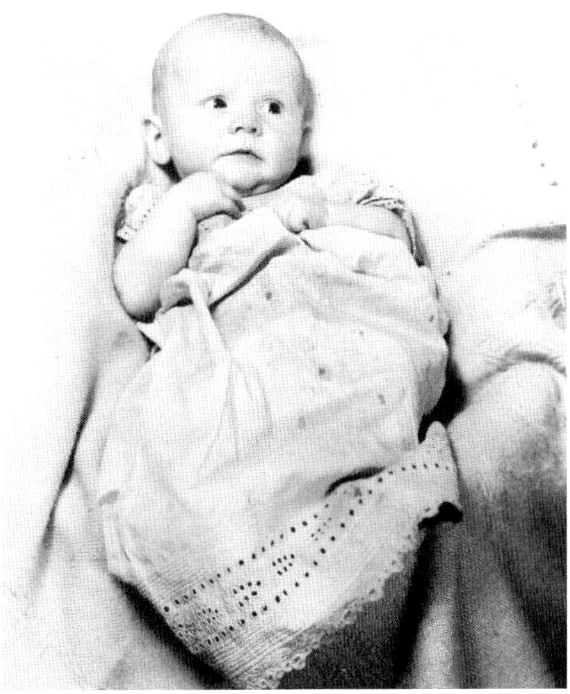

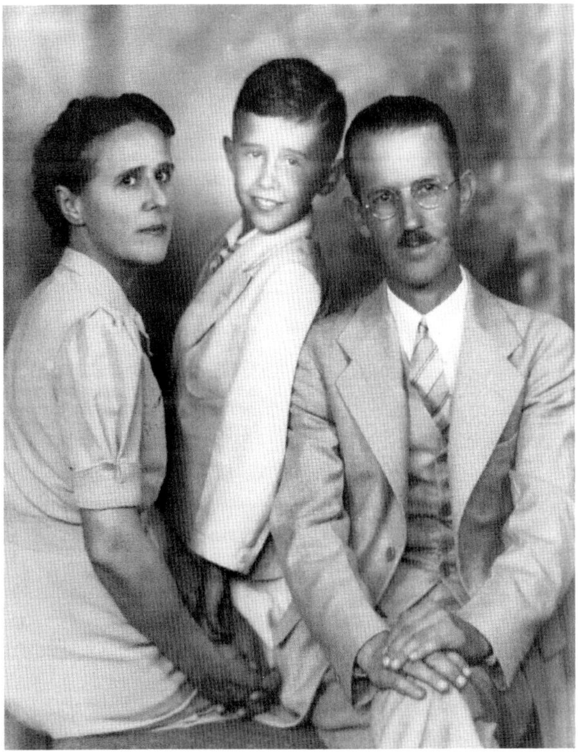

Watson Wilkinson

Watson Wilkinson, posing with his parents, graduated from Wake Forest College and served as president of Wake Forest Federal Savings & Loan. Wilkinson grew up in town in one of a pair of twin houses on South Main Street built by his father and uncle, both local doctors. Wilkinson's grandfather founded one of Wake Forest's earliest businesses, Wilkinson Department Store.

Roy Lynam and Judy Lynam Wish

Growing up in the mill village in a family of six children, Roy Lynam and Judy Lynam Wish recall their father, "Smiles" Lynam (see page 30) as friendly, strict, and fair. The proprietor of one of Wake Forest's most popular neighborhood stores, he expected all his children to help stock merchandise and make deliveries.

Roy Lynam recalls that his father developed a unique system for teaching his children about honesty, good character, and patience. When one of them badly misbehaved, he would generally respond simply, "I'm going to have to whip you for that." But then he would wait—sometimes for weeks—before doling out the punishment. Lynam says, "He'd never forget, and would always do it. But he made you think about it a lot. He never did it when he was angry. He'd wait it out until he wasn't angry anymore—so you'd get just the lesson, not the rage." (Courtesy of Roy and Donna Lynam.)

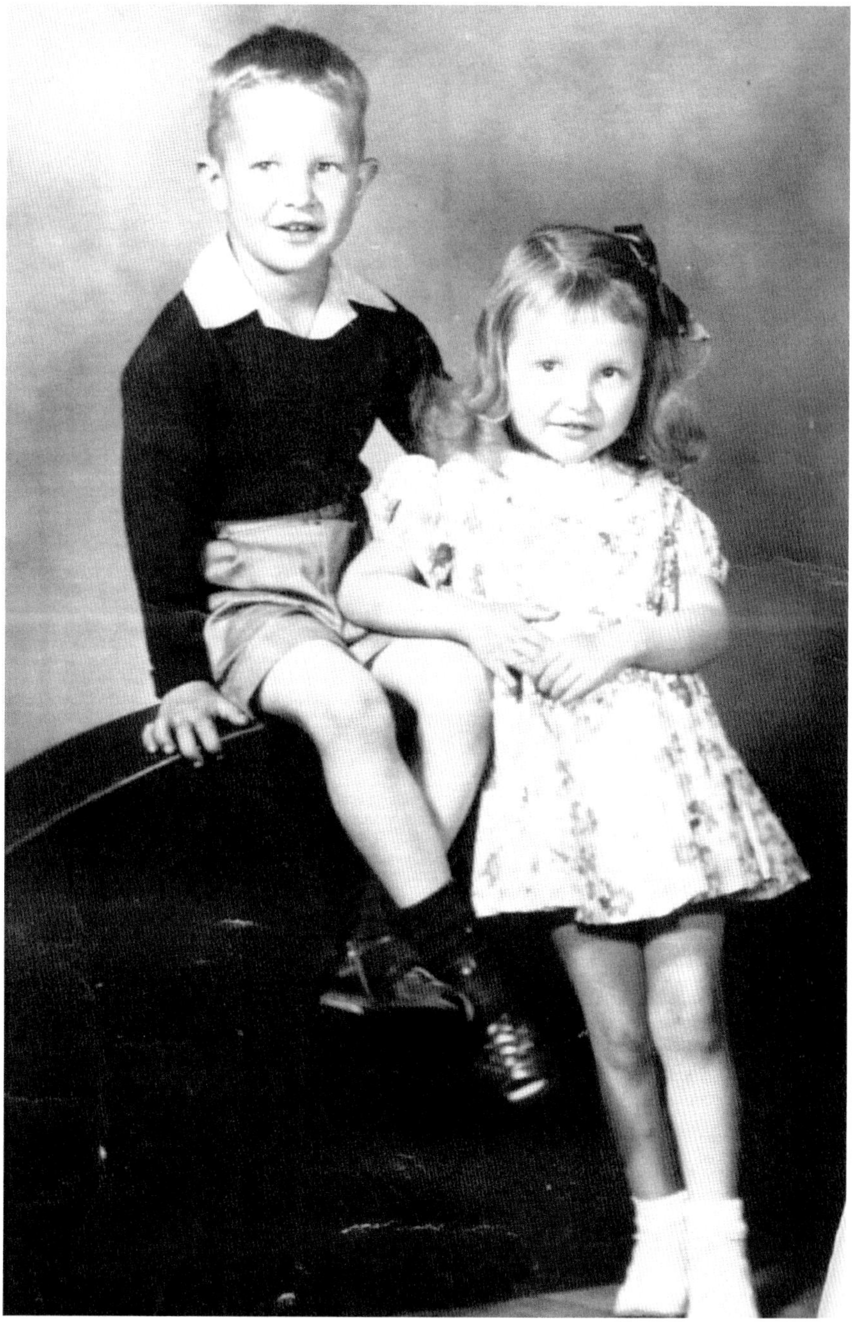

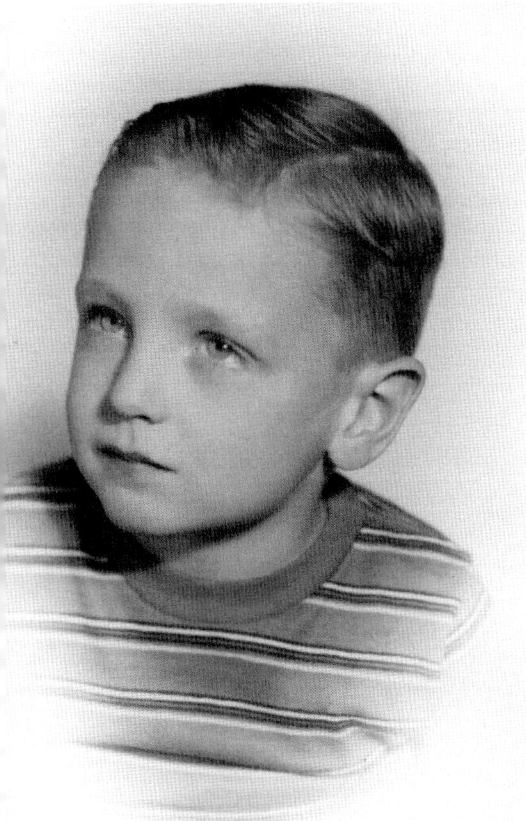

Durward Matheny
Born in Forest City, Matheny grew up in Wake Forest and married his high school sweetheart, Shirley East. Retired from the State Bureau of Investigation, Matheny is now a nationally sought-after forensic documents examiner. As a remarkable citizen and civic volunteer, Matheny has received the town's Peggy Allen Lifetime Achievement Award. (Courtesy of Durward Matheny.)

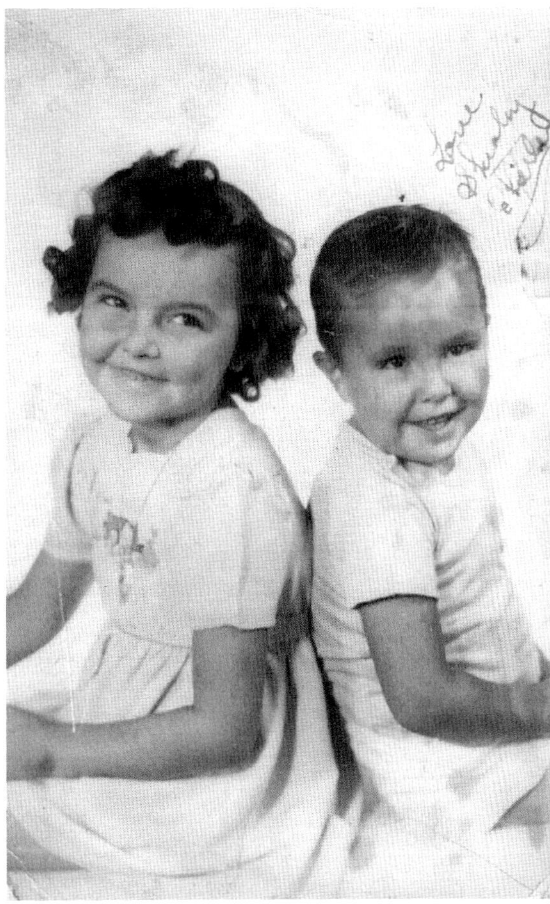

Shirley East Matheny and Charles East
Arriving in Wake Forest in the late 1940s, Shirley and Charles East were the children of North Carolina State Highway Patrolman Robert R. East (see page 90). Charles East became a successful businessman and noted collector of duck decoys. Shirley East, who married her high school sweetheart, Durward Matheny, trained as an artist at Richmond Professional Institute (Virginia Commonwealth University). Her work is regularly exhibited in Wake Forest, and her original designs appear on annual holiday cards from the Wake Forest Historical Museum. (Courtesy of Shirley Matheny.)

John Garland Mills III and Suzanne Mills Erskine

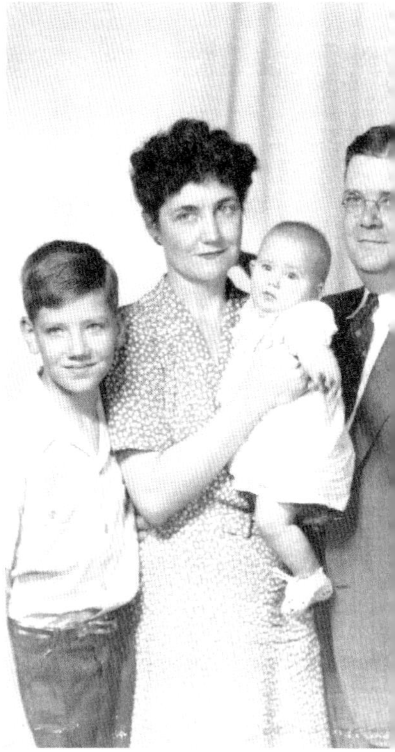

As children, John and Suzanne Mills lived on Faculty Avenue. Theirs was an old Wake Forest family; their father was a highly regarded local attorney, their mother ran a kindergarten, and their playmates were the children of business owners and college professors. Both became pillars of the Wake Forest community. They are pictured in this c. 1946 photograph with their parents, Ethel and John Garland Mills Jr. (Courtesy of Suzanne Mills Erskine.)

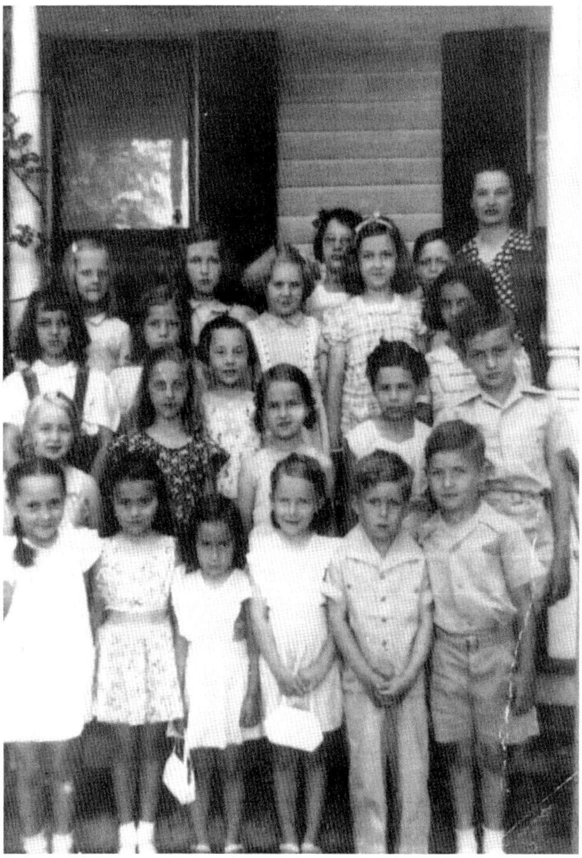

The Sunbeams of Wake Forest Baptist Church

The Southern Baptist Missions organization for boys and girls who'd grown old enough to leave the Sunday school nursery and were ready for instruction at the beginner and primary level for younger school age children, the Sunbeams would sing the children's hymn, "Jesus wants me for a sunbeam, to shine for Him each day..." This particular group, pictured around 1942, includes Peggy and Sally Patterson (first row, third and fourth from left), the daughters of Wake Forest College Registrar Grady Patterson, and James Mackie (front row, far right), son of town doctor George Mackie.

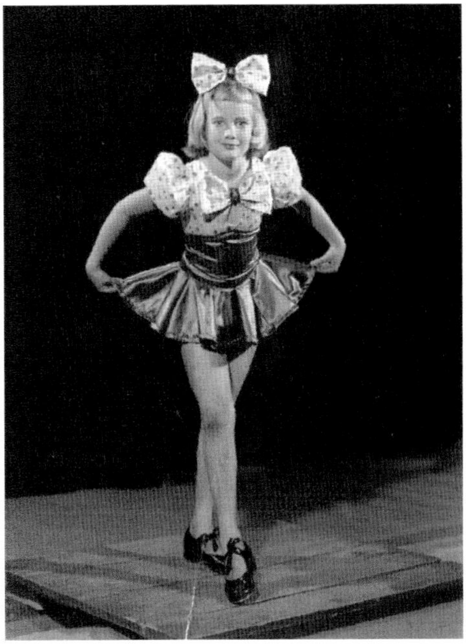

Judy Underwood Gould
Daughter of the local dentist, Gould grew up in Wake Forest and married real estate developer Steve Gould, known for renovating a number of historic properties in town. Gould became a career educator, teaching at Ravenscroft School, the private Episcopal academy in Raleigh. In this 1958 image, she poses in costume for her recital at Betty Holding's dance studio.

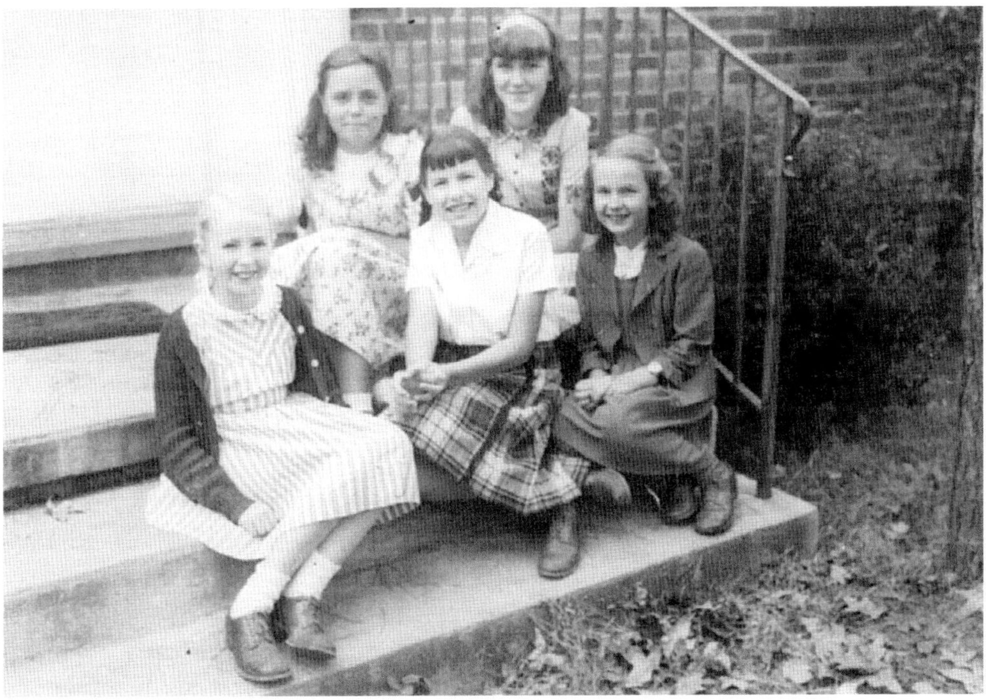

Staff of the Woodland News
In the 1940s, a group of school friends decided to report, write, and distribute a publication featuring stories of interest about neighbors living along Faculty Avenue and other streets surrounding the Wake Forest College campus. Pictured from left to right are Melinda Speas Buchanan (who handled delivery), with newspaper reporters and editors Virginia Pearson Tharrington, Alice Speas Wilkinson, Margaret Brown, and Virginia Cocke.

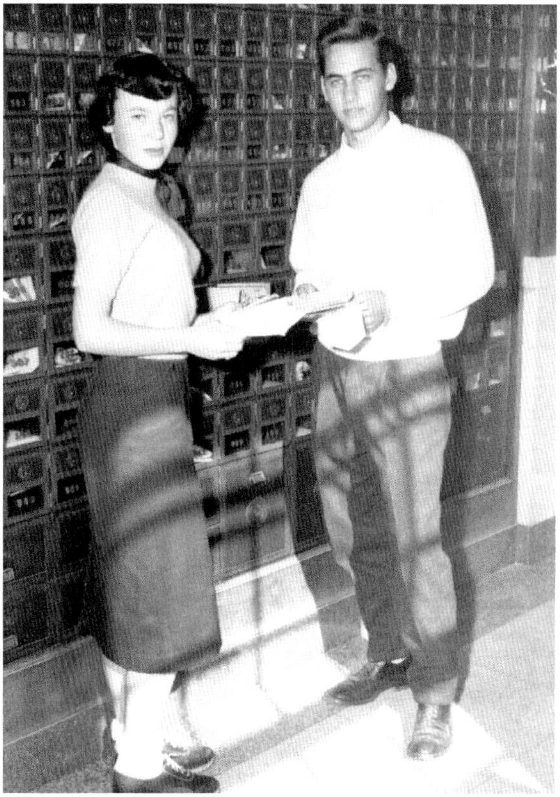

Rose Lake and John Lyon

Voted "Best Looking" in the class of 1955, Rose Lake and John Lyon represented the old and the new. Lyon's father had just taken a job as superintendent of the cotton mill. A big-city boy, he wore pegged pants with jingling keys and styled his hair like Elvis. He eventually became town mayor. Lake belonged to Wake Forest's collegiate past, with ancestors on the faculty dating back to the 19th century. (Courtesy of Barbara Hollowell Lyon.)

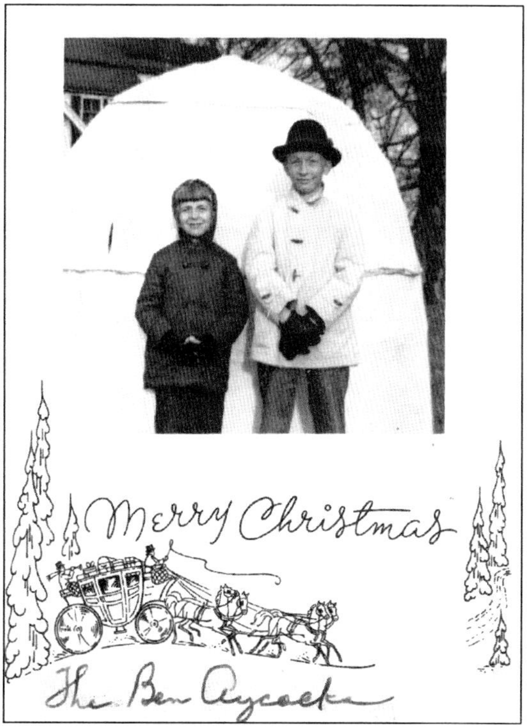

Minta Aycock McNally and Ben Aycock Jr.

In this c. 1960 Christmas card, Minta and Ben Aycock pose in front of a canvas igloo that had been used as Santa's house for Wake Forest's downtown holiday celebration. As their father was mayor, it is likely he purchased the tent for the backyard of his historic home across from Wake Forest Baptist Church. McNally went on to become an assistant vice president at Wake Forest University. (Courtesy of Margaret McClure.)

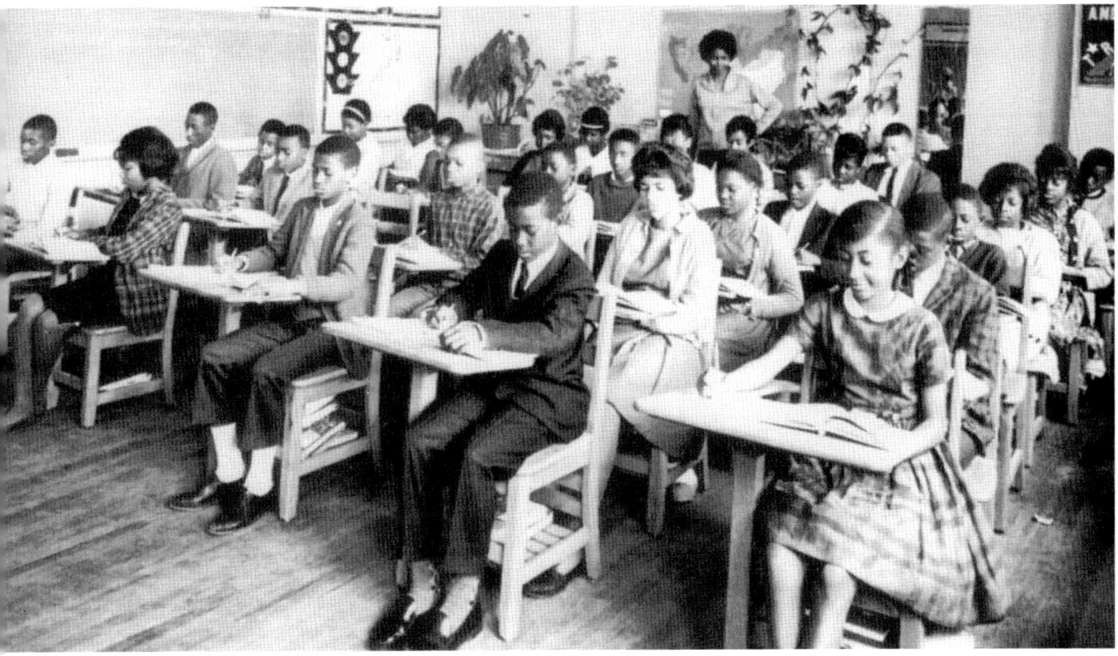

The Last Segregated Class
These seventh graders posing for a 1965 yearbook photograph in their classroom at the DuBois School would make history just five years later as Wake Forest's last segregated graduating class. In the fall of 1970, the town officially integrated its public schools and turned the DuBois campus into a junior high. The officers of this seventh-grade class included Verdie Barbour (president), Vernese Towns (vice president), Patsy Allen (secretary), and Joyce Price (treasurer). (Courtesy of the National Alumni Foundation DuBois School.)

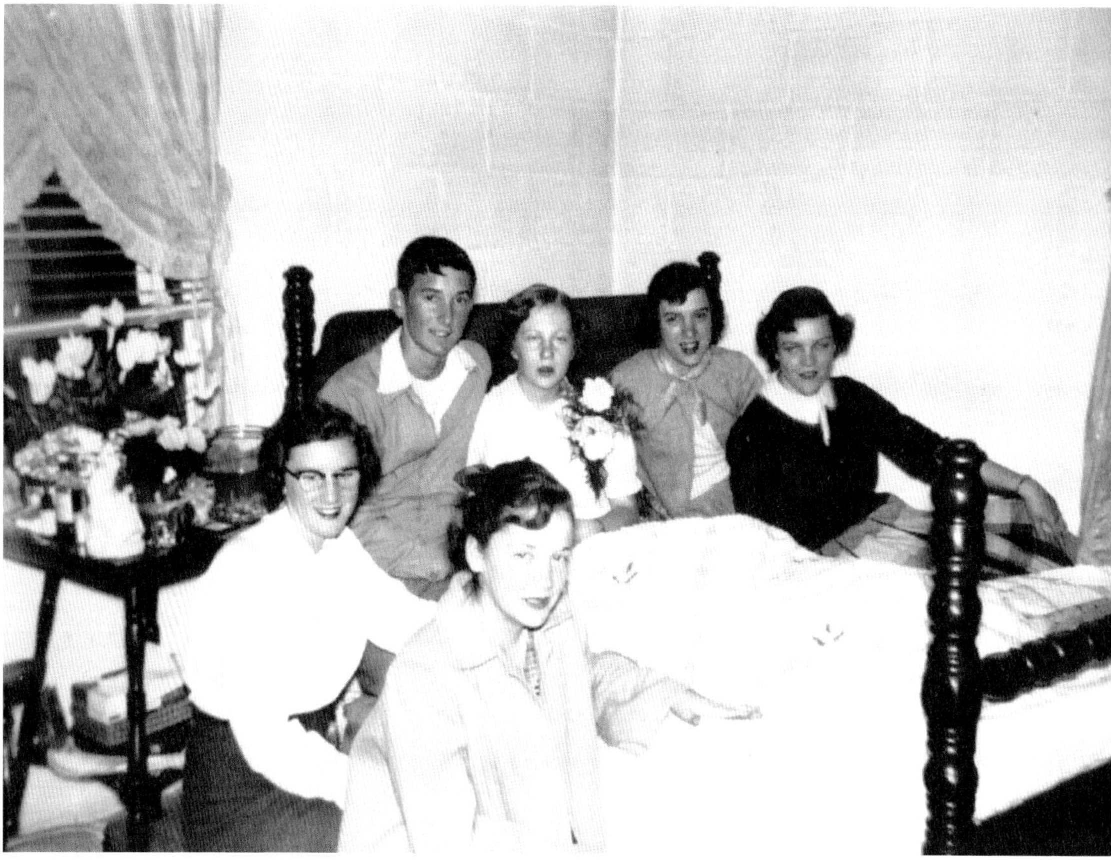

Audis Jean Phillips

A teenager living near Purnell Road in the area known as the Harricane, where her grandfather ran a store, Audis Jean Phillips was diagnosed with leukemia in early 1954. In this era, when contemporary cancer research was in its infancy and treatment options were limited, childhood leukemia was considered a death sentence. When news got around, Wake Forest residents rallied around the young girl, sending hundreds of "get well soon" cards. Phillips fought the disease for eight long months, but despite the town's heartfelt support and her own heroic efforts, she lost the battle and died on December 6, 1954, at age 15. This photograph of friends visiting her bedside was one of the last taken before her death.

CHAPTER TWO

The Town

In many ways, Wake Forest was the brainchild of John Purefoy, a local leader who wanted a greater number of well-educated Baptist ministers preaching in rural areas. With energy and determination, Purefoy persuaded the North Carolina Baptist Convention to purchase approximately 600 acres of land—along with a c. 1820 farmhouse and a handful of outbuildings—from Dr. Calvin Jones, a physician and former mayor of Raleigh who was selling his plantation in order to move west. This is how, in a rather remote section of northern Wake County, the story of Wake Forest College (now Wake Forest University) and the town of Wake Forest began.

The school was a success. Within a few years, Wake Forest College was teeming with students and faculty. However, the town did not really take off until 1874, when the Raleigh & Gaston Railroad agreed to move its depot from Forestville to Wake Forest so disembarking passengers—many of them students—would be spared the trouble of lugging their trunks the final mile to campus. From that moment on, storefronts along South White Street filled with restaurants, shops, and banks. The district expanded in later decades to include movie theaters, department stores, and service stations. Neighborhoods began to develop, starting with Faculty Avenue (now North Main Street), which was home to many professors, business owners, and student boarders. On the north edge of town, the Royall Cotton Mill opened in 1899, with homes for textile workers and their families. And the historically African American neighborhood on the other side of the railroad tracks, now called the East End, had its own churches, shops, and schools. Finally, there was a community northwest of town, a region known as the Harricane. Named for an ancient storm, this area consisted of small farms owned by families known for their close relationships, resilience, determination, and loyalty.

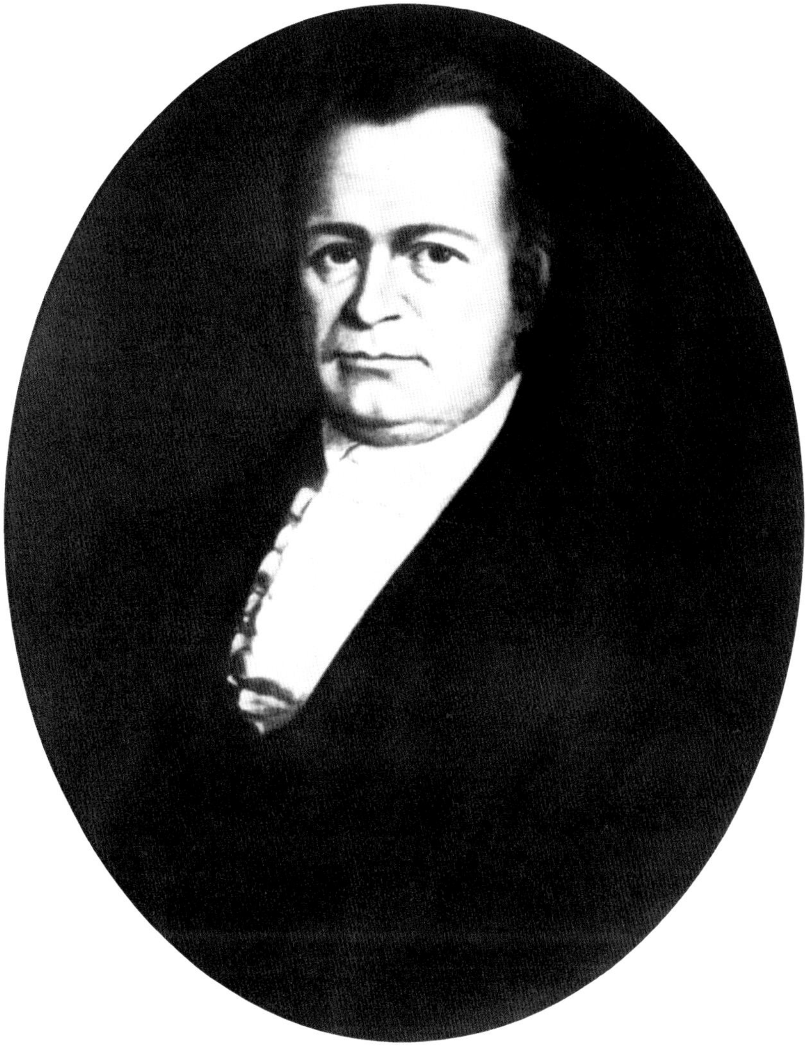

Calvin Jones

By the time Dr. Calvin Jones sold his house and 615 acres of land to the North Carolina Baptist Convention in 1832, he was already one of the state's most prominent citizens. Born in Sheffield, Massachusetts, in 1775, Jones received his medical education by apprenticing with an established physician. He soon migrated south and opened an office in Smithfield, North Carolina, where he practiced medicine for eight years before moving to Raleigh in 1803. Jones has the distinction of being among the first physicians to perform cataract surgery on patients. He also went on to found the North Carolina Medical Society, serve as mayor of Raleigh, become a state legislator, publish the *Raleigh Star*, serve on the board of trustees at the University of North Carolina, work as an educator, postmaster, and farmer, and serve as a general in the War of 1812. When he was 41 years old, Jones married widow Temperance Boddie Williams Jones of Franklin County. Daughter of a wealthy Warren County planter, she brought to the relationship several enslaved African Americans and a son by her first marriage. The Jones family and their slaves lived in the area that Jones named Wake Forest, taken from the original designation, "the Forest of Wake." After selling his property to the Baptists, who paid $2,000 and planned to use the site to establish a school, the Jones family moved to central Tennessee. By the time Jones died in 1846, his Tennessee estate encompassed 30,000 acres.

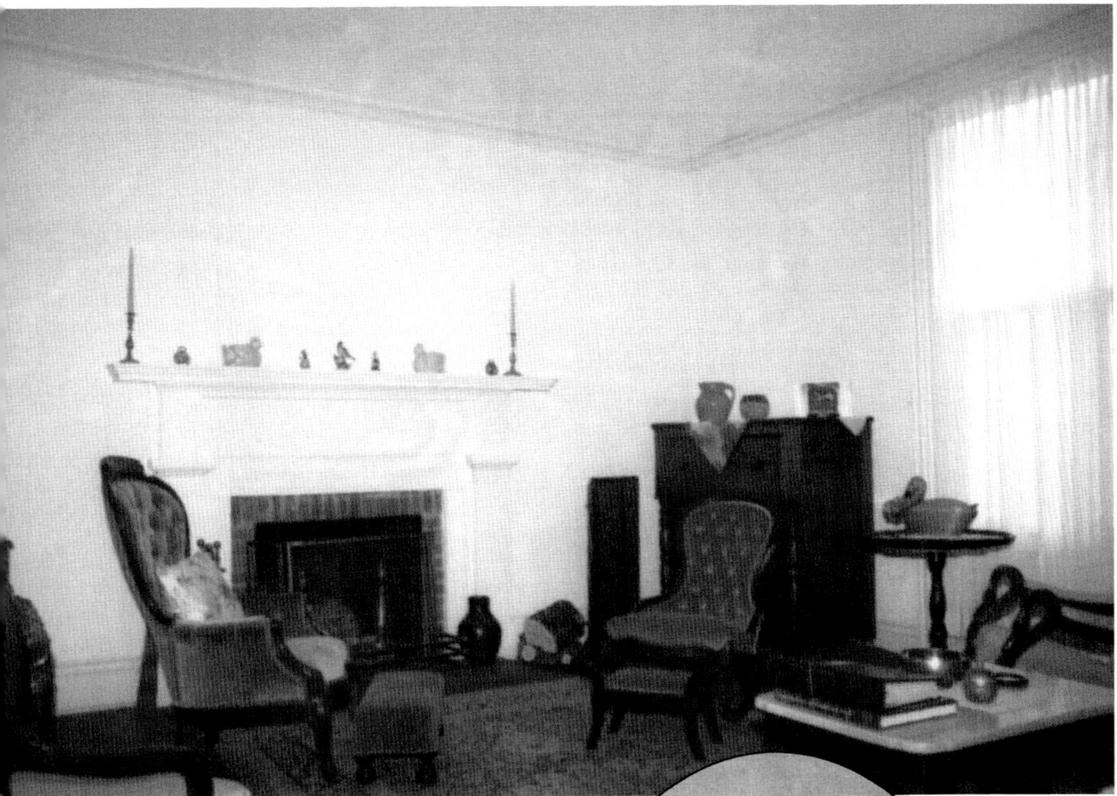

John Purefoy
The Purefoy-Dunn House was owned by minister John Purefoy, whose concern over the lack of proper educational opportunities for Baptist ministers led the North Carolina Baptist Convention to purchase property from Dr. Calvin Jones and create what would become Wake Forest College. (Courtesy of the State Archives of North Carolina.)

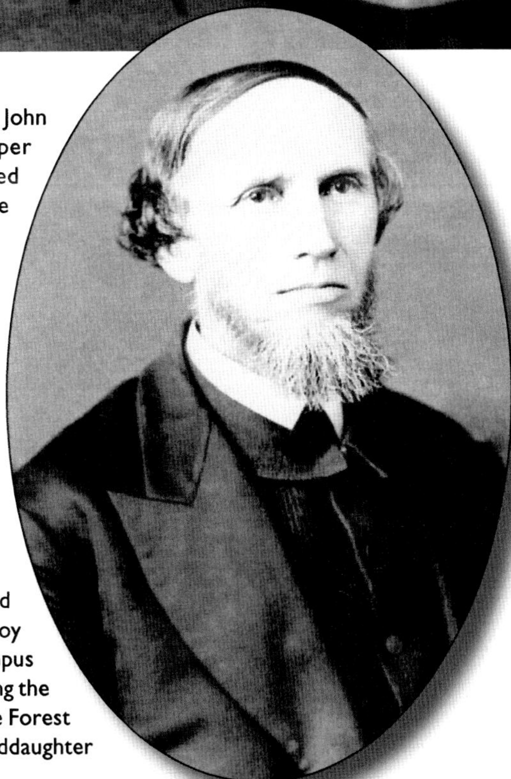

James Purefoy
The son of John Purefoy, James was born in 1846 and worked as a minister, farmer, and merchant. Purefoy built the College Hotel near the Wake Forest campus and helped raise funds to support the school following the Civil War. One of his granddaughters married Wake Forest College president William Poteat, and another granddaughter married professor and poet Benjamin Sledd.

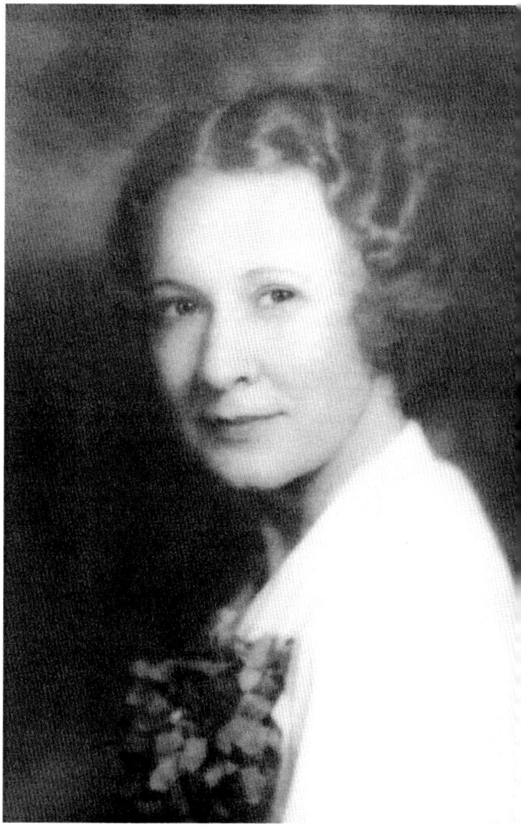

Nancy Cullom Harris

Nancy Cullom Harris, the daughter of beloved Wake Forest College religion professor W.R. Cullom, served as the town's first female postmaster. A talented wife, mother, and career woman, she gave the *Wake Weekly* its name, briefly edited the paper, and ran a successful 1950s-era personal-shopping business. The auditorium at the Wake Forest Historical Museum is named in her memory.

Louise Williams

Always known as "Miss Lou," Louise Williams was born in 1889 and lived most of her life at Crenshaw Hall, home of her grandmother and her step-grandfather, Maj. John Crenshaw. At age 39, she learned to dance, and she soon became a prominent dance teacher with schools in Wake Forest, Henderson, and Raleigh. During World War II, Williams founded the Wake Forest USO. A local icon, she was a longtime member of St. John's Episcopal Church and lived 102 years.

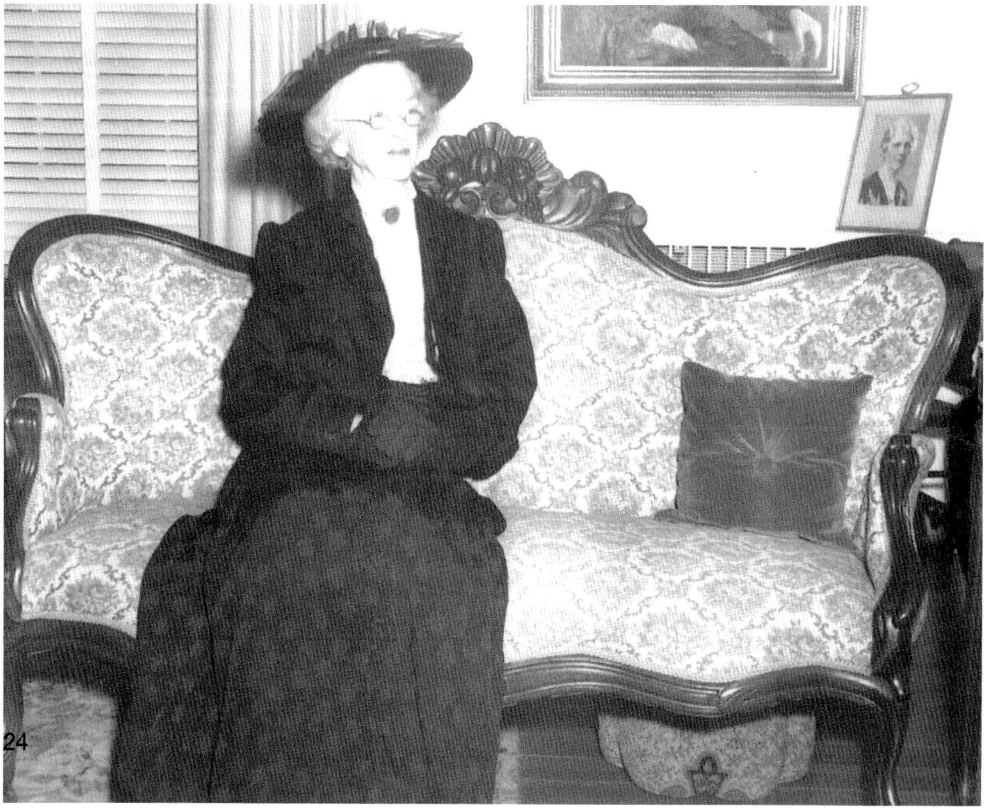

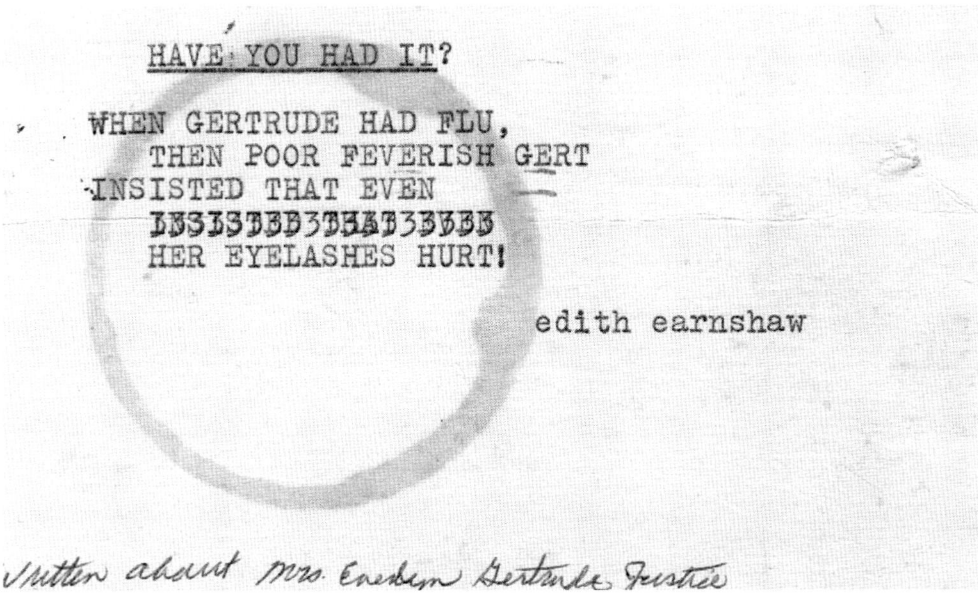
HAVE YOU HAD IT?

WHEN GERTRUDE HAD FLU,
THEN POOR FEVERISH GERT
INSISTED THAT EVEN
HER EYELASHES HURT!

edith earnshaw

Edith Taylor Earnshaw
A daughter of Wake Forest College president Charles Taylor, Edith Taylor Earnshaw was a published poet known for her light verse. She and her husband worked for the college, and in 1945, they bequeathed to it their entire estate—a then-princely sum of $44,000. Earnshaw's last poem, published after her death, includes the lines, "Wake Forest, blessed village of my birth, you evermore will be my Heaven on earth."

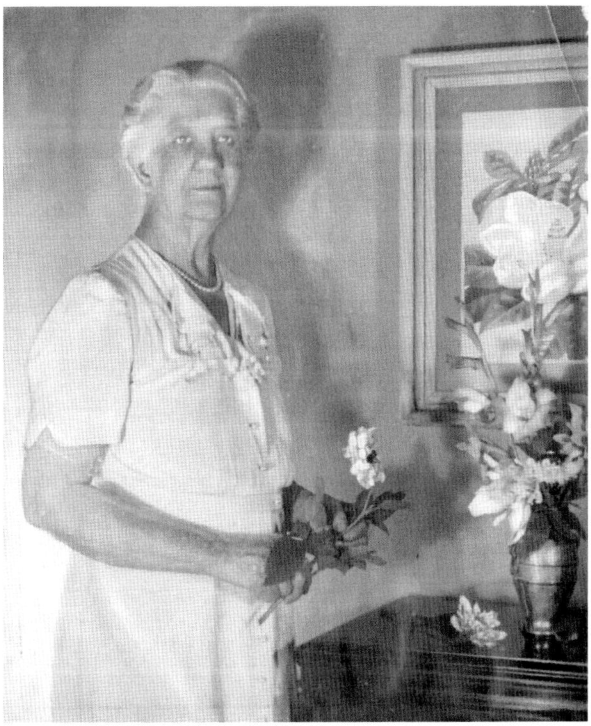

Ethel Taylor Crittenden
Another daughter of Wake Forest College president Charles Taylor, Ethel Taylor Crittenden was a preservationist, volunteer, and community activist who was instrumental in saving the Calvin Jones House and moving it from campus to North Main Street. Crittenden was also mother of well-known state historian Christopher Crittenden.

Robert Best

Robert Best, son of a noted principal of the DuBois School, graduated in 1947 with a prestigious Pepsi-Cola Scholarship, scoring second highest in the South in the academic scholarship contest before earning a degree in medicine from Columbia University. As an internist in Los Angeles, California, Best was one of the few black physicians granted hospital privileges at Cedars-Sinai Medical Center. Noted as well for his striking appearance, his school nickname was "Pretty Boy." (Courtesy of Eric Best.)

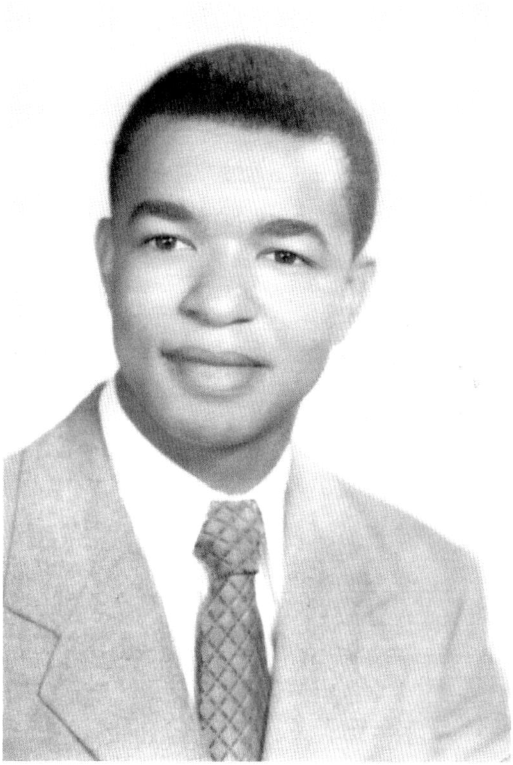

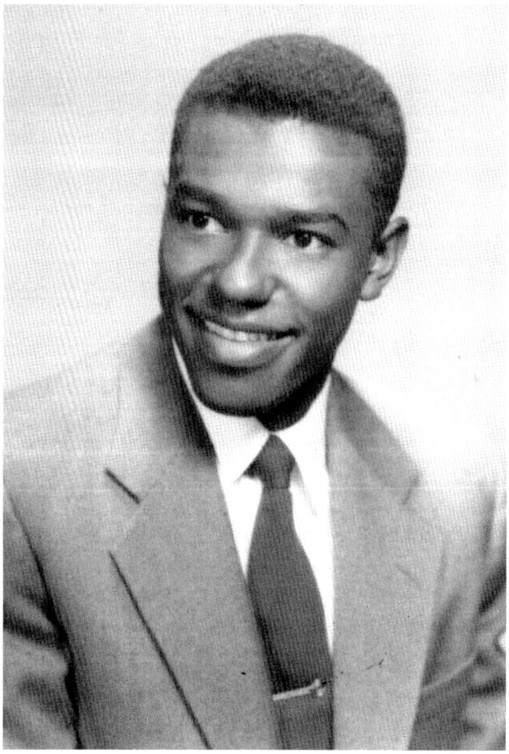

Eric Best

The Bests' second son, Eric, benefited from North Carolina's brief "separate but equal" law that required the state to provide equivalent educational opportunities for blacks. As North Carolina had no medical school that admitted African American students, Best received free tuition for a full year of training at Columbia University before the law was declared illegal in 1954. A specialist in internal medicine, he retired in Albuquerque, New Mexico, in 2000. (Courtesy of Eric Best.)

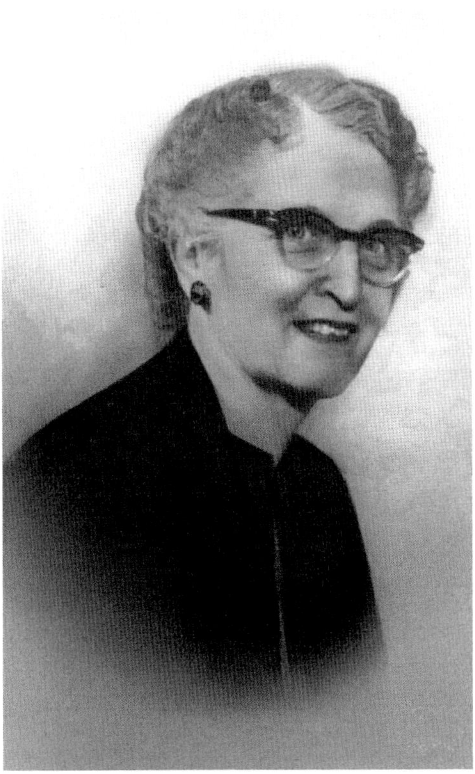

Rosa Winston

The first policewoman in Wake Forest, Rosa Winston started with the town's water and light department, handling service and billing for approximately 2,500 residents. She also acted as clerk of court. When the town required a bondsman, Winston took that job, too. This led to a position as a police officer. Winston made many arrests and earned widespread respect, working until her death in 1957. (Courtesy of Willis Winston.)

Marie Joyner

A native of Enfield, North Carolina, Annie Marie Whitehead married Millard E. "Shorty" Joyner of Shorty's Famous Hot Dogs. She represented the best of Wake Forest and was particularly known for making Christmas ornaments and decorating the tree each year at the town's annual Christmas Tea. On the day of her funeral, the hearse drove down South White Street to take Joyner past Shorty's Famous Hot Dogs one last time.

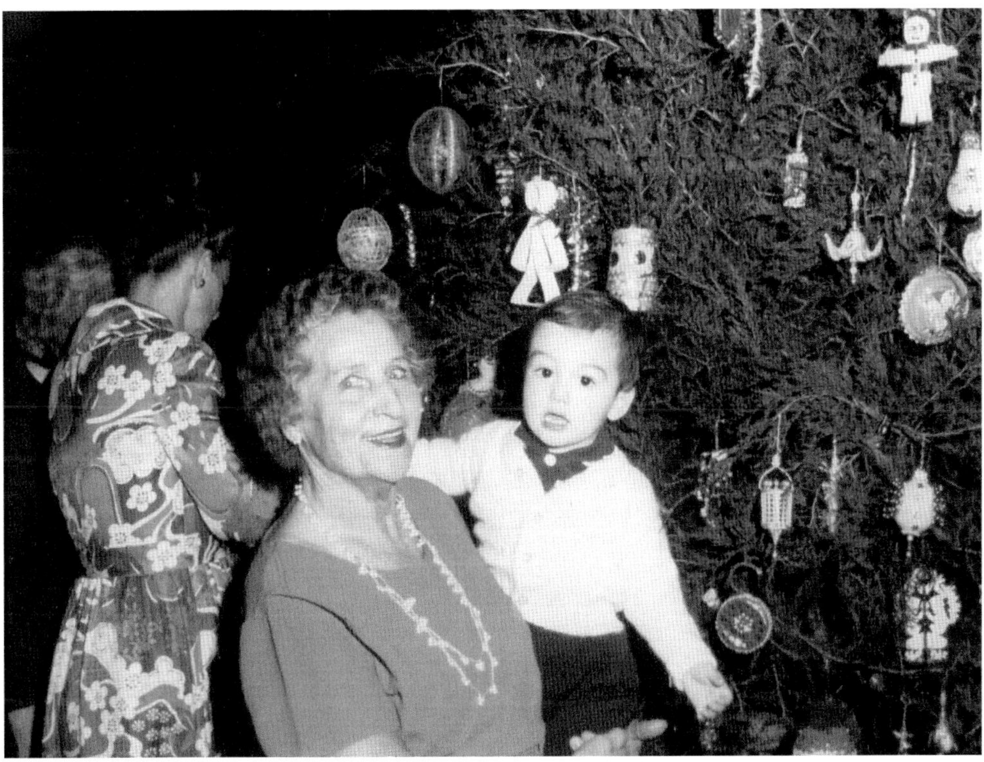

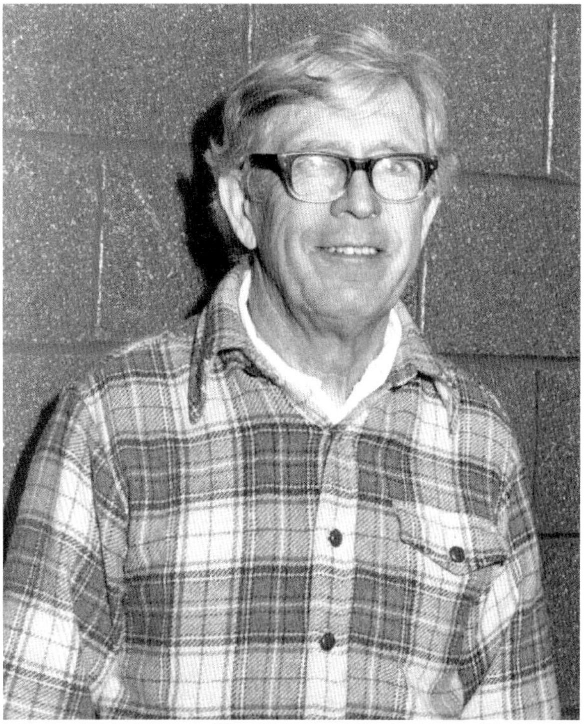

James L. Warren

James L. Warren, born in Sampson County in 1917, graduated magna cum laude from Wake Forest College and served with the Army Air Corps in World War II, planning bombing missions and drawing maps for pilots. But it was in banking and community service that Warren made his mark. He started the town's Little League Baseball program and, following a heart attack in 1969, became a pioneering marathon runner. (Courtesy of James S. Warren.)

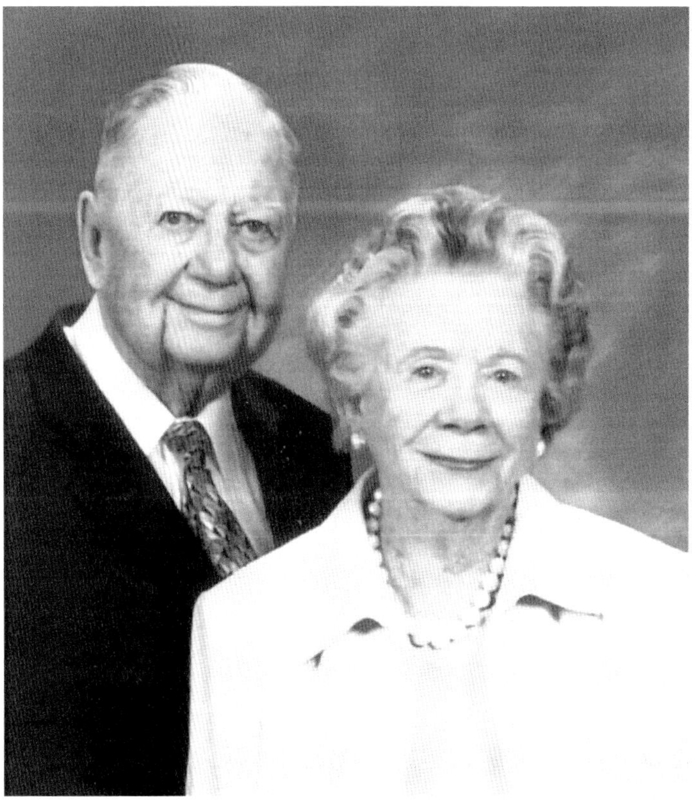

John and Shirley Wooten

John Wooten was instrumental in reviving the Wake Forest economy after the college left in 1956. As a member of the 1964 Industrial Development Corporation, he worked to bring Schraeder Brothers, the Athey Plant, and other manufacturers to Wake Forest. Shirley Wooten joined her husband in making enormous contributions as members of Wake Forest Baptist Church and nearly all the town's civic organizations.

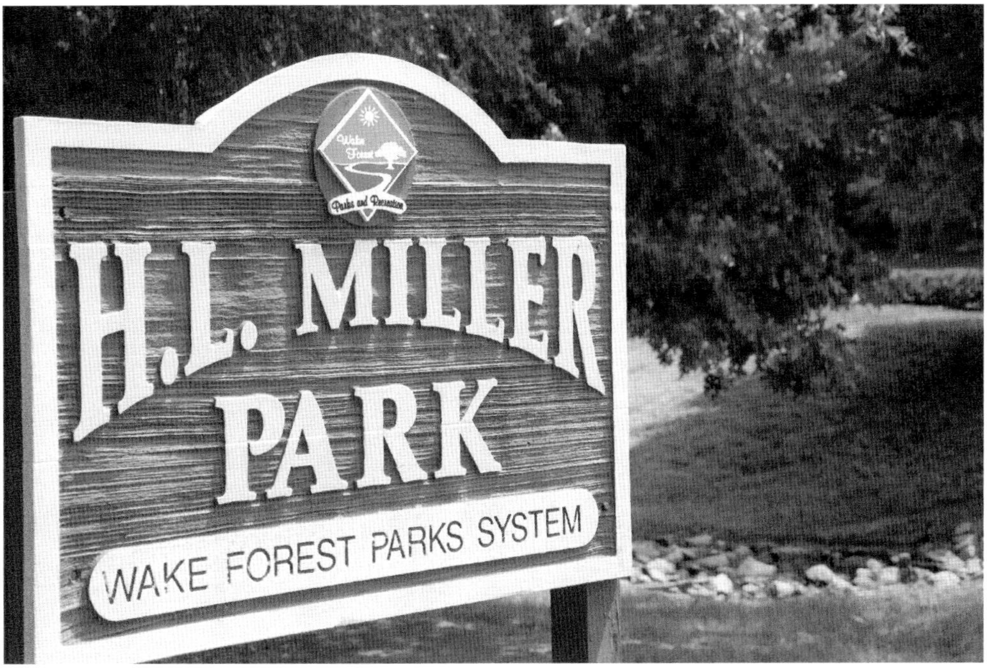

Henry Miller

Henry Miller was born in 1899 in Allen, Oklahoma, and arrived in Wake Forest in the mid-1920s. In 1940, he bought the local Ford dealership on South White Street, and he eventually added other ventures: an oil company, a car wash, a funeral home, a Laundromat, and real estate. Miller helped found a church, was a board member at Wake Forest Federal Savings & Loan, and served as town mayor. H.L. Miller Park on Franklin Street is named in his memory.

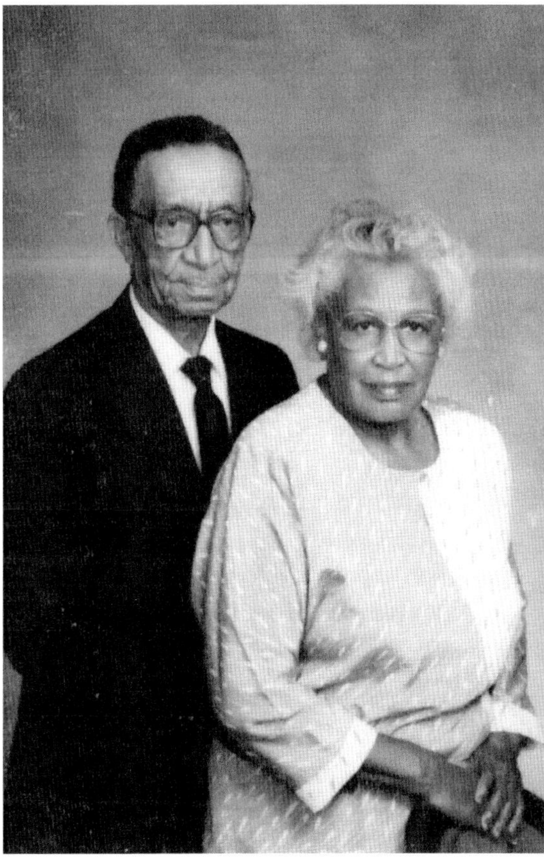

Luther and Hazel Yarborough Watkins

Married in 1941, Luther and Hazel Yarborough Watkins were friends with Allen Young, founder of the Normal and Industrial School, a private academy for African American children. Watkins drove the bus on school days and chauffeured Young to meetings with potential donors. Hazel served on the DuBois School Parent-Teacher Association and worked in the nursery at Wake Forest Baptist Church. (Courtesy of Theresa Watkins.)

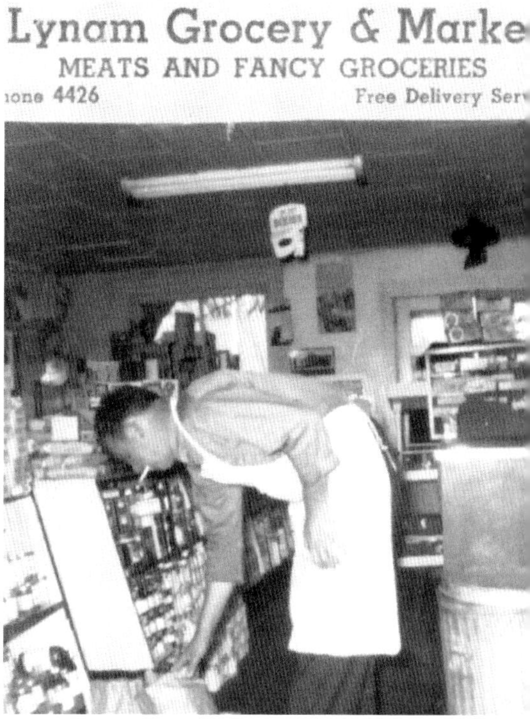

William Melius Lynam
The proprietor of Lynam Grocery and Market, William Melius Lynam began working as a child at Glen Royall Cotton Mill and in 1938 built the cinderblock strip of shops at the end of North Main Street. A self-taught butcher, Lynam supported his wife, Mary Doris, and six children by slicing and selling exceptional cuts of meat that drew hundreds of customers. Nicknamed "Smiles," Lynam was known for never going back on his word and for delivering free food and supplies to needy Wake Forest families every Christmas. Lynam was working at the store when he died of a heart attack on November 29, 1966. The family immediately shuttered the business and sold the remaining inventory to Dr. George Mackie, who would similarly die of a heart attack while at work in his medical office on the same street just three years later. The loss of Lynam's store was a blow to the town, particularly the residents of the mill village. (Courtesy of Roy and Donna Lynam.)

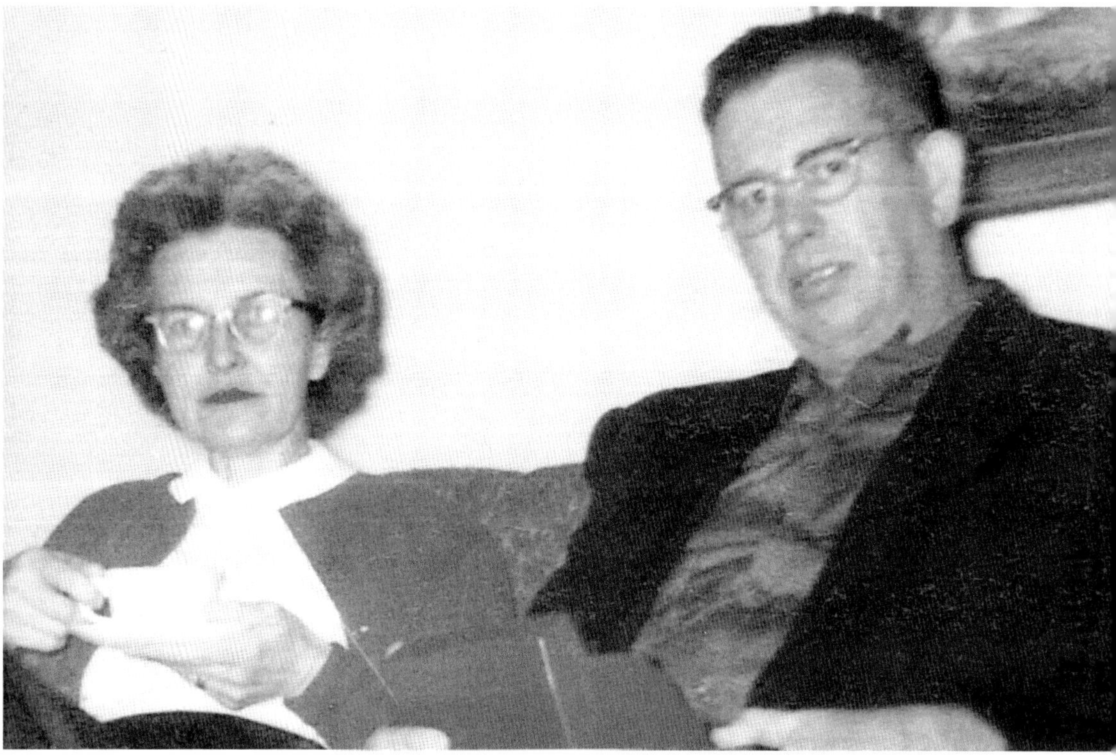

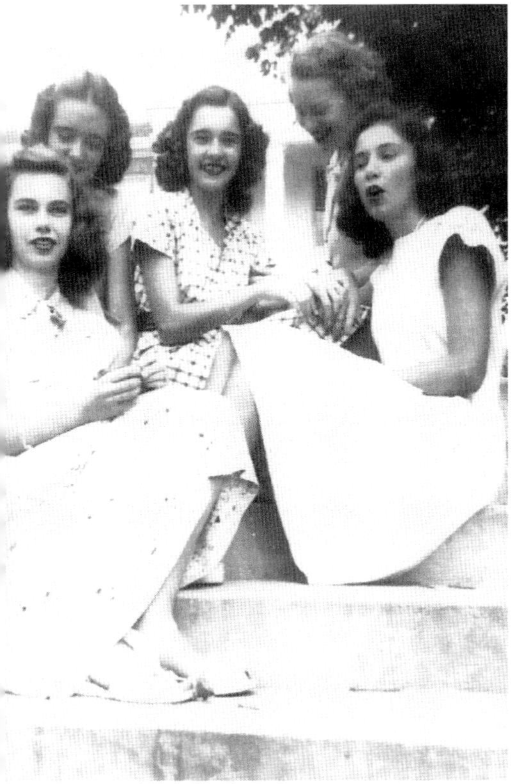

Bettie Marable Patterson Dowda

Local beauty and valued civic volunteer Marable Patterson Dowda was the daughter of Wake Forest College registrar Grady Patterson. She married Wake Forest College football star Harry Dowda (see page 49) and traveled many years with her family before returning to Wake Forest in the 1990s. Sitting on the high school steps in this c. 1945 photograph are, from left to right, Billie Bryan, Betty Rose, Peggy Nelson, Eleanor Easley, and Bettie Marable Patterson Dowda. (Courtesy of Cristie Dowda.)

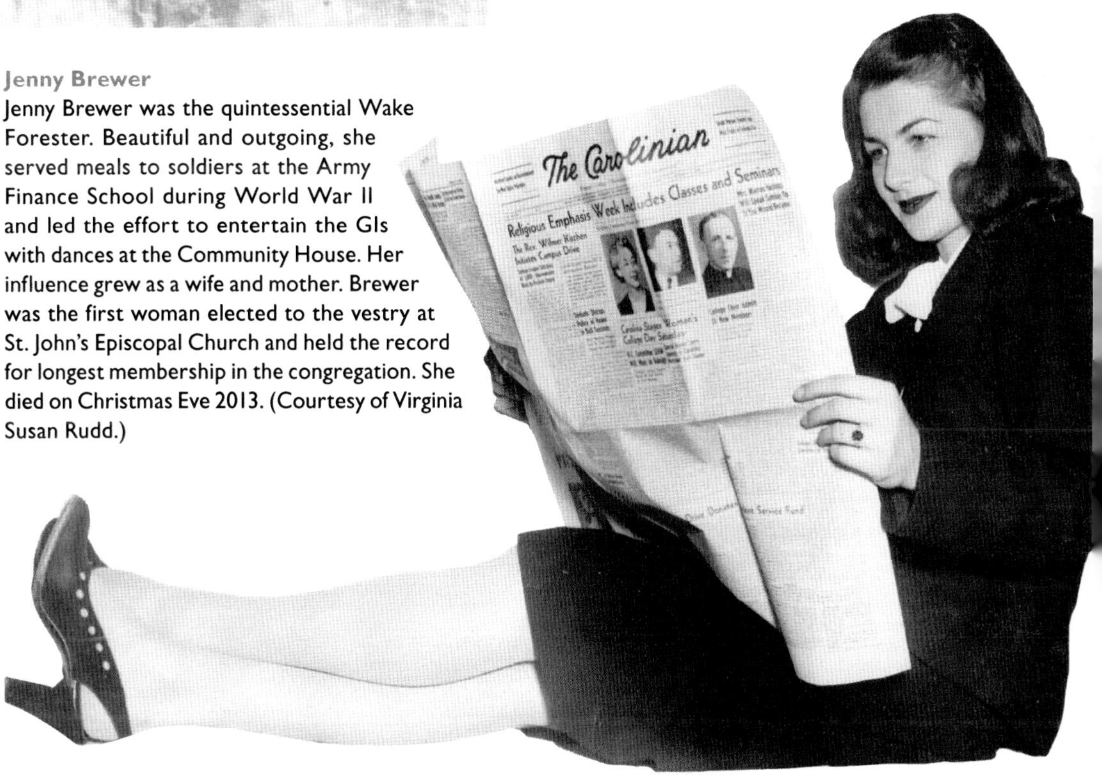

Jenny Brewer

Jenny Brewer was the quintessential Wake Forester. Beautiful and outgoing, she served meals to soldiers at the Army Finance School during World War II and led the effort to entertain the GIs with dances at the Community House. Her influence grew as a wife and mother. Brewer was the first woman elected to the vestry at St. John's Episcopal Church and held the record for longest membership in the congregation. She died on Christmas Eve 2013. (Courtesy of Virginia Susan Rudd.)

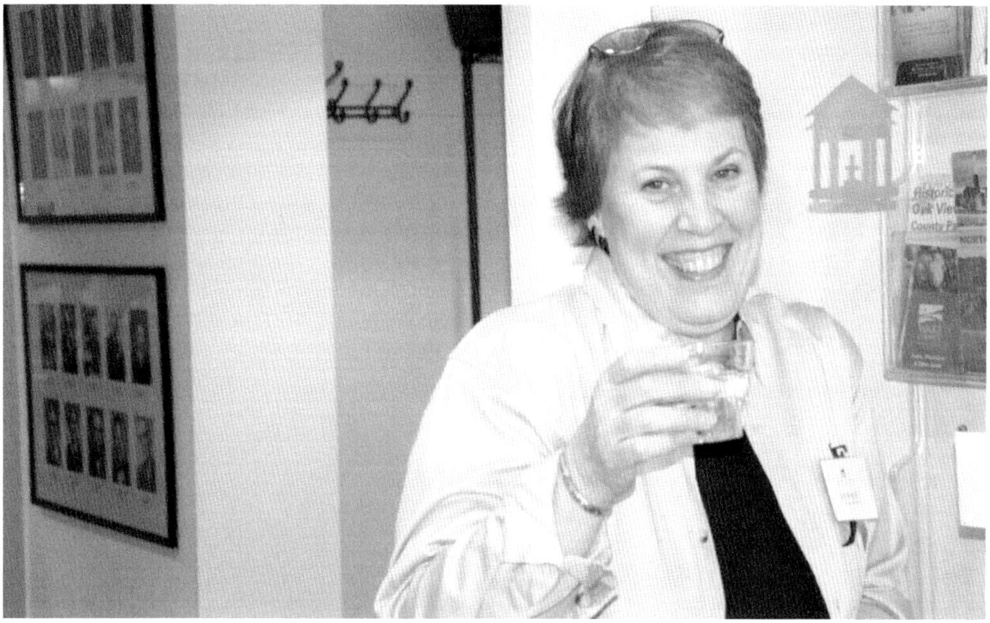

Jill Bright

Jill Bright not only works at the family business, Bright Funeral Home, but she is also a mainstay of the Wake Forest Chamber of Commerce, the Wake Forest Historical Museum, and the Wake Forest Fire Department. Bright lends a hand to everything from the Fire Department's fish fry to the town's Christmas Historic Home Tour and Fourth of July parade. Bright was honored as the 2012 Wake Forest Citizen of the Year.

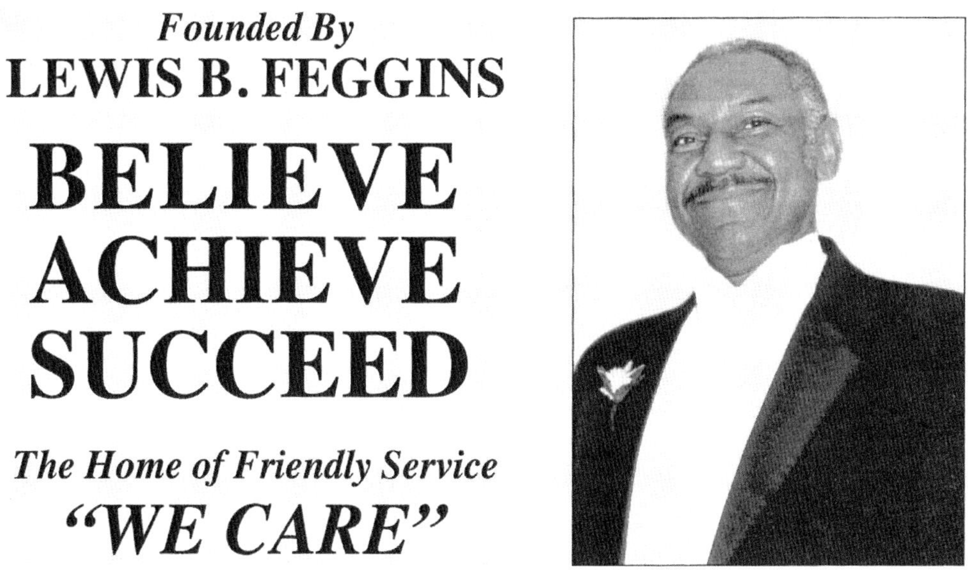

Feggins & Feggins

This photograph was printed as part of a calendar giveaway by Feggins & Feggins Funeral Home in Wake Forest. The father-and-son operation, located beside the town cemetery on North White Street, has served the East End community for generations.

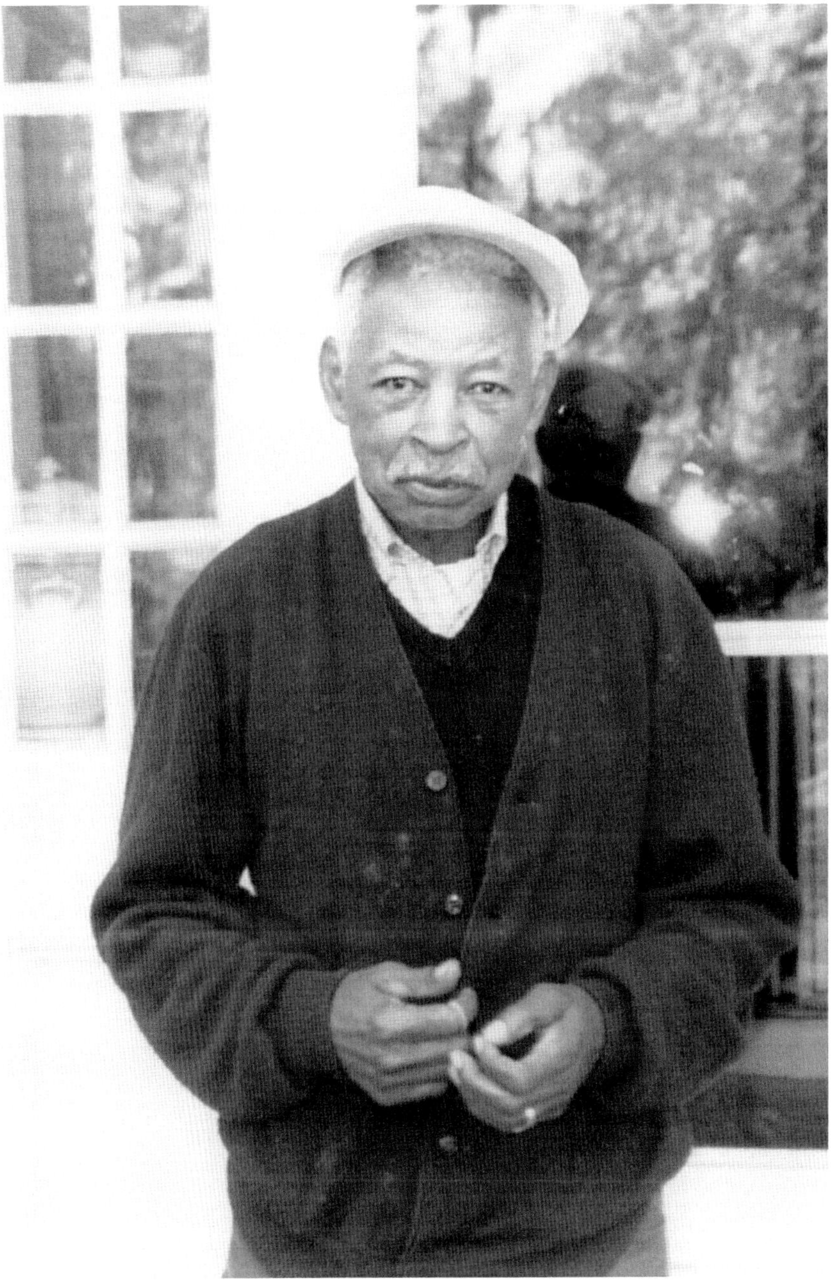

Willie Fleming

Named Wake Forest's 1988 Citizen of the Year, Willie Fleming was a well-known cook at Wooten's Hometel on South Main Street during a period when it was one of the town's most popular restaurants. A proficient pastry chef, Fleming also managed the facility's kitchen. He was a trained bartender, worked at many of the private social events around town, and was never seen without his pipe. After leaving his job at Wooten's to serve with distinction in World War II, Fleming returned to Wake Forest and began volunteering in the community. He was known for making routine visits to the sick and elderly, doing free yard work and chores, and walking from his home in Forestville. Fleming never drove a car.

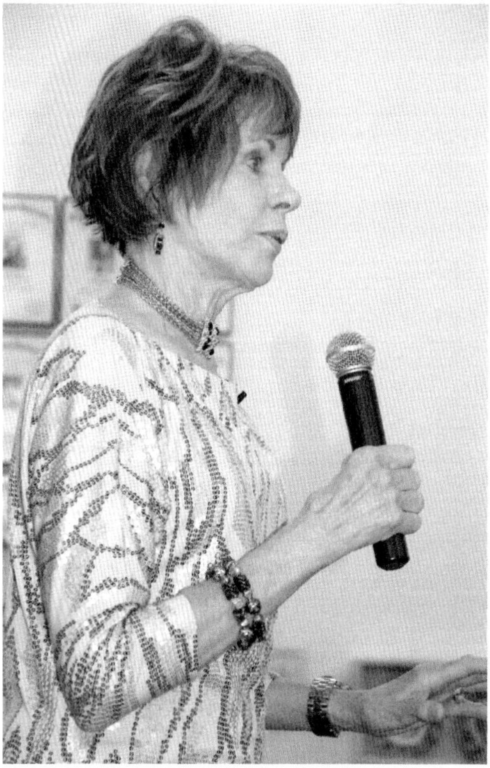

Emory Earp Austin

Daughter of Wake Forest College classics professor Cronje Earp (see page 118), Emory Earp Austin's humor and wisdom have made her a famous motivational speaker. "Every time I had a problem . . . one [of my parents] would exclaim, 'Isn't that fascinating! I wonder how many ways you can deal with this?' And off we would go, exploring possibilities and turning problems into adventures."

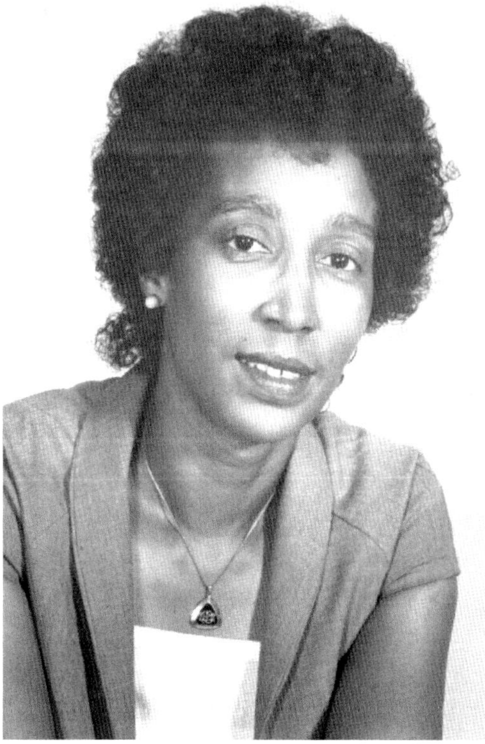

Dianne Watkins Laws

Born in Wake Forest, Dianne Watkins Laws attended the Normal and Industrial School, graduated from the DuBois School in 1959, and spent her career working for the US Department of Agriculture and the Environmental Protection Agency. Specializing in the area of civil rights, Laws eventually managed a staff of 1,600 before retiring to Wake Forest and serving as president of the National DuBois Alumni Association. (Courtesy of Dianne Laws.)

Jimmy Keith

Jimmy Keith was a third-generation chief of the Wake Forest Fire Department, and it seemed only natural when he stepped into the role previously held by his father and grandfather. He joined the department while still a student at Wake Forest High School, becoming its hugely popular leader in 1987. During his 17 years at the helm, Keith persuaded the town to purchase better fire trucks, build two new stations, and more than double the force of 30 volunteers to a group of 70 professional and volunteer firefighters. Keith was just 53 years old when he died of cancer in 2004; his funeral was attended by firefighters from across Wake County and as far away as New York City. Nearly 700 mourners paid their respects, many calling it the largest funeral remembered in recent town history. In the photograph, Bruce and Margaret Keith stand beside a memorial bust of their son outside the Wake Forest Fire Department's stationhouse at the corner of Franklin Street and Elm Avenue.

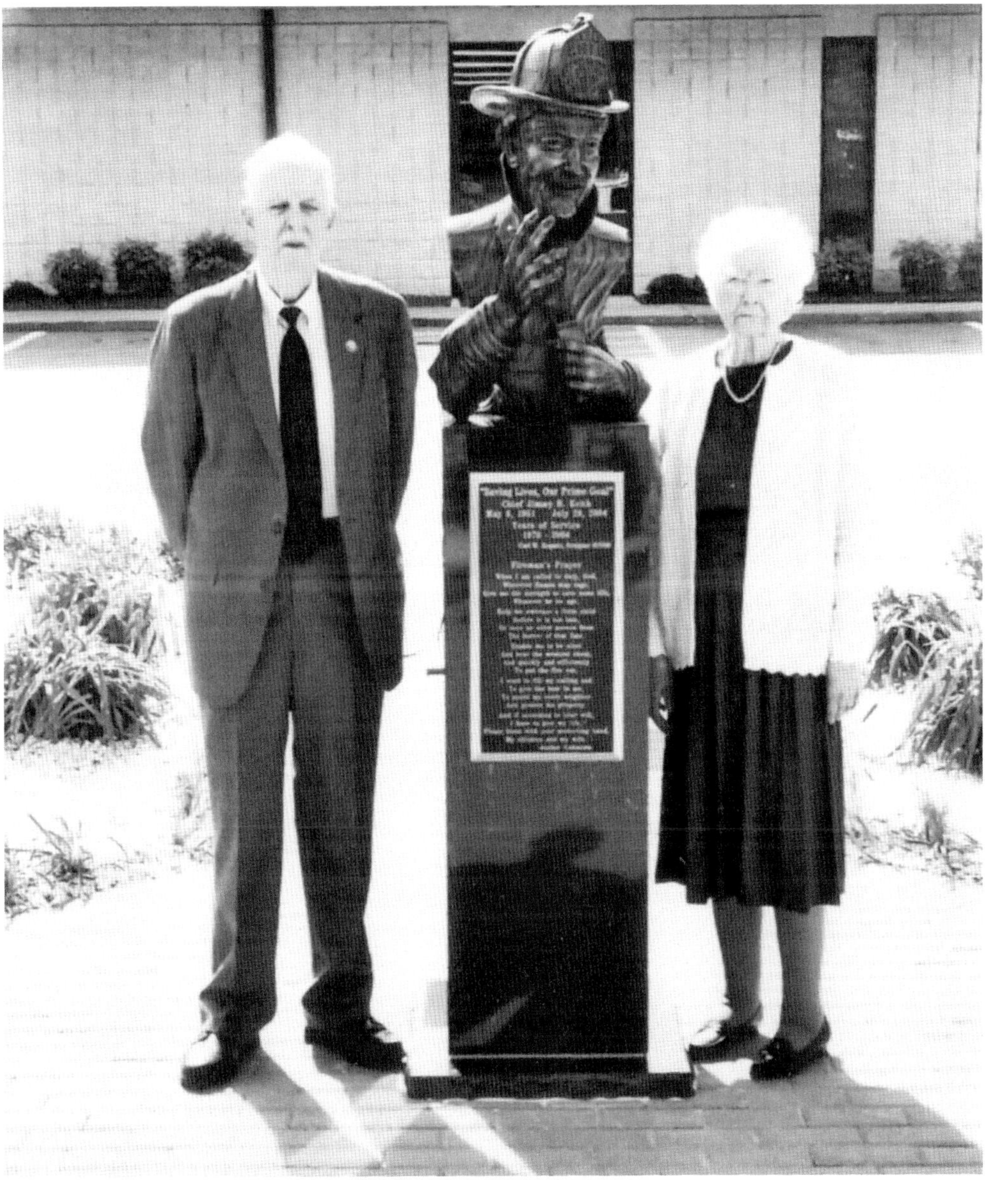

Donna Rollins Pace

In the mid-1960s, Wake Forest native Donna Rollins Pace made history in the Miss North Carolina pageant by becoming the only contestant ever to represent Wake County two years running. After Pace first won the Wake County title in 1965, she inspired such confidence in pageant organizers that all agreed she should keep the crown for another go-round. Pace was honored to return in 1966 and compete for additional scholarship awards, which she used to pay her tuition at East Carolina University. A bright student with a beautiful smile, Pace remains something of a legend among the 1960s-era graduates of Wake Forest High School, where her achievements included head cheerleader, Miss Football, Miss Wake Forest High School, and "Best All-Around" in the class of 1964. Pace makes Wake Forest her home and is a board member of the Wake Forest College Birthplace Society. (Courtesy of Donna Rollins Pace.)

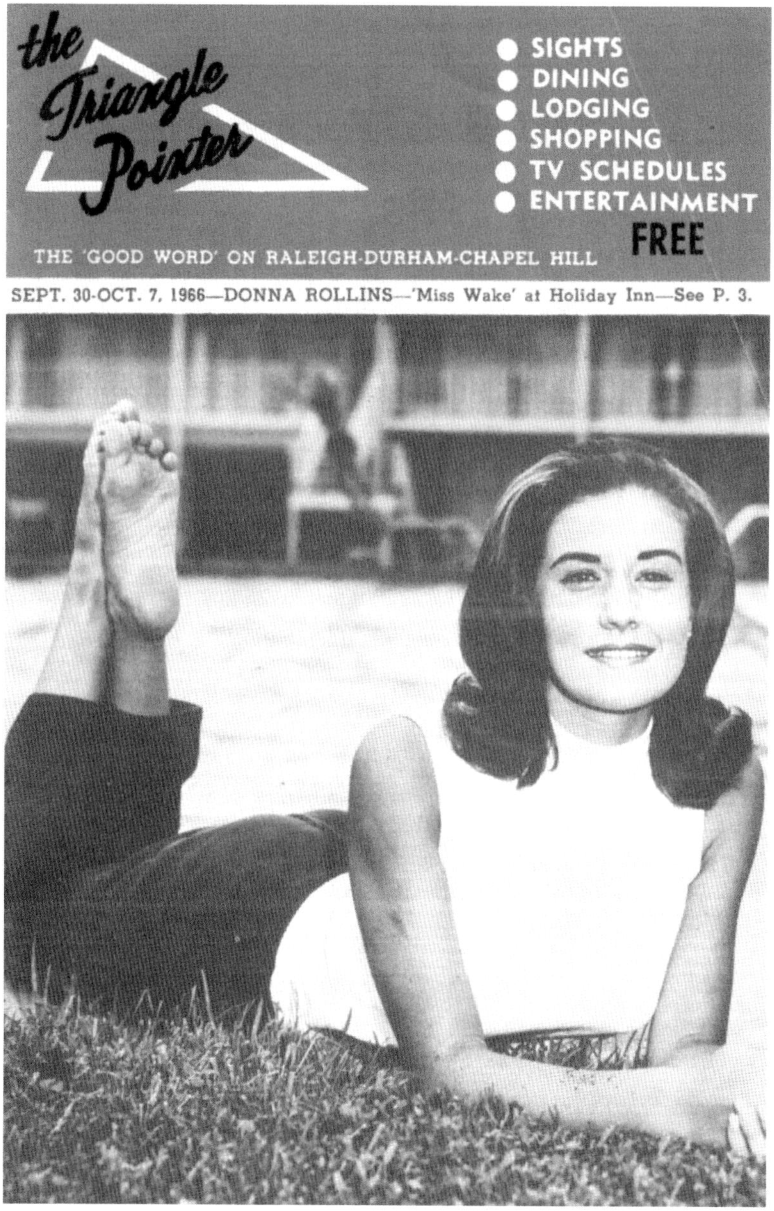

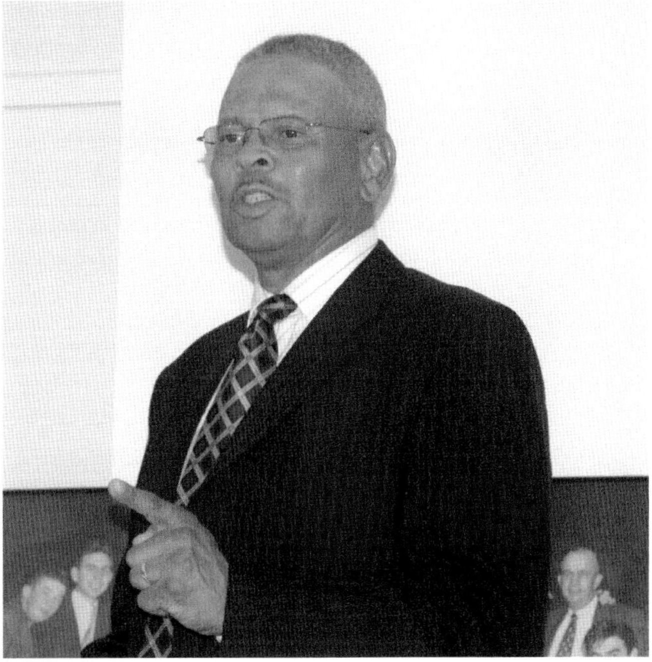

Al Merritt
A native of Wake Forest, Al Merritt grew up in the East End community, where he attended the DuBois School as a standout athlete and scholar. In his 50 years as production foreman at the *Wake Weekly*, Merritt has helped shape the growth and prosperity of his hometown by guaranteeing the newspaper gets printed and delivered to all its regional subscribers and many local businesses. (Courtesy of David Leone and the *Wake Weekly*.)

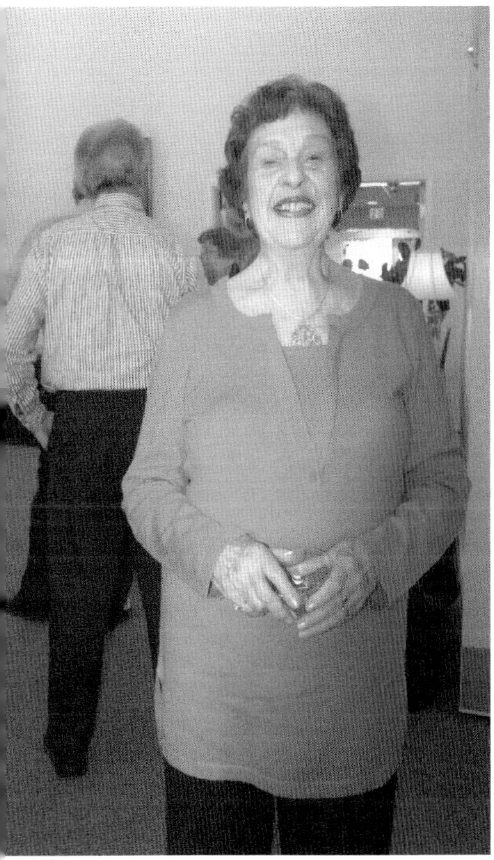

Carol Pelosi
A native of upstate New York, Carol Pelosi moved to Wake Forest with her family in the summer of 1970. As an intuitive researcher and determined journalist, Pelosi worked as a reporter and editor for the *Wake Weekly* before launching Wake Forest's first online newspaper, the *Wake Forest Gazette*. Pelosi also served as the longtime president of the Wake Forest Historical Association and is the author of a comprehensive town history, *Connections*.

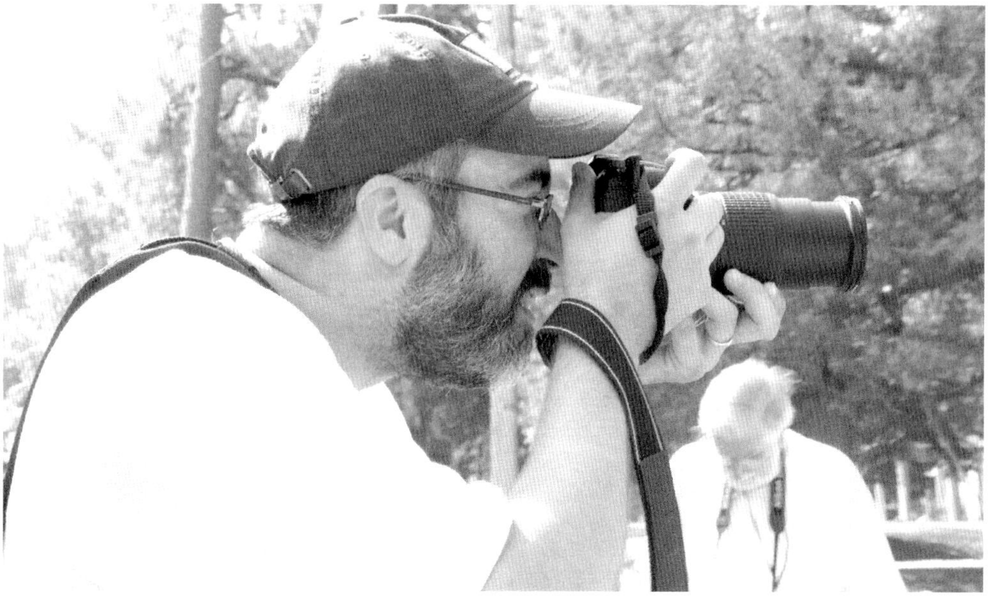

David Leone

As associate editor at the *Wake Weekly*, David Leone is seen at virtually every local news event. He has written articles about the 1996 destruction of Hurricane Fran, the downtown's regular Art After Hours events, and everything in between. An accomplished reporter and photographer, Leone is also locally famous for the smart asides and amusing observations he posts on his Twitter feed.

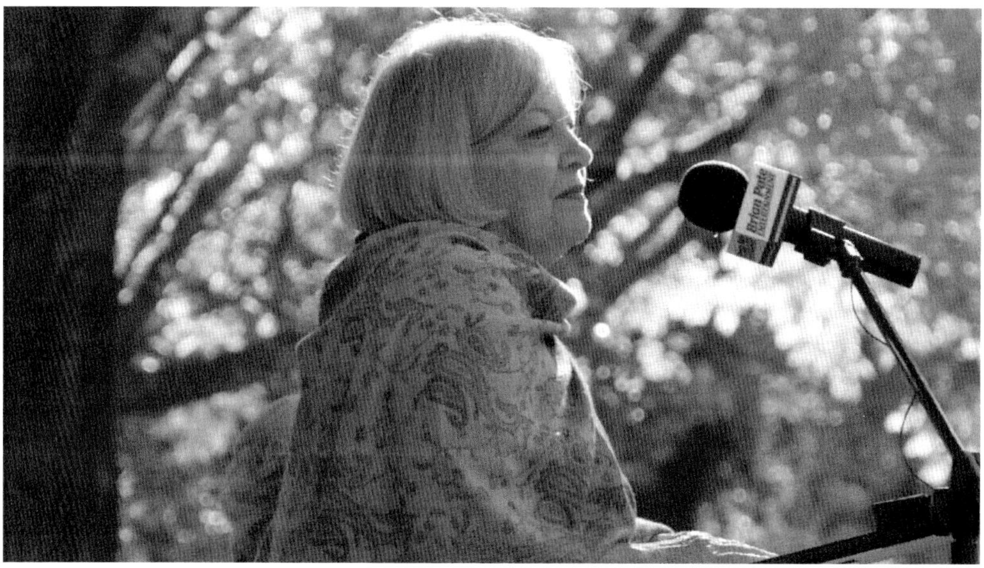

Vivian Jones

Vivian Jones is the longest-serving mayor in Wake Forest history and the first woman to be elected mayor. A smart strategist who has guided the town through a period of enormous growth, Jones has overseen the development of new roads, neighborhoods, factories, and schools while helping the community retain its unique small-town atmosphere. This photograph was taken during her speech at the Wake Forest Historical Museum's grand opening in 2010.

CHAPTER THREE

The College

Founded in 1834 as the Wake Forest Manual Labor Institute, Wake Forest College was among the first colleges established in North Carolina and was one of the 40 oldest in the United States. Initial growth happened quickly, with the school installing a brick campus of three original buildings and an expanded faculty within its first decade. By the turn of the 20th century, Wake Forest College was a respected academic training ground for Baptist ministers, academics, and educators, and its faculty members were busy developing the freshly created schools of law and medicine.

As an intellectual enclave surrounded by rural farmland, the college community was far from ordinary. The professors lent the town a glow of academic achievement, and the names of its leading families, often connected by marriage, remain prominent. These include Wait, Wingate, Brewer, Poteat, Lanneau, Powell, Royall, Holding, and Mills. Meanwhile, the prevailing climate of intellectual curiosity produced exceptional results. Wake Forest College cultivated an atmosphere in which young men and women were expected to think critically about social issues, and the town of Wake Forest and its college were completely synonymous—considered by all to be one and the same.

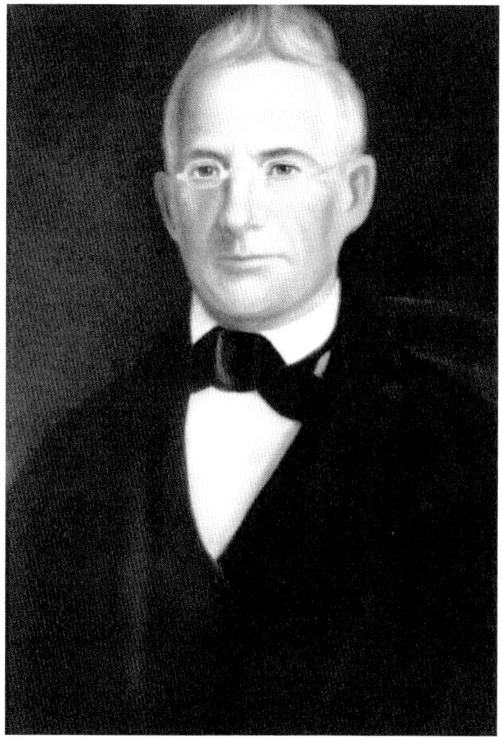

Samuel Wait

When Wake Forest Institute opened on February 3, 1834, Samuel Wait was its first president. Along with the expected farm labor, he accepted as tuition items such as flour, butter, beef, soap, and feathers—all handwritten beside each of the original 16 pupils' names in the official student account book. A Baptist minister from upstate New York, Wait shaped the school's vision, curriculum, and mission.

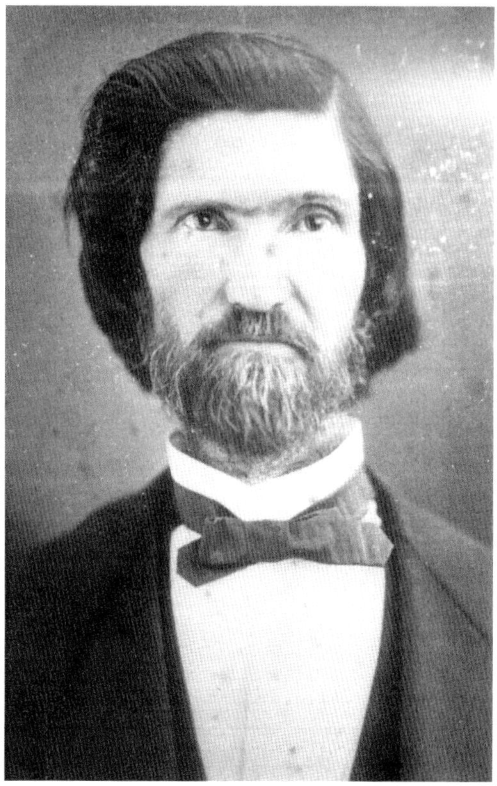

Washington Manley Wingate

The president of Wake Forest College before and after the Civil War, Washington Manley Wingate saw the college temporarily close, its buildings turned into a hospital for wounded soldiers, and much of its savings invested in Confederate bonds. When the war ended, Wingate brilliantly dispatched James Purefoy to raise money up North. He expanded the campus and hired more professors. One biographer wrote, "He was so bright and cheerful and lovable."

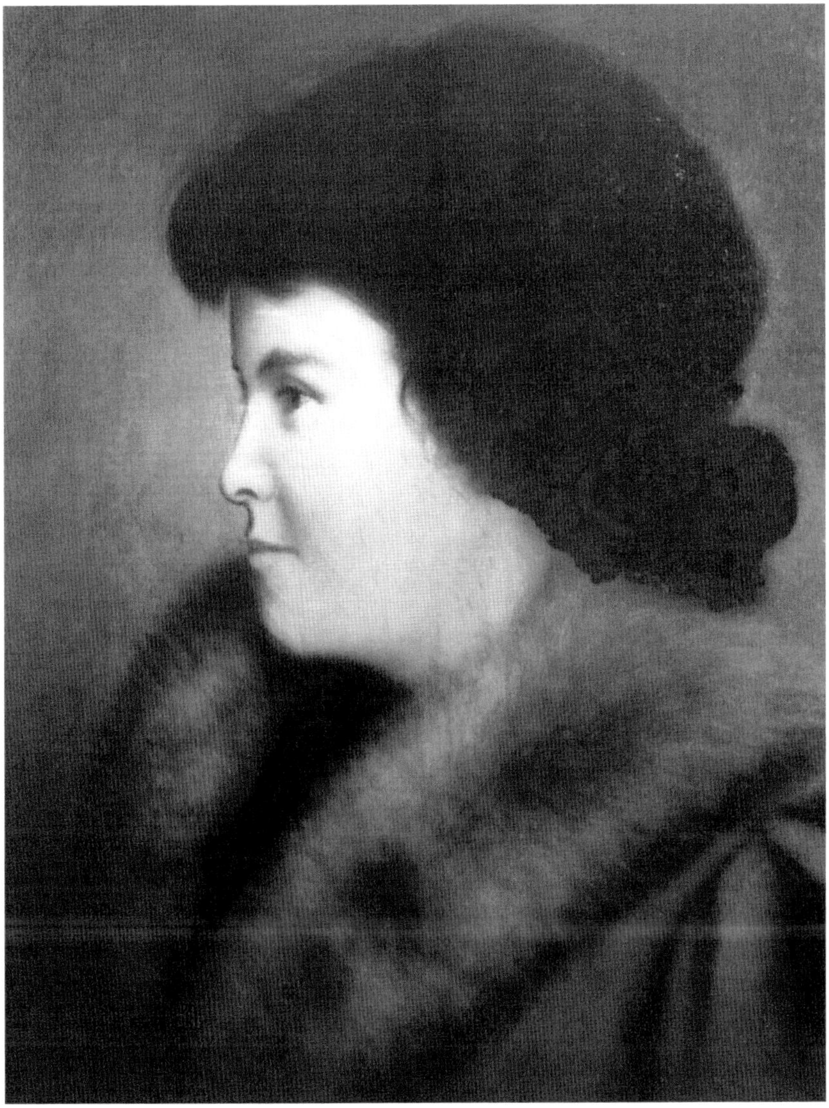

Evabelle Simmons
As a daughter of faculty member William G. Simmons, Evabelle Simmons was allowed to enroll with her brother Henry at Wake Forest College in 1883. She was a girl of 14, and she stuck close to Henry during their classes on campus. Simmons was an outstanding student and participated in the life of the college. She contributed anonymous poetry to the *Student* magazine and was the first female member of the Philomathesian Literary Society. In recognition of her achievements, the board of trustees even passed a resolution making her the sole exception to a rule forbidding females from participating in class recitations. However, when she completed her course work in 1888, Simmons was initially denied a diploma. Following a campaign by fellow students and faculty members, the trustees again relented, passing a resolution that read, "On the recommendation of the faculty the degree of B.A. is conferred upon Miss Evabelle Simmons." After graduation, Simmons taught school in Wake County and at a female seminary in Alabama until her untimely death in 1898. Her body was returned home and buried in the Wake Forest Cemetery, and she will always be remembered for blazing a trail of equality at Wake Forest College.

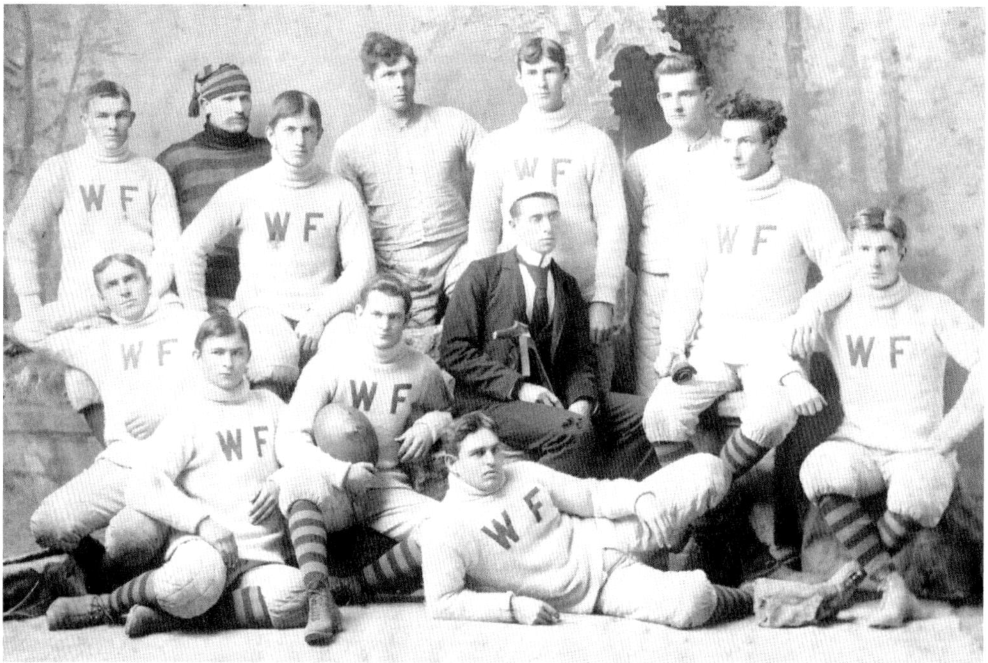

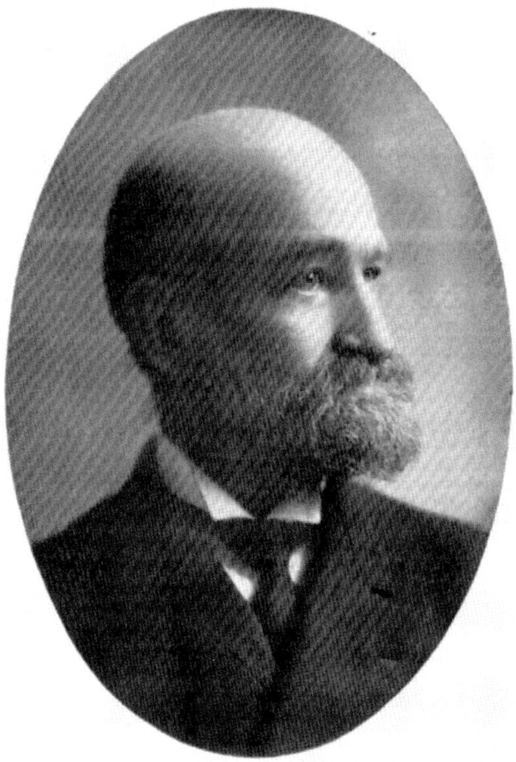

DR. CHARLES E. TAYLOR.

The First Wake Forest College Football Team

The first college football game played in North Carolina pitted Wake Forest against the University of North Carolina at the state fairgrounds in Raleigh. Wake Forest won by a score of 3-2. The date was October 18, 1888, and team members included William Dowd, Enoch Sikes, and James McDaniel. To overturn a later ban on the sport, Herbert Peele, editor of the *Student*, wrote, "Why should Wake Forest students be . . . held back from a sport that is manly and clean?"

Charles Taylor

A former Confederate spy, Charles Taylor arrived at Wake Forest College in 1870 to teach Latin and German. He soon became an ordained minister, frequently preaching at Wake Forest Baptist Church and for surrounding congregations. Becoming college president in 1884, Taylor tripled the school's $100,000 endowment, grew the curriculum, established the Schools of Law and Medicine, erected new buildings, landscaped the grounds, and more than doubled student enrollment.

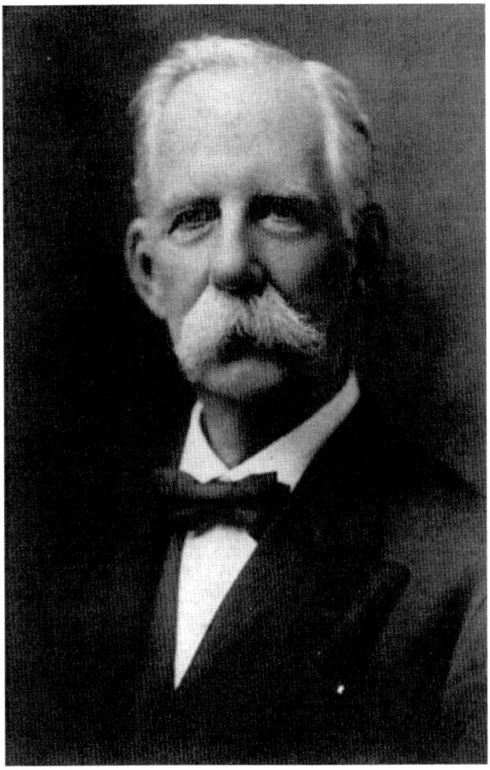

John Francis Lanneau

John Francis Lanneau was an instructor in physics, applied mathematics, and astronomy. He joined the Wake Forest College faculty in 1890. Lanneau's outstanding contribution as a scholar was in the field of astronomy, authoring articles published in various periodicals. It was through his influence that a telescope was made to order and mounted in the observatory on top of Lea Laboratory, where students took measurements still used by NASA today.

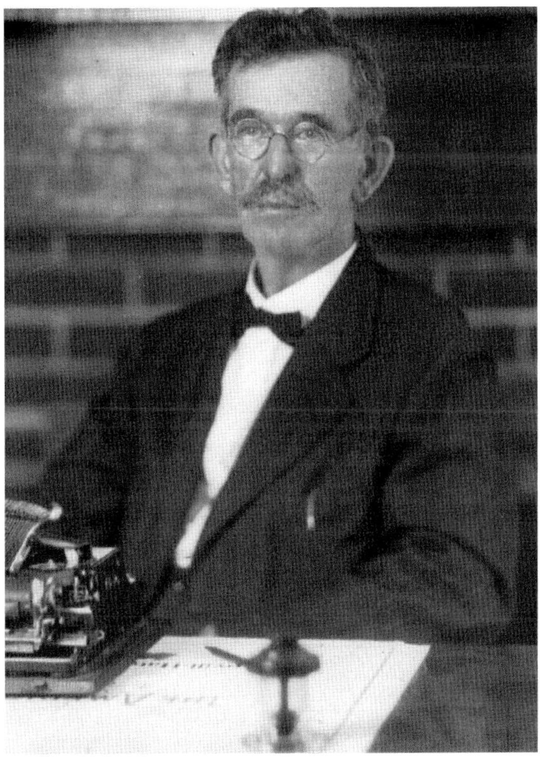

James Edgar Johnson

Born four years after the Civil War, James Edgar Johnson was one of the first students to receive a law degree from Wake Forest College. Eventually becoming a newspaperman, Johnson bought the *Mount Airy News* in 1904 to "help in the moral, intellectual and material development of our part of the state." His family owned and operated the paper for 70 years.

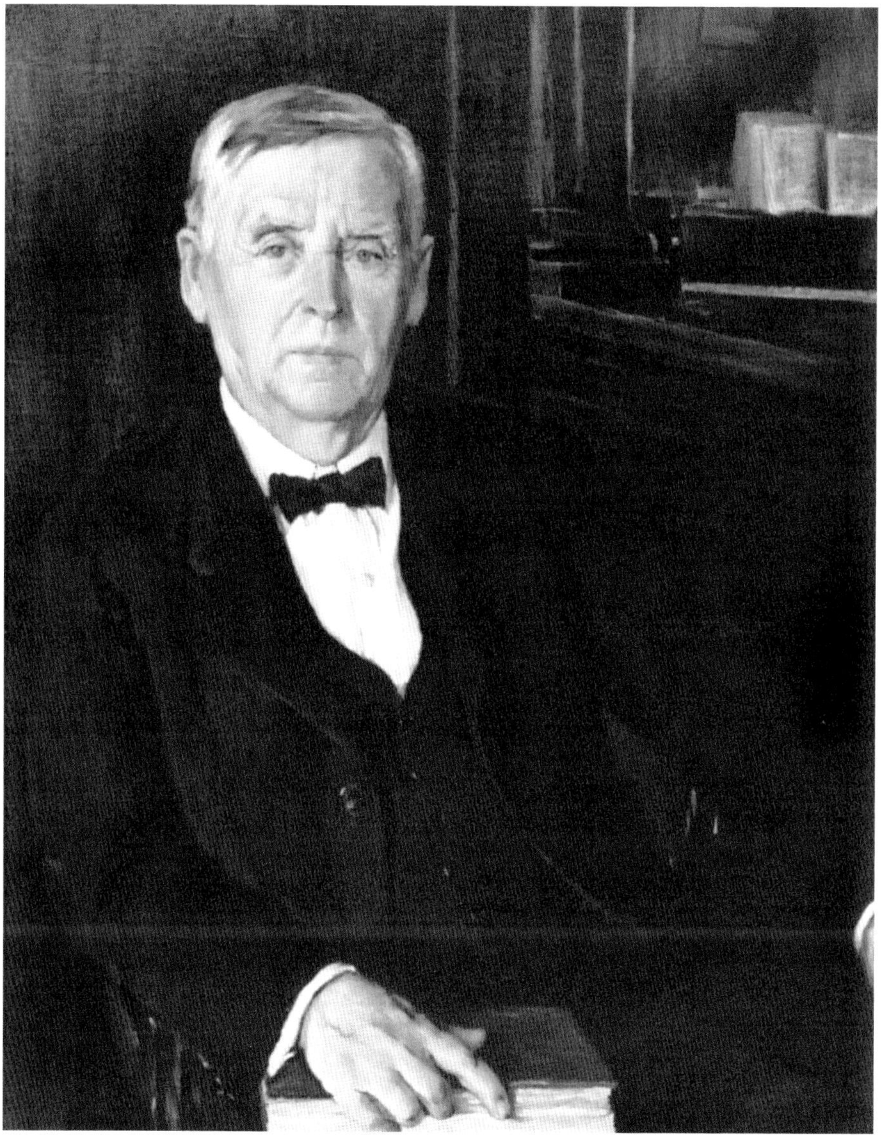

George Washington Paschal

A noted scholar and the town's official historian, George Washington Paschal was born in Chatham County in 1869. He had a twin brother, Robert Lee, and legend has it the boys were so identical the family could only tell them apart by tying a red ribbon around George Washington's neck. Graduating from Wake Forest College in 1892, he was ranked second in his class and quickly went on to earn a PhD in Greek from Chicago University before returning to Wake Forest as a professor. A biographical article written about Paschal in 1939 remarked, "Somehow Wake Forest holds men all their lives." In his case, this was certainly true. Paschal remained in town the rest of his life, dedicating himself to the community and writing Wake Forest's definitive history—a full three volumes—published between 1934 and 1943. Paschal loved town and college equally, and remained active in both until 1950, when he broke his hip while hurrying home from a Wake Forest baseball game to hear a news program on the radio. He died at age 86 in 1956, just one month after his beloved college left for Winston-Salem. Paschal Golf Course bears his name.

The Demon Deacon

The Demon Deacon was invented in 1923. Students felt the previous nicknames for the college athletic teams—the *Baptists* or *Old Gold and Black*—did not convey quite the right character, dignity, menace, or humor. It was sportswriter Mayon Parker who first described the school's football players as "Demon Deacons" while describing a matchup with Trinity College, later known as Duke University. Almost 20 years passed before the name evolved into a regular mascot thanks to a 1941 fraternity dare. That is when Jack Baldwin ('43) donned the top hat, coat, and cane and ran out onto the field to taunt the University of North Carolina. The Deacon soon became an institution, frolicking on fields, courts, and in the stands. This early caricature version, when the mascot was not yet a Deacon but known as "the Baptist," was drawn by Jack Beal, class of 1916. The cartoon appeared in the 1913 student yearbook.

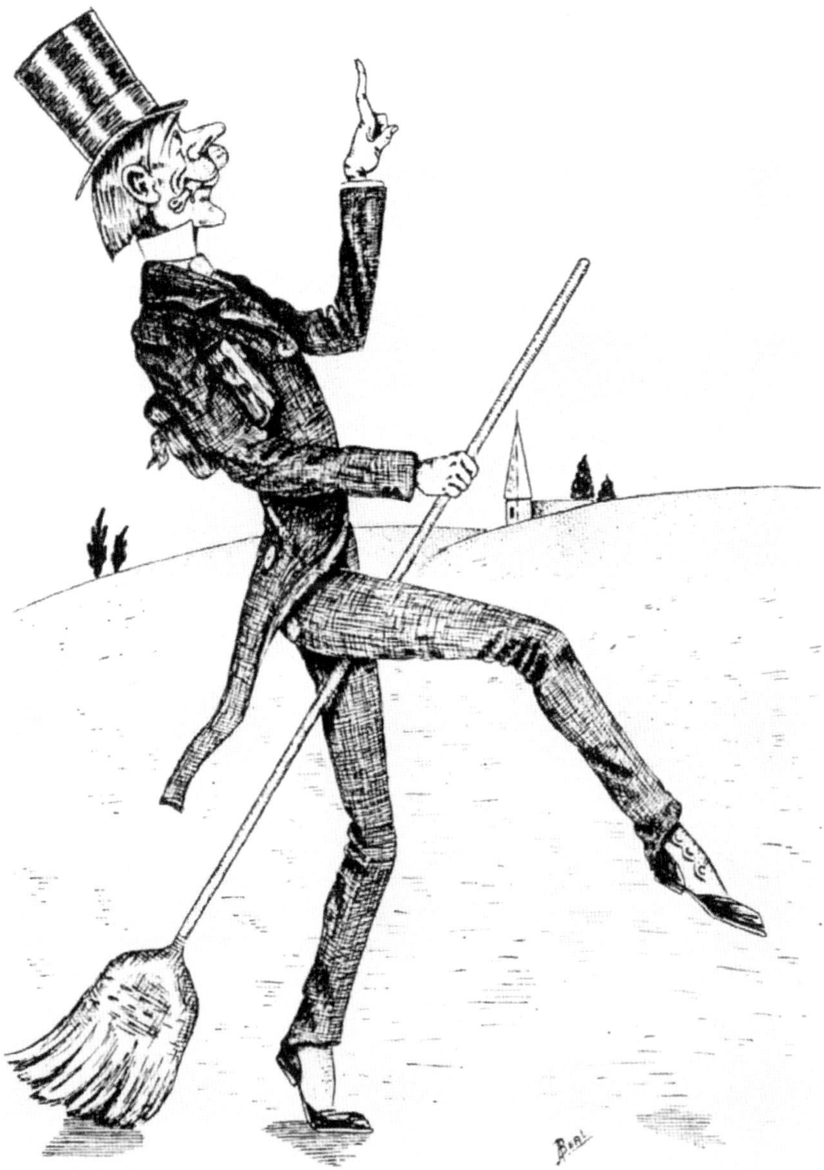

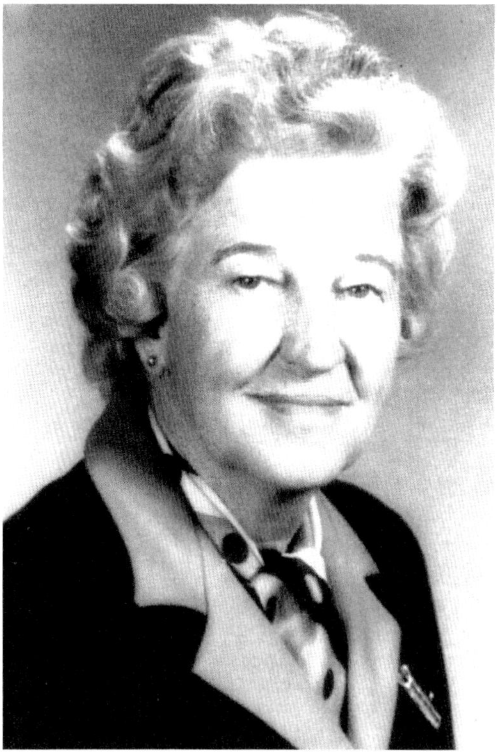

Marjorie Crisp

Wake Forest hired its first full-time female faculty member in 1947, an act that opened important doors for college athletes and women. Marjorie "Marge" Crisp established the school's physical education program, intramural sports program, and guided its entrance into women's intercollegiate athletics. A member of the Wake Forest University Sports Hall of Fame, Crisp also received the Appalachian State University Distinguished Alumni Award in 1979.

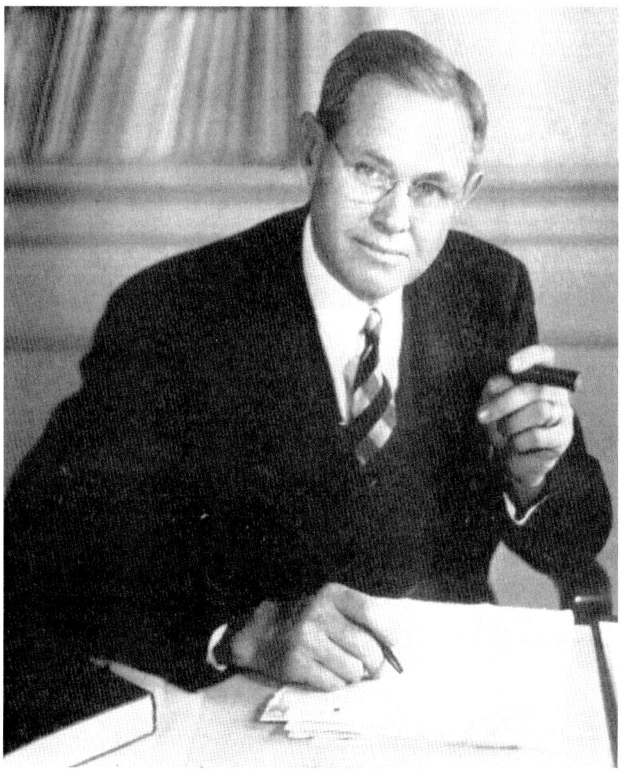

Daniel B. Bryan

For more than three decades, Daniel B. Bryan served as dean of Wake Forest College, guiding the academic careers of thousands of students. He resolved conflicts, provided counseling, and recommended admitting women to the college beginning in 1942. A $50 tuition scholarship from Bryan allowed Dr. William Friday—future leader of North Carolina's state university system and guiding hand in the regulation of intercollegiate athletics—to become the first in his family to attend college.

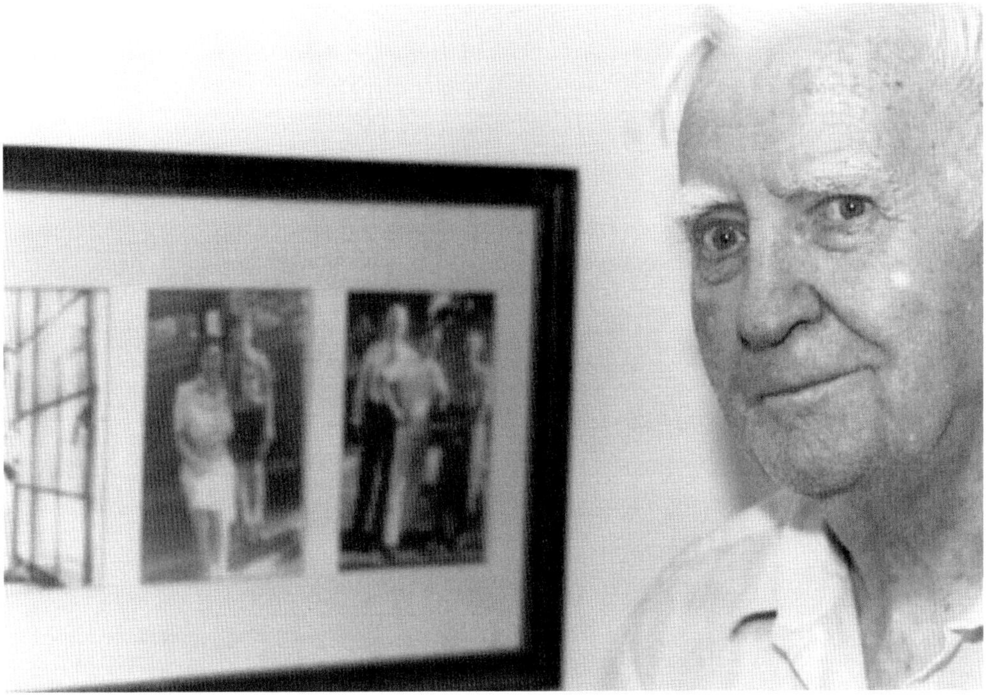

Jasper Memory
Jasper Memory graduated from Wake Forest College in 1921 and returned as a professor in 1929. He taught education for 42 years, served as a college fundraiser, editor of the alumni magazine, director of the news bureau, and even helped establish the school's first tennis team. Memory once said, "Yes, I've done a lot of different things for Wake Forest. I liked doing them." (Courtesy of the *Wake Weekly*.)

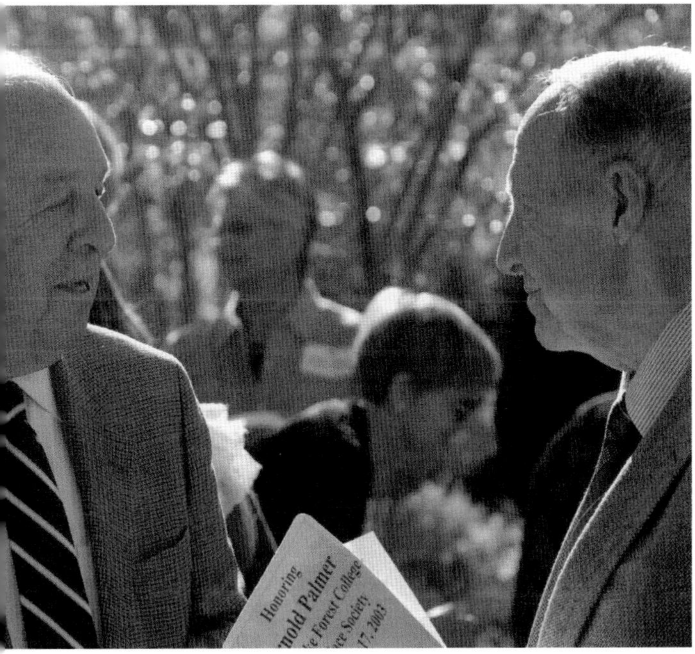

Edwin G. Wilson and I. Beverly Lake Jr.
Edwin G. Wilson enrolled at Wake Forest College in 1939, returned to teach in 1946, and moved to Winston-Salem in 1956. Known as "Mr. Wake Forest," Wilson has served as university provost and is now provost emeritus. I. Beverly Lake Jr. grew up in Wake Forest, graduated from the college, served as chief justice of the North Carolina Supreme Court, and established the NC Actual Innocence Commission to investigate wrongful criminal convictions across the state.

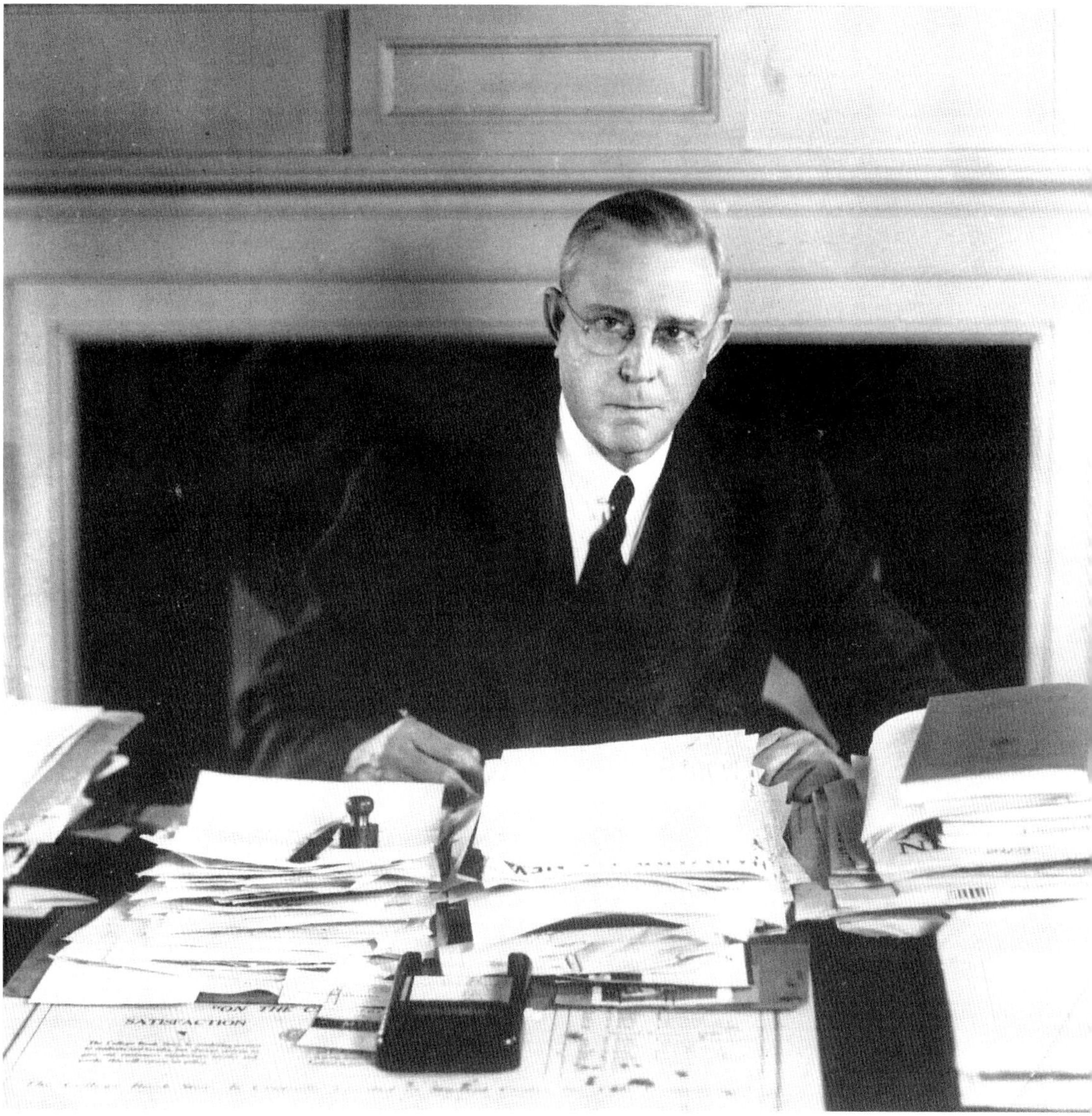

Thurman Kitchin

The only local ever to become president of Wake Forest College, Thurman Kitchin was born and raised in town. He went on to graduate from Wake Forest College and eventually to helm its medical school. Kitchin was a successful doctor when he was offered the office of president in 1930; he gave up a thriving medical practice to accept the position. Unfortunately, his first years leading the college were among the most difficult in its history. Not only was the dreadful austerity of the Great Depression shaking the campus and broader community, but in the mid-1930s, an unidentified arsonist unleashed a terrifying string of fires across Wake Forest. Although no one was ever injured in these mysterious blazes, two vital campus buildings and many other important structures all over town were destroyed. The criminal was never apprehended. Kitchin's term in office lasted 20 years, extending beyond those early hardships to include a period of rapid growth in finances, enrollment, and construction for Wake Forest College, along with the beginning planning stages of its move to Winston-Salem following a promise of millions of dollars and acres of land from the family of tobacco giant R.J. Reynolds.

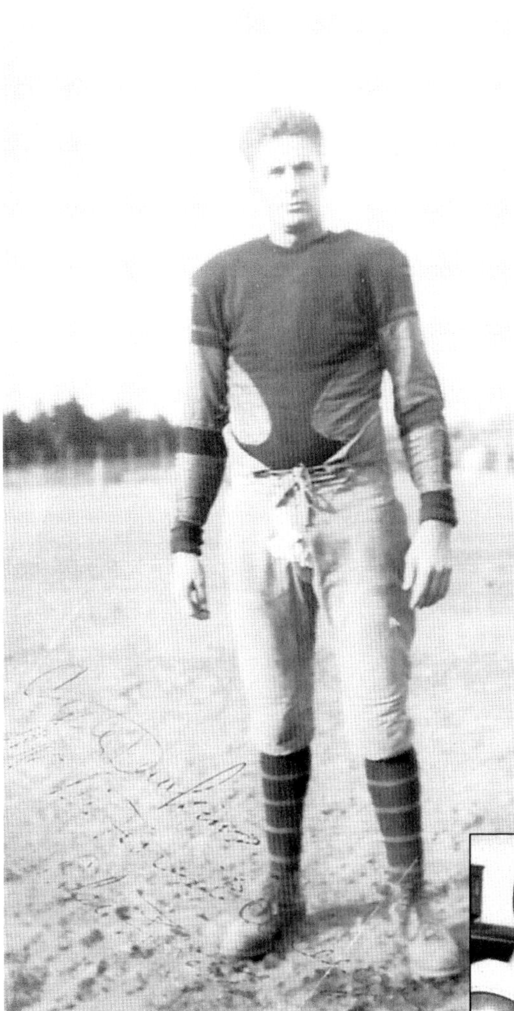

Clyde Dawkins

Clyde Dawkins played football at Wake Forest College in the 1920s, and he gave his black and gold Wake Forest College scarf to his first love, a girl named Gladys. Although they eventually parted ways, Gladys always remembered Dawkins. Many decades later, when she passed away, her son found the scarf among her belongings and donated it, along with this photograph, to the Wake Forest Historical Museum.

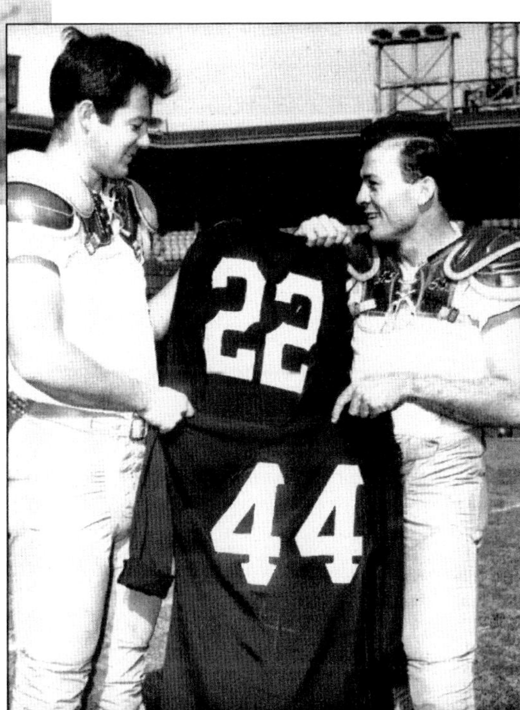

Harry Dowda

A World War II paratrooper with the 82nd and 101st Airborne Divisions, Harry Dowda (left) made two jumps into the Battle of the Bulge. He attended Wake Forest College on a football scholarship, and one of his finest athletic moments was defeating top-ranked University of Tennessee in 1946. Dowda married Marable Patterson (see page 31) and played for the Washington Redskins and Philadelphia Eagles. Here, he is exchanging jerseys with legendary University of North Carolina tailback Charlie "Choo Choo" Justice.

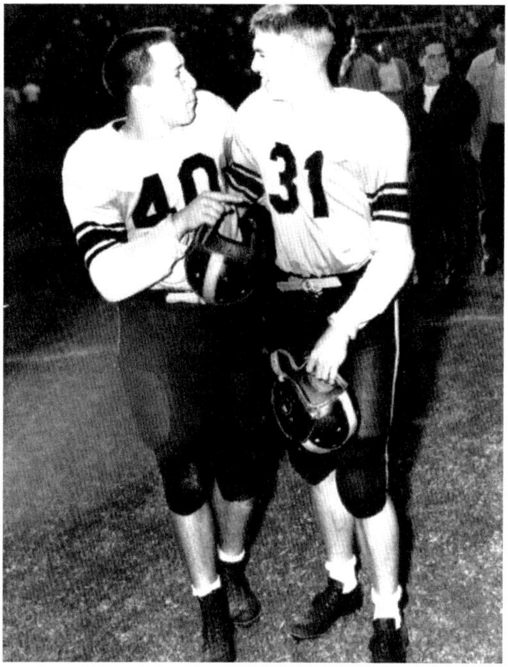

Dickie Davis

A skinny six-footer, weighing just 138-pounds, Davis arrived at Wake Forest College in 1948 and went on to distinguish himself on the gridiron, starting as a quarterback and punter on the freshman team. Davis led his team to the mythical "Big Four" title in 1950 and 1951, and he was inducted into the Wake Forest University Sports Hall of Fame in 2003. He is pictured here (at right) with teammate Ed Kissen.

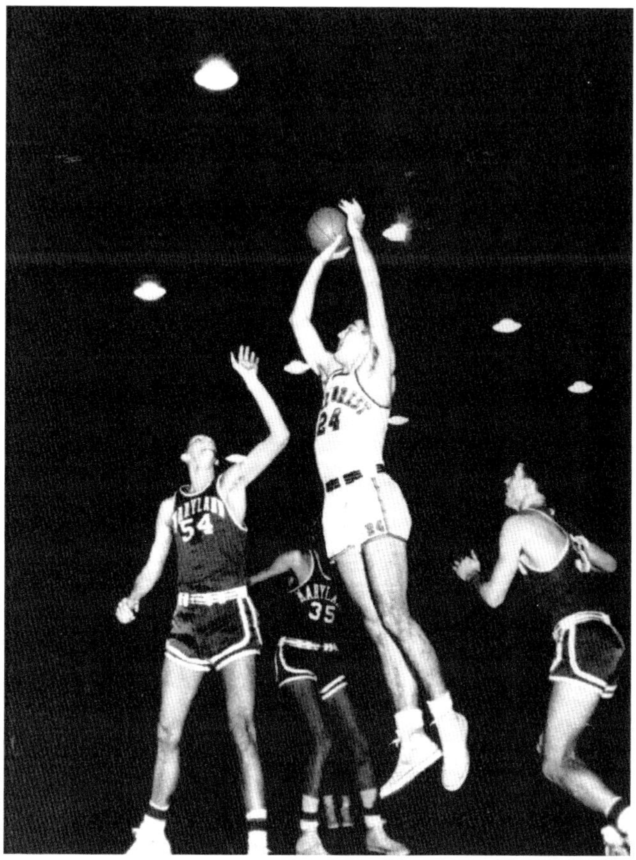

Dickie Hemric

One of the most dominating players in Wake Forest and Atlantic Coast Conference history, Dickie Hemric led the Deacons from 1952 to 1955 and held the record as all-time leading scorer for 50 years. One of the few college players to score more than 2,000 points and grab more than 1,000 rebounds, he played two seasons for the Boston Celtics.

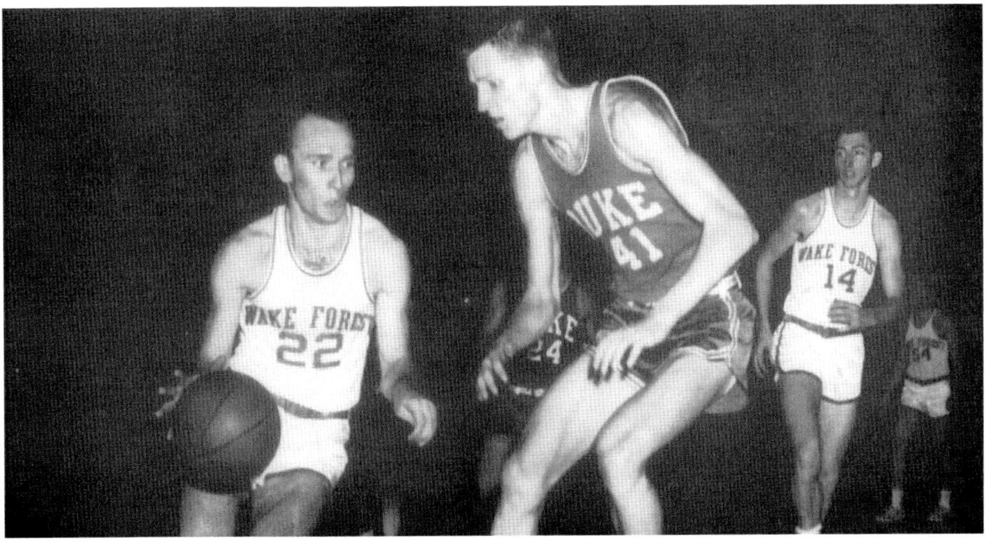

Marshall Winston "Twig" Wiggins

"Athletics teach if you work hard, you can succeed," said "Twig" Wiggins (No. 14), whose freshman-year failure to make the Youngsville High School basketball team led to years of intense practice that ended with a pair of full scholarship offers from Wake Forest College and North Carolina State University. Wiggins played for coach Bones McKinney and went on to a career in coaching, business, and support of youth recreation programs.

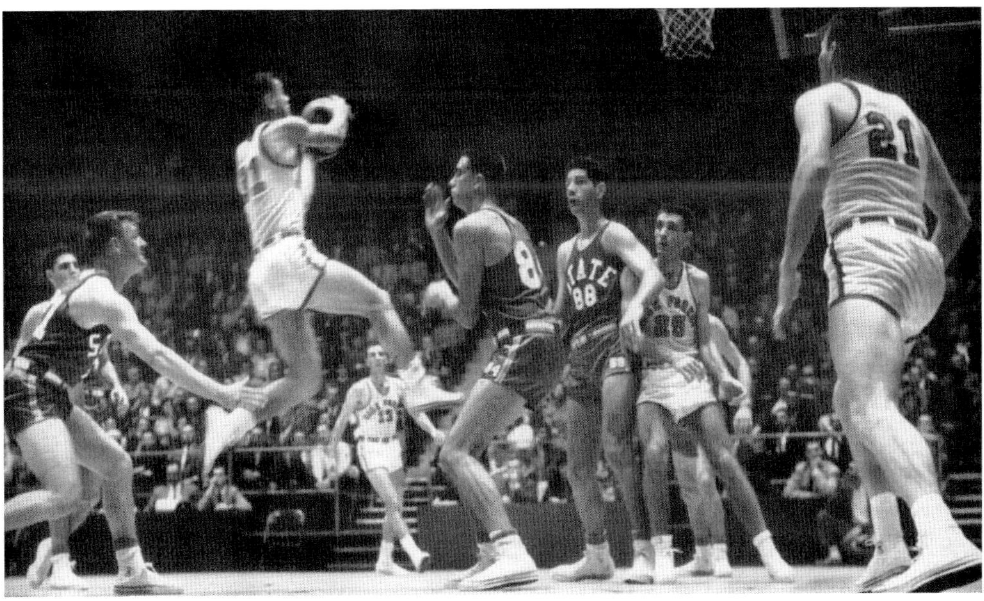

Jack Murdock

A member of the Wake Forest University Hall of Fame, Jack Murdock grew up in Raleigh and played basketball for Wake Forest College during its transition to Winston-Salem. A 5-foot-10-inch guard, Murdock (shown high above the hardwood) averaged 85 percent of free throws and once converted an ACC-record 39 straight, finishing his college career with 1,239 points. Murdock briefly coached at WFC before accepting a position with the North Carolina Department of Transportation.

Sara Page Jackson Lewis

This high-stepping strutter made a magnificent splash in the 1950s as Wake Forest College's head majorette. When *Holiday* magazine published a story about the school's marching band, the editor showcased Sara Page Jackson Lewis in a huge layout. Not surprisingly, she instantly became a nationwide sensation. Invitations to perform at a wide variety of far-flung conventions and athletic events began flooding into the college, with every request specifying, "Please be sure your head majorette accompanies the group." Lewis's biggest moment arrived when she led the band down Fifth Avenue in New York City as part of the International Lion's Convention, winning third-place musical honors in a competition that included groups from around the globe.

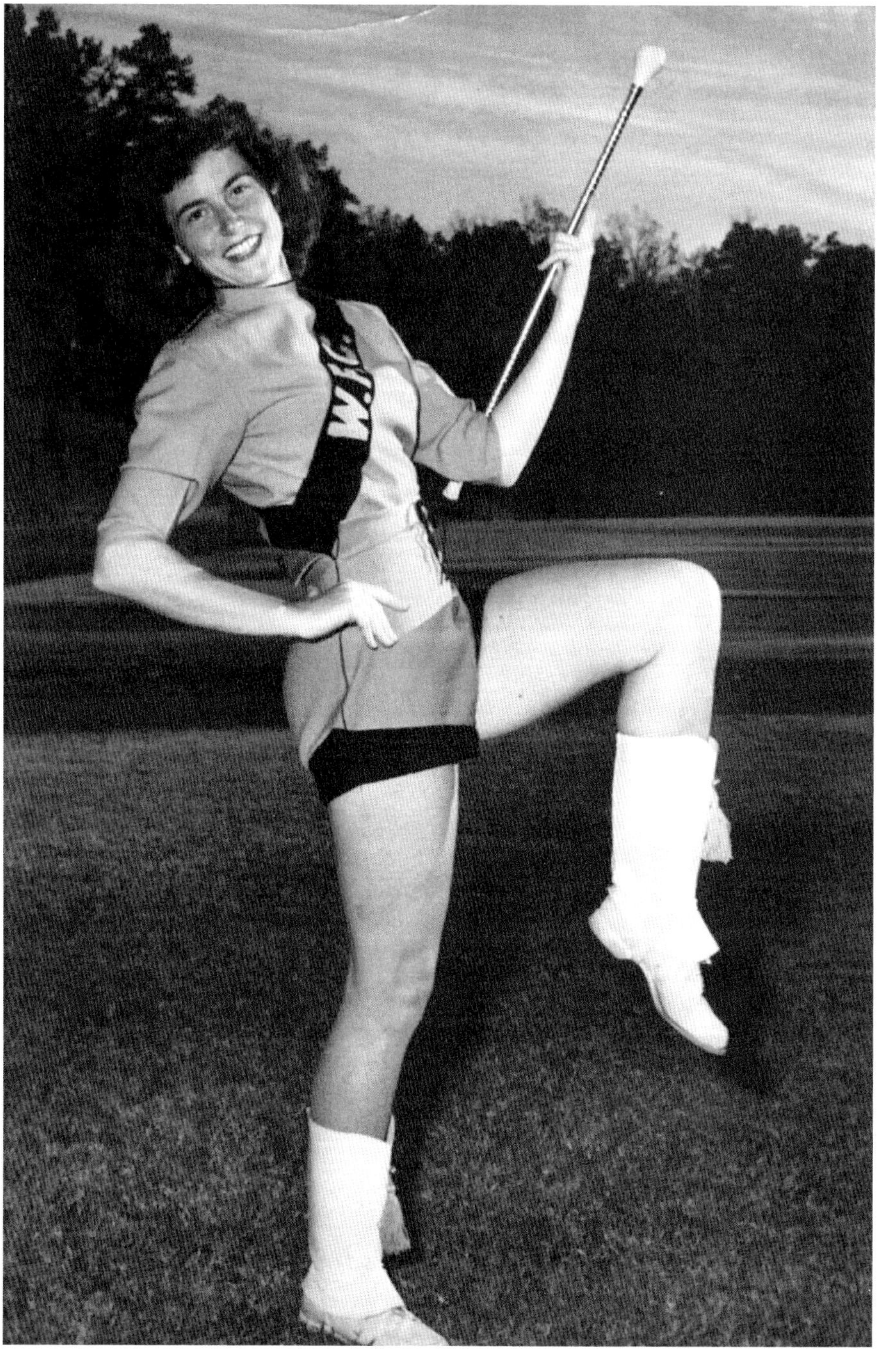

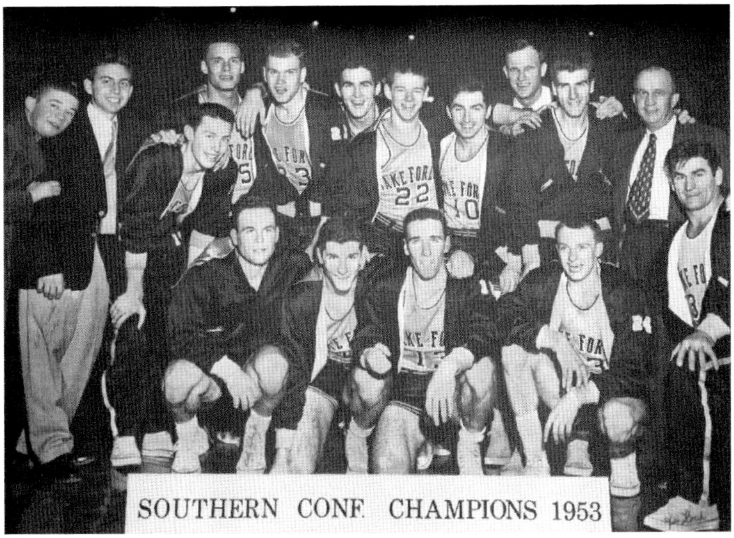

Southern Conference Champions, 1953
The Southern Conference had 17 colleges in 1953—the last year before the formation of the Atlantic Coast Conference—and the top eight teams qualified for that year's tournament. North Carolina State University was nationally ranked and heavily favored to win its seventh straight title. But Wake Forest College defeated the Wolfpack in a thrilling 71-70 victory, capturing its first basketball championship in conference history.

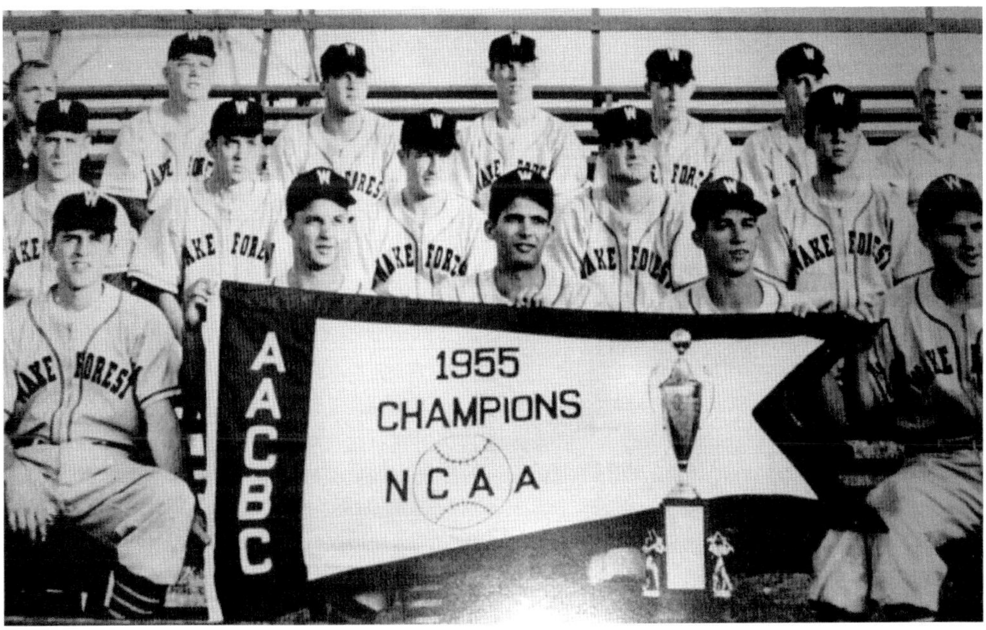

The 1955 National Championship Baseball Team
Wake Forest College won the National Championship in 1955 after defeating Western Michigan 7-6 in the title game. Although the athletes took some heat for playing on Sunday, coach Taylor Sanford was voted national coach of the year, and catcher Linwood Holt was named All-American. To date, they are the only ACC baseball team to win the NCAA College Championship.

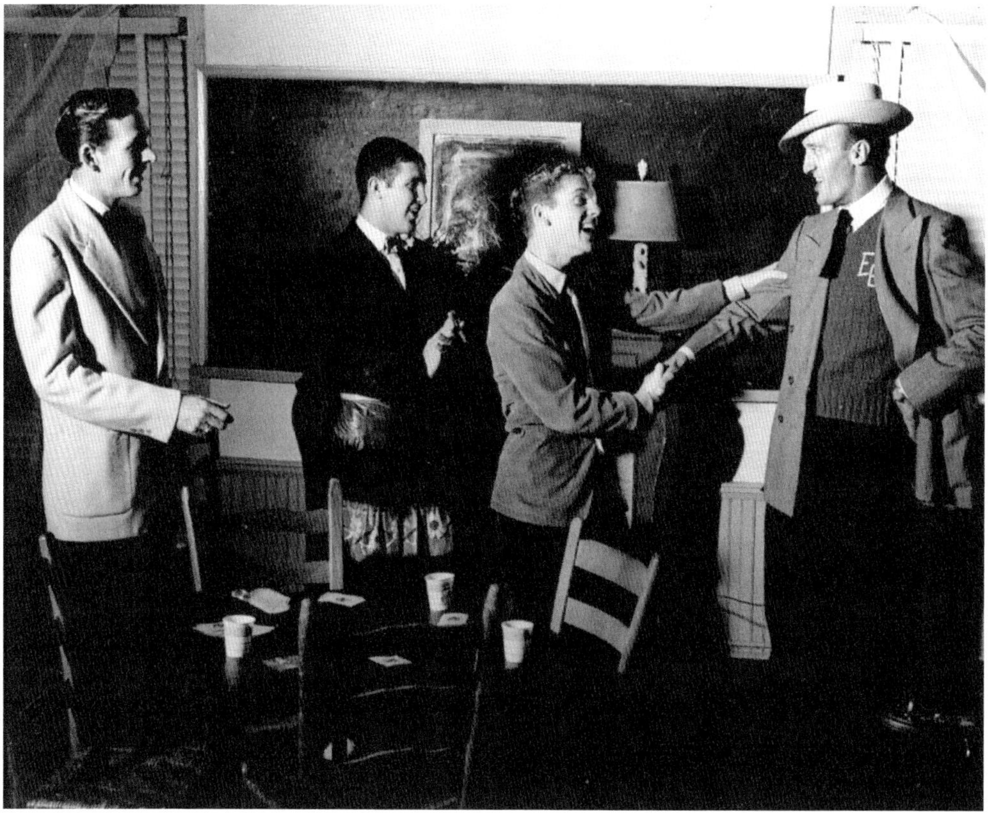

W.E. "Doc" Murphrey

W.E. "Doc" Murphrey, of Roanoke Rapids, North Carolina, was Wake Forest College's Herculean hollerer at all sports events for several decades. With no official title or approval, Murphrey donned his hat and cane to begin trash talking and cheering from the stands way back in the 1950s. A great humorist, Murphrey reported that he had donated his body to the Wake Forest University School of Medicine so he could stay there even after death. He is shown above (second from right) in a 1951 student play and at right in his older years.

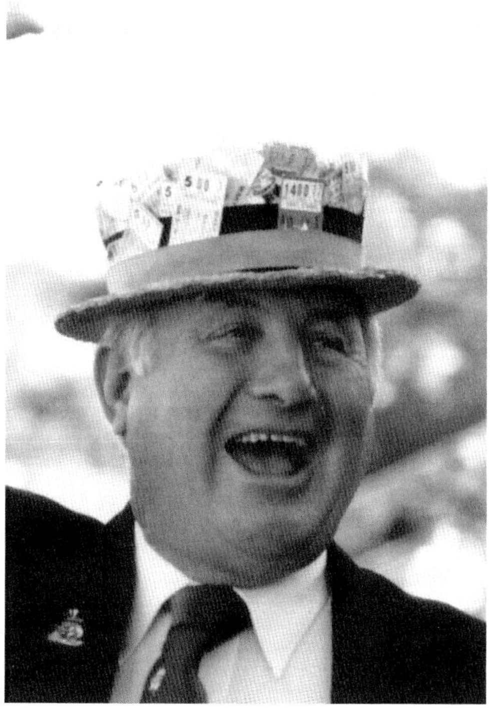

CHAPTER FOUR

Teachers, Mentors, Coaches, and Ministers

It only makes sense that a community founded on religious and academic achievement would have more than the usual number of extraordinary instructors. From preaching in the pulpit to coaching on the sidelines, many of Wake Forest's most memorable citizens have been the teachers, mentors, coaches, and ministers who provided the guidance and wisdom that have traditionally made Wake Forest a strong, moral, and intelligent community.

But a good number of these beloved authority figures could also be called "characters." For instance, there was basketball's Bones McKinney, whose courtside rants and compulsive cursing were nearly as impressive as his coaching. Quirky Benjamin Sledd was known to generations of Wake Forest College students as "Slick," and high school teacher Catherine Lee was infamous for insisting her biology students copy and memorize a blackboard's worth of fresh notes each and every day.

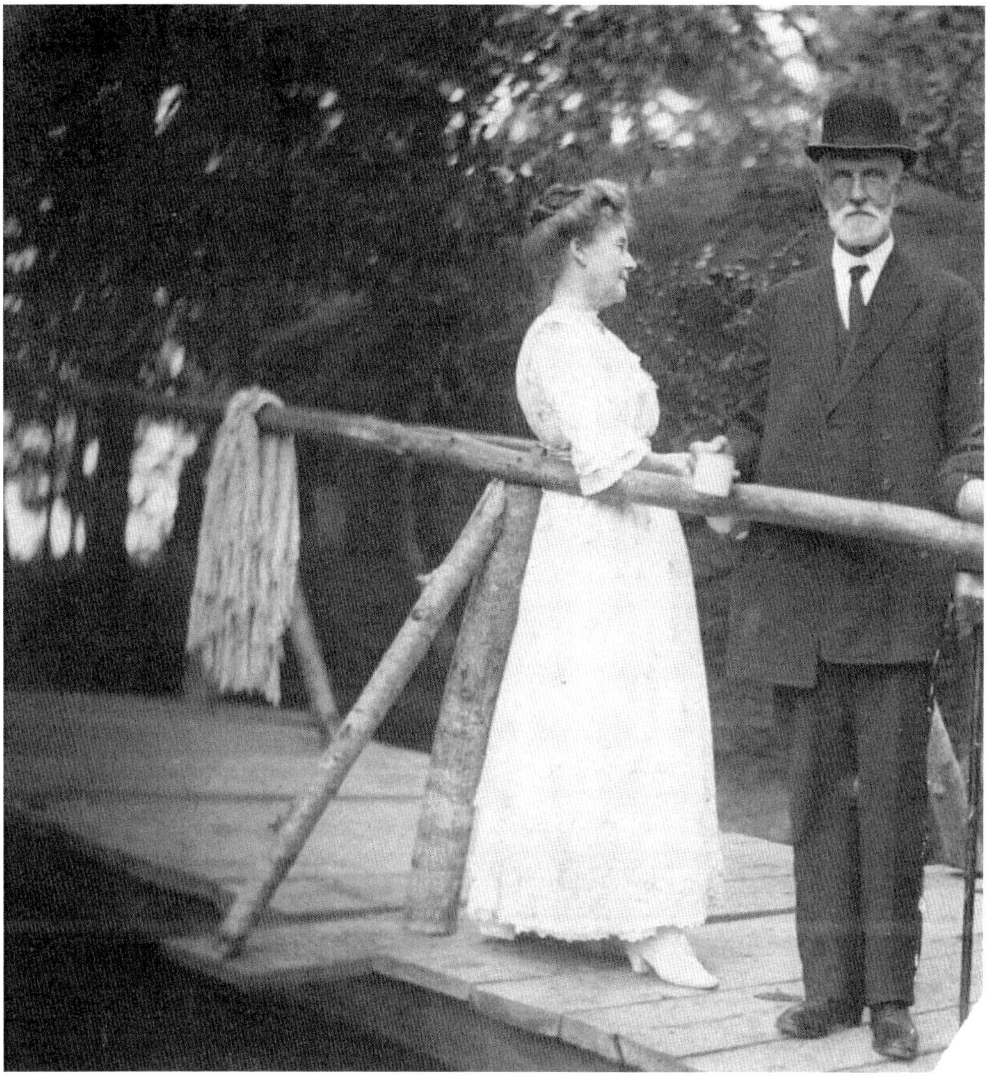

William Bailey Royall

A resident of Faculty Avenue, William Bailey Royall was among Wake Forest College's most notable instructors. His father had also been a Wake Forest College professor, and Royall graduated from the school at age 17 in the spring of 1861, joining his classmate Thomas Toon (see page 99) and a few other new graduates who immediately joined up to fight the Civil War. Royall served as commissary sergeant with the 55th North Carolina Regiment and, after the South's surrender, returned to Wake Forest to begin his career as a teacher of Greek. He was only 21 years old, and he would continue to teach for 60 years. To this day, Royall remains the longest-serving faculty member in the history of Wake Forest University. Described as a man of dignity and grace combined with scholarship, culture, and intelligence, he died at age 83 following a two-year illness that stole his strength and sight and left him bedridden. His colleagues were utterly destroyed by his death. WFC president William Louis Poteat was quoted as saying, "Dr. Royall was light. Its beauty was in his face; its gentleness was in his voice; its clearness was in his words." As a young man, Royall had established a church in the Harricane on the outskirts of town. He was a lifelong member of Wake Forest Baptist Church. In this photograph from the turn of the 20th century, he poses with his wife, Sarah Hall Royall. (Courtesy of Margaret McClure.)

Benjamin Sledd

English professor Benjamin Sledd was one of the most beloved and respected teachers in the history of Wake Forest College. He arrived in 1888, and his career spanned half a century. His students, some of whom became the country's leading journalists and literary figures, honored him with the nickname "Slick," in recognition of his prematurely balding pate and as a reflection of their fondness for his compassion and intelligence.

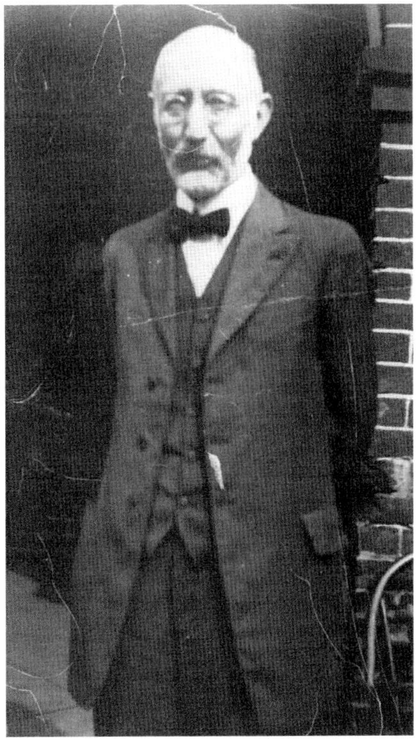

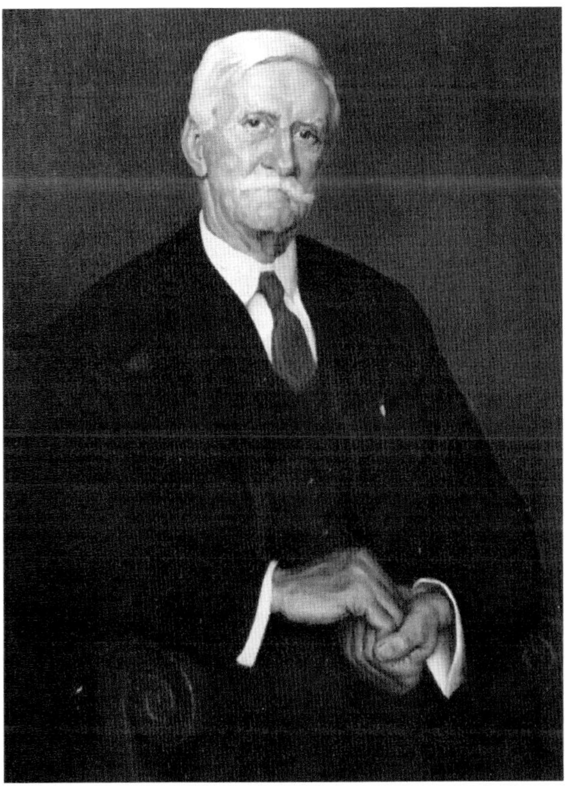

Needham Yancey Gulley

Needham Yancey Gulley's life was split evenly between the centuries. As a boy, he saw Sherman's troops march toward Raleigh. In 1894, he founded the Wake Forest College Department of Law. By 1931, he had taught approximately half of North Carolina's attorneys–including future governors, senators, congressmen, and state supreme court justices. Shortly before dying at 91, he said, "It's just too much trouble to live to be a hundred."

William Louis Poteat

Known across campus as "Dr. Billy," William Louis Poteat was arguably the school's most influential leader, beginning as a teacher and then serving as college president from 1905 to 1927. Poteat was a man of enormous contradictions and even greater intellect. A deeply committed Christian and biology professor, he believed in exposing students to scientific theories, including the teaching of evolution. He successfully worked to defeat an antievolution bill in the North Carolina State Legislature with the argument that "God was the creator but his method was evolutionary." As a leader, Poteat spoke out in favor of education, scientific progress, mental health care, improved prison facilities, stricter child-labor laws, and interracial cooperation. When he died at age 81 in 1938, famed essayist and social satirist H.L. Mencken reportedly wrote that Poteat had made North Carolina "the most intelligent" of all Southern states.

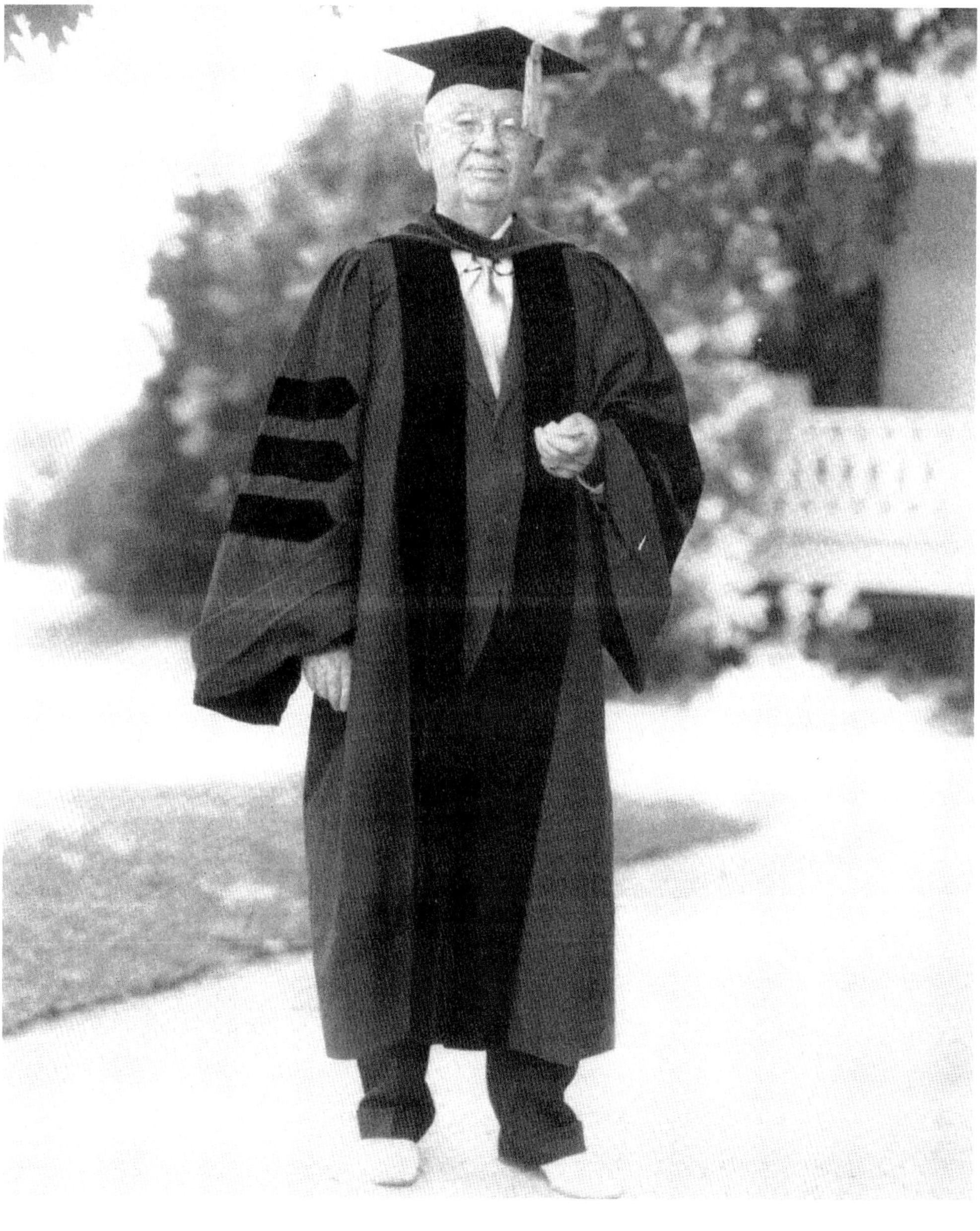

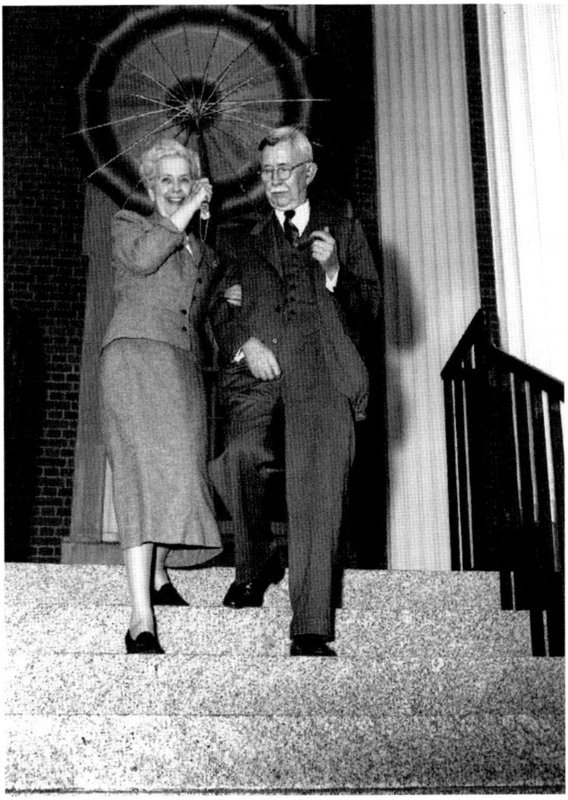

Lois Johnson

Lois Johnson made history in 1942 as Wake Forest College's first dean of women. During her 30-year tenure, she fashioned the standards and rules governing female students while witnessing a sevenfold increase in their enrollment. Johnson Dormitory at WFU honors her legendary leadership, kindness, and wit. She is pictured here with her brother Gerald Johnson, who graduated from WFC in 1911 and went on to an illustrious literary career.

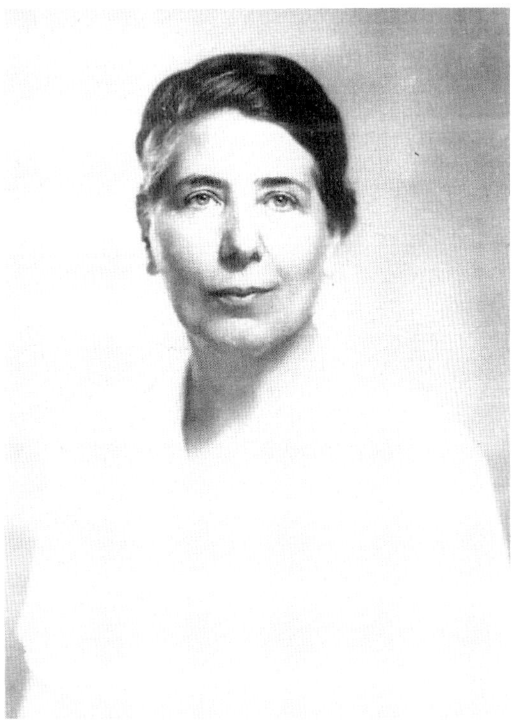

Sophie Stephens Lanneau

Sophie Stephens Lanneau moved to Wake Forest at age eight, graduated from Meredith College, and served as a Baptist educational missionary to China from 1907 to 1950, founding the Wei Ling Girl's Academy in Soochow. Interned by the Japanese in 1942 and repatriated to the United States, she returned to China in 1946. The Chinese Communists seized her school four years later, and she came home to Wake Forest to stay.

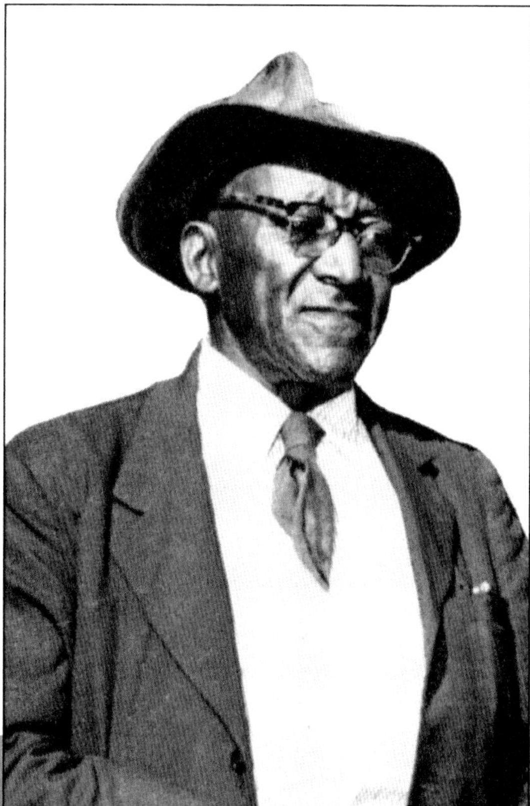

Allen Young

Allen Young was an educational visionary, running a private school for African American students from 1905 to 1957. Once considered the most important facility of its kind in Wake County, the Wake Forest Normal and Industrial School offered classes in Latin, French, and civil government. Young's intellect was widely recognized; as a young man, he was privately tutored by Wake Forest College professors.

Ailey Mae Young

Daughter of Allen Young, Ailey Mae Young was born in Wake Forest and became a noted teacher and community leader. She also made a lasting mark in local politics, paving the way for equal representation of women and minorities by becoming only the second woman and the first African American to serve on the Wake Forest Town Commission. This photograph was taken in 1974.

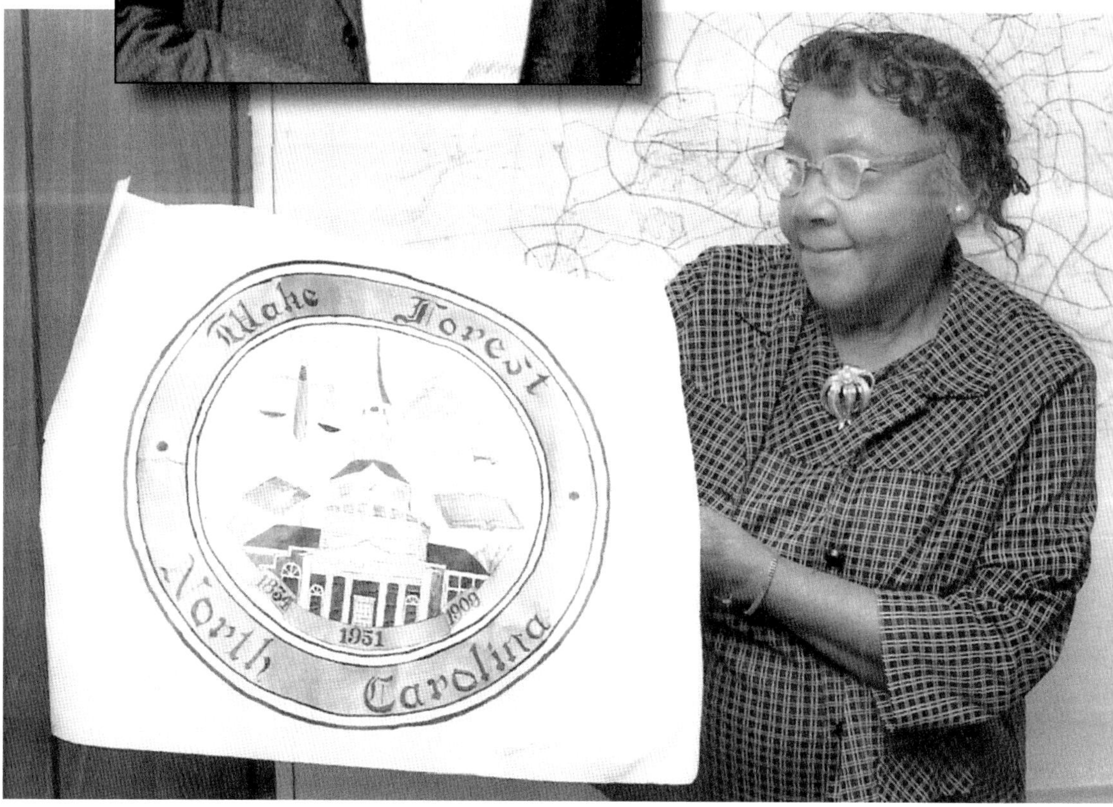

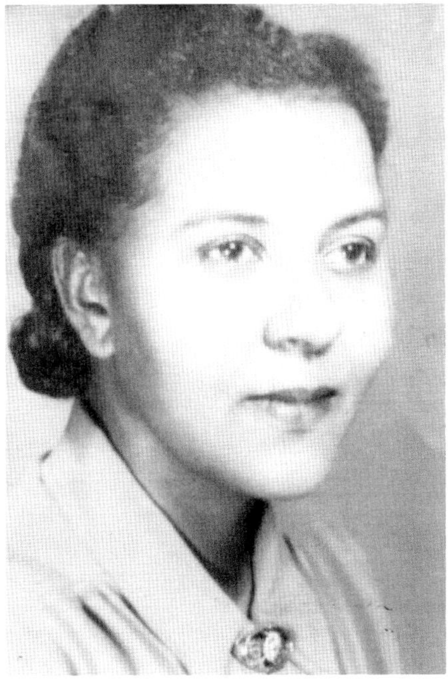

Doris Best

As home economics teacher at the DuBois School, Doris Best demonstrated household skills and points of etiquette: how to behave at a party, hold a cup of tea, and set a table. Born in Charleston, West Virginia, Best was first sent to school to become a maid. Administrators noticed her exceptional intelligence and transferred her to academic classes. She met her husband, Lincoln Robert Best, soon after graduation. (Courtesy of Eric Best.)

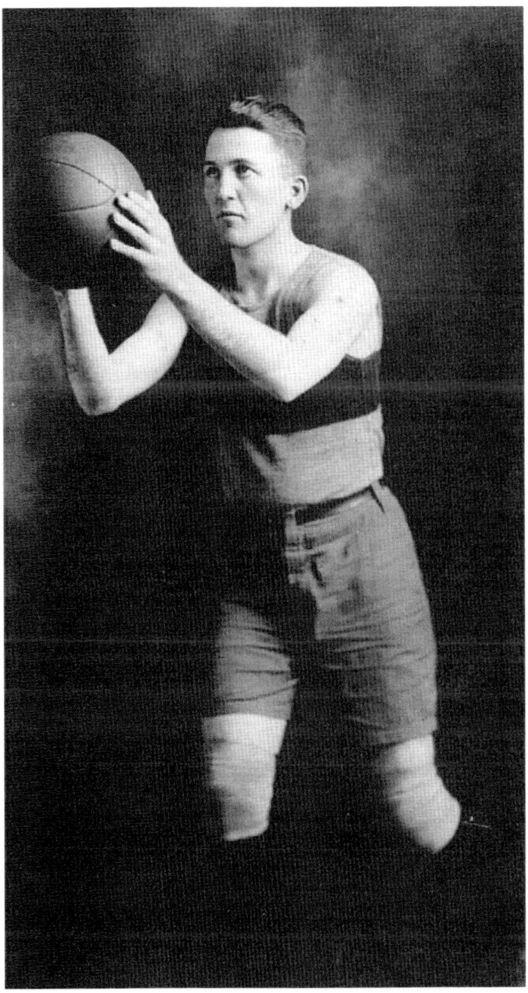

William W. Holding Jr.

Born in 1895 on Christmas Eve, William Willis Holding Jr. went on to become one of the greatest athletes in Wake Forest College history. Holding lettered in four sports, and after graduating in 1916, he spent a few years coaching the school's basketball and baseball teams. A veteran of World War I, he died in 1962 and is buried in the Wake Forest Cemetery.

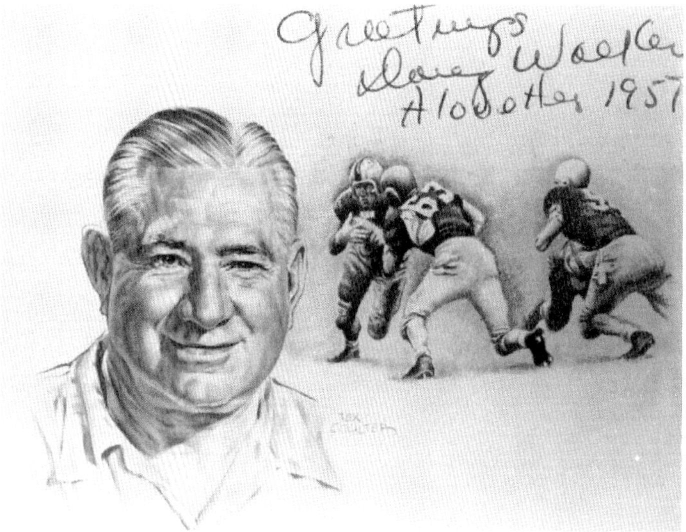

Douglas Clyde "Peahead" Walker

Douglas Clyde "Peahead" Walker left Wake Forest College almost against his will. Beginning in 1937, he coached the football team to a series of victorious seasons with a combination of brilliant recruiting, technique, and discipline, and he led WFC to the first ever Gator Bowl in 1946. But in 1950, amidst loud protests, Walker departed for Yale University after WFC president Harold Tribble refused him a $1,500 raise.

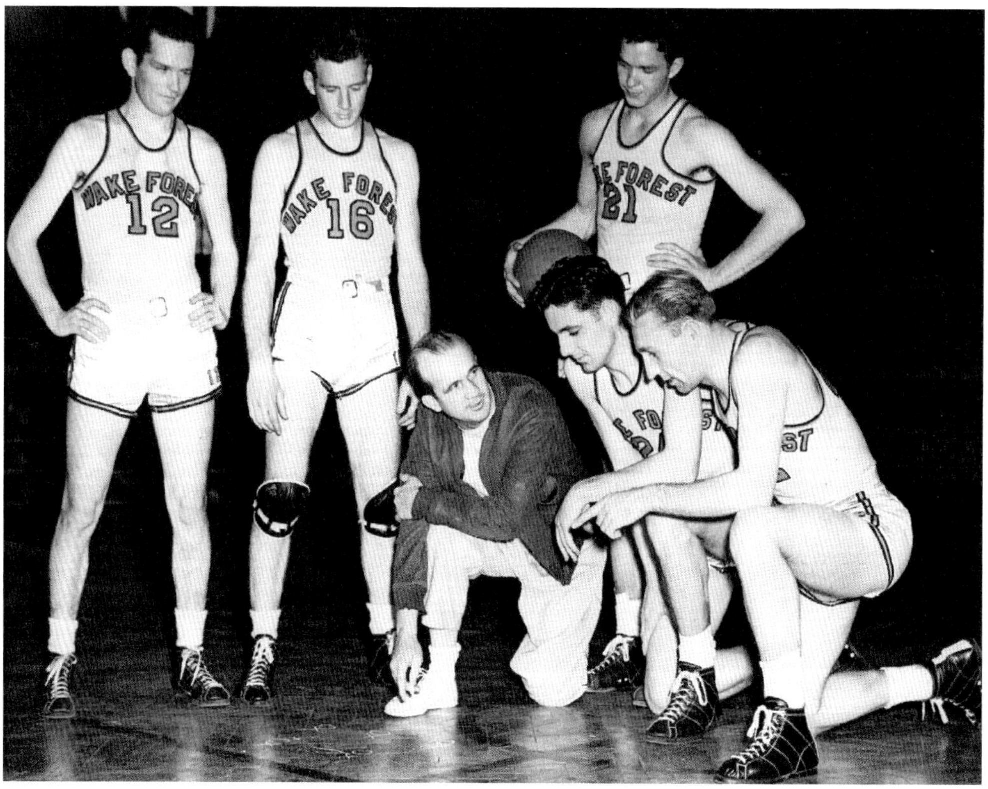

Murray Greason Sr.

People loved Murray Greason "for his ability to take defeat with the same grace that he enjoys victory." A Wake Forest College athlete in the 1920s, Greason coached the school's basketball team from 1933 to 1957. Named Southern Conference Coach of the Year in 1953, he led WFC into the newly formed Atlantic Coast Conference in 1954 and was ACC Coach of the Year in 1956. Greason was killed in a car accident on January 1, 1960.

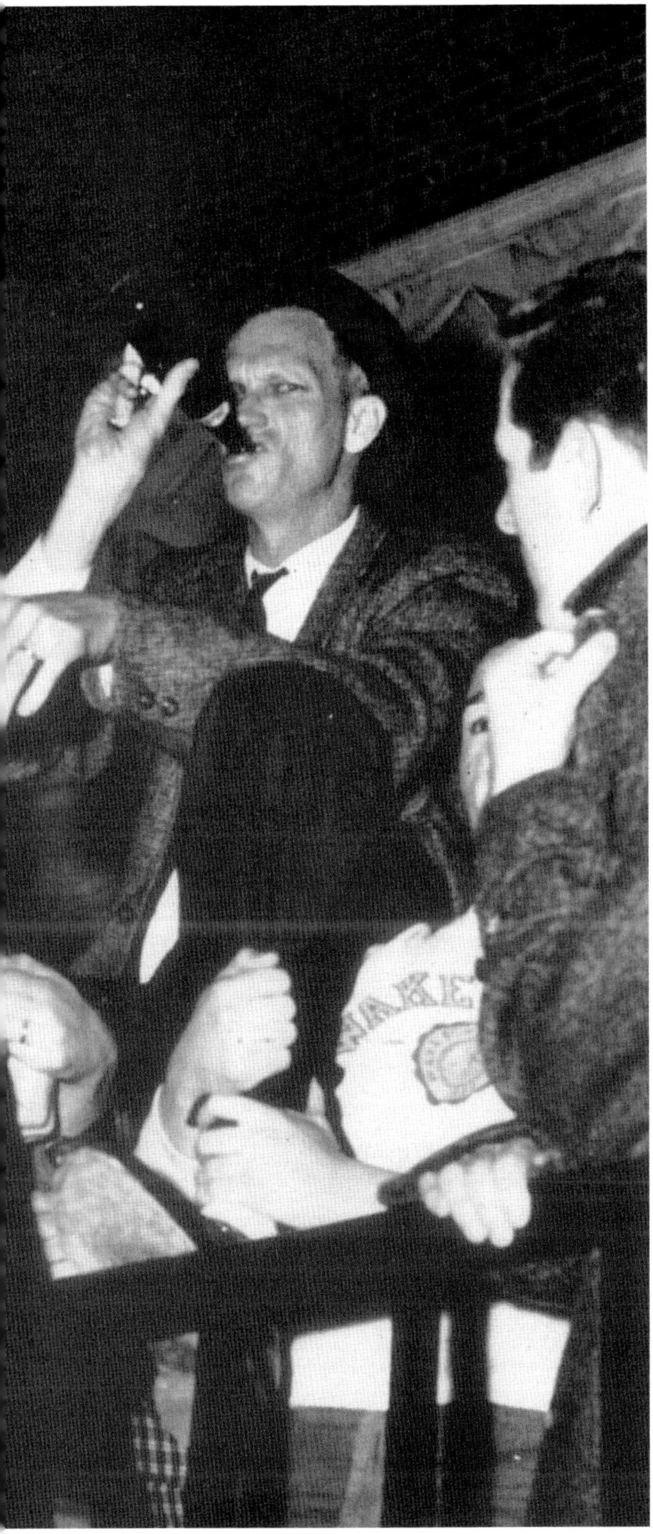

Bones McKinney

Horace "Bones" McKinney was a charismatic preacher with the mouth of a sailor and the heart of a warrior. Tough and strong from childhood, McKinney helped lead his Durham High School team to a state championship before going on to play basketball for North Carolina State University, serving in World War II, and returning to finish his education and college ball career at the University of North Carolina at Chapel Hill. McKinney then signed on with the Boston Celtics before retiring in 1952 and enrolling at Southeastern Baptist Theological Seminary, which was then sharing the Wake Forest College campus, to train for the ministry. By this time, he had a wife and four children, so when Wake Forest basketball coach Murray Greason offered a position as coaching assistant, McKinney jumped on it. He went on to succeed Greason, going down in history as a showman whose colorful sideline antics inspired his athletes and entertained thousands of fans. In one famous incident, McKinney viciously cursed the officials until one finally shouted, "I thought you were a minister!" McKinney reportedly earned a technical foul by yelling back, "Yeah, and I thought you were a referee!" Noted North Carolina State University coach Everett Case once said, "Bones can take a bunch of water boys and a manager, and beat most teams in the country." McKinney stayed at Wake Forest from 1957 to 1965, later finding additional work as a radio and television commentator. He died in 1997, but the legendary basketball program that he helped to build continues to live on.

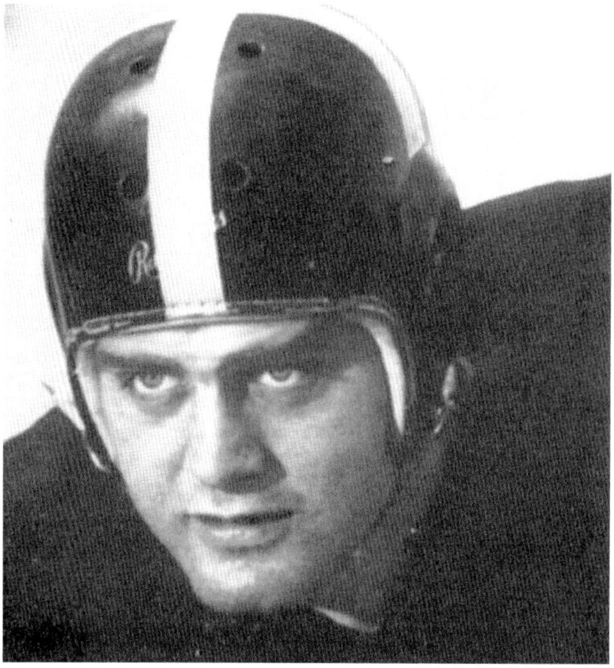

Tony Trentini

Tony Trentini, who played football for Wake Forest College, went on to establish a strong athletic tradition as the first football coach at Wake Forest High School. The stadium there is now named for Trentini, as is a charitable foundation that provides student scholarships each year in his honor. Trentini later coached at Wake Forest University and Temple University before passing away at a very young age.

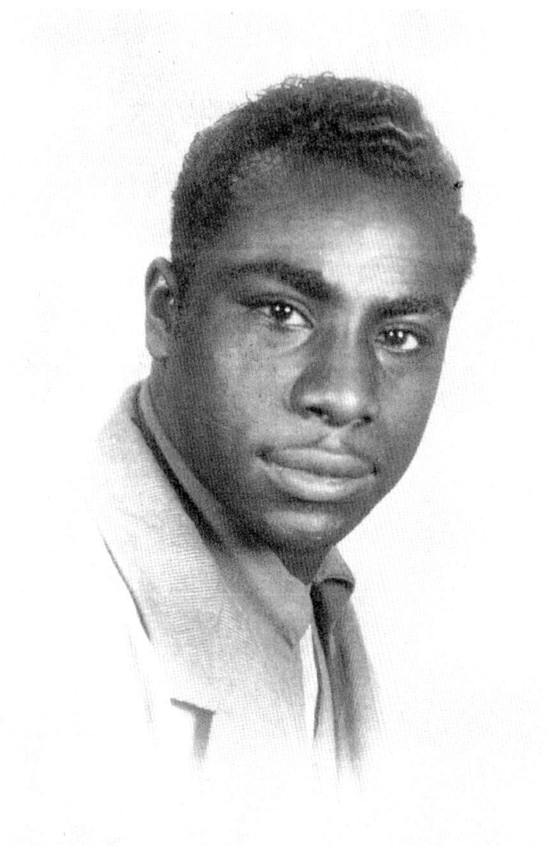

John Hall Jr.

Driving home from his job at the Durham Veterans Administration Hospital in 1968, John Hall Jr. hit an icy stretch of asphalt, lost control, and ran off the road. The accident left him paralyzed. In the following years, Hall mentored dozens of boys in the East End community. From his wheelchair, he taught them to repair bicycles—sometimes with as many as five working on bikes all at the same time. (Courtesy of Geraldine Hall-Taylor.)

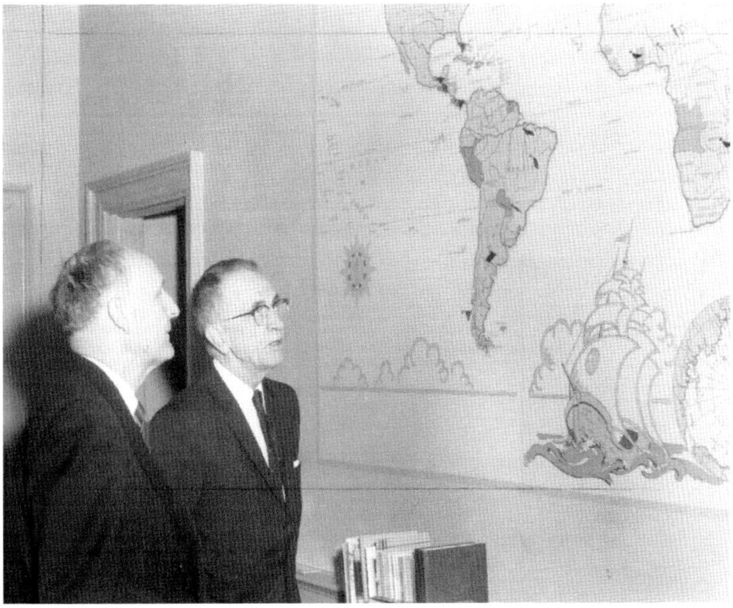

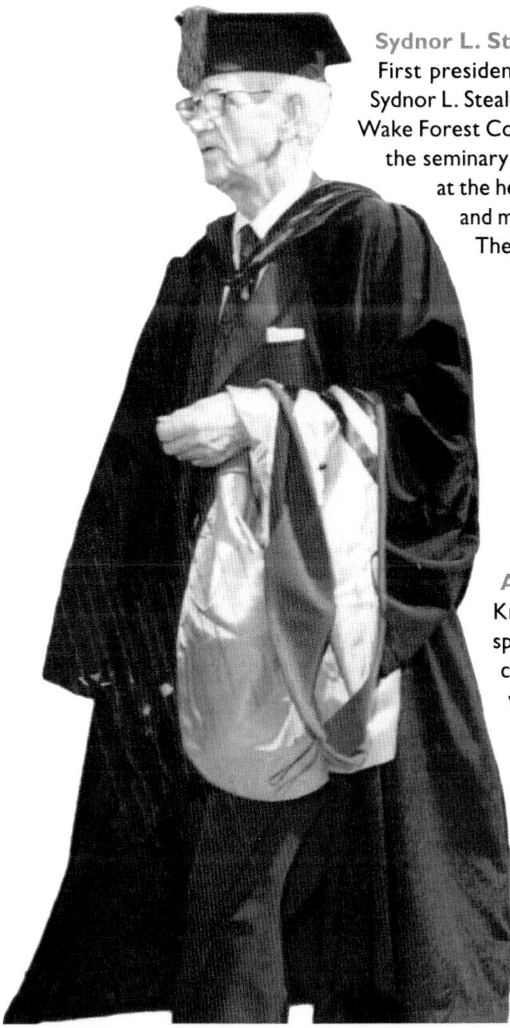

Sydnor L. Stealey

First president of Southeastern Baptist Theological Seminary Sydnor L. Stealey (right) arrived in town in 1951, five years before Wake Forest College moved to Winston-Salem. During that time, the seminary and college shared the campus. Stealey remained at the helm until 1963, guiding the seminary's early growth and missionary work. (Courtesy of Southeastern Baptist Theological Seminary.)

Albert Clayton Reid

Known for driving a long Cadillac with fins at a top speed of 10 miles per hour and occasionally misjudging curbs to park in the middle of the street, A.C. Reid was a 1917 graduate of Wake Forest College and became one of its most adored professors. One student recalled him stopping a lecture to say, "I don't mind you looking at your watch, but don't, for goodness sakes, hold it up to your ear and shake it to see if it's stopped running."

George Stokes

The Reverend George Stokes led Friendship Chapel Baptist Church from 1931 to 1972, through the Great Depression, construction of the new church sanctuary, and the civil rights movement. Although he ministered four churches on a rural circuit, Friendship Chapel was his home. Formally established in 1866, Friendship Chapel still has a large and devoted congregation. (Courtesy of Friendship Chapel Baptist Church.)

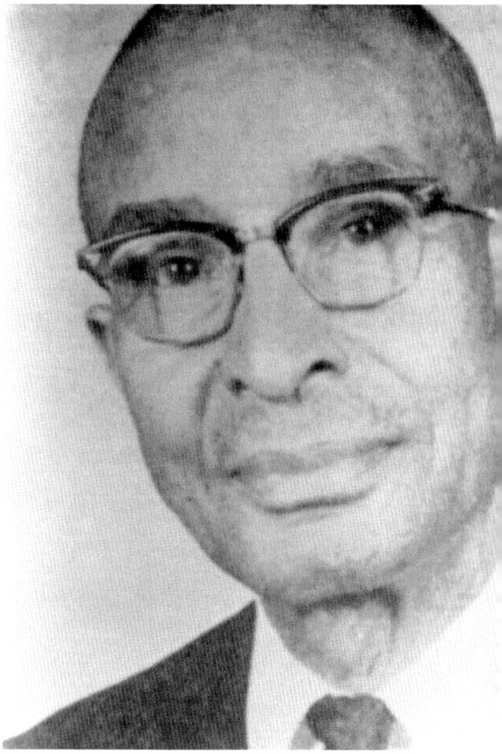

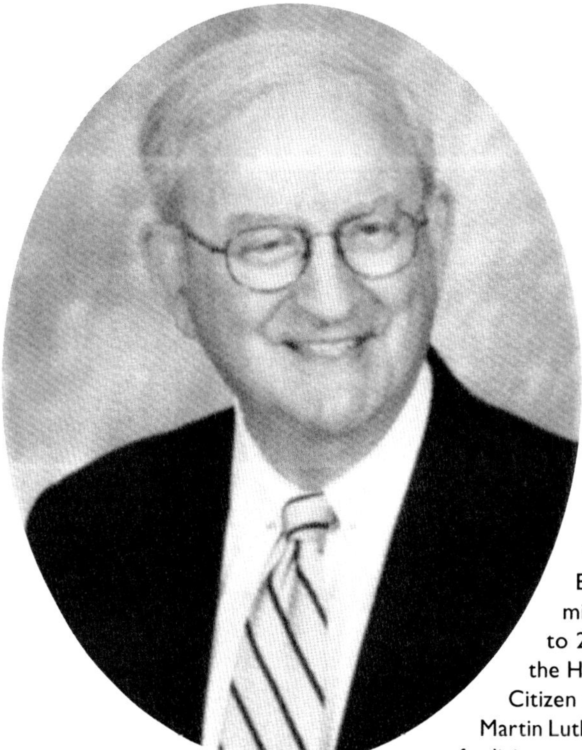

Tom Jackson

As pastor emeritus at Wake Forest Baptist Church, Tom Jackson helps lead one of the town's largest congregations. He earned a theological degree from Southeastern Baptist Theological Seminary, served as minister at Wake Forest Baptist from 1988 to 2004, and has organized and led tours to the Holy Land since 1978. Named Wake Forest Citizen of the Year in 1998, he also received the Martin Luther King Jr. Award and is a noted composer of religious anthems.

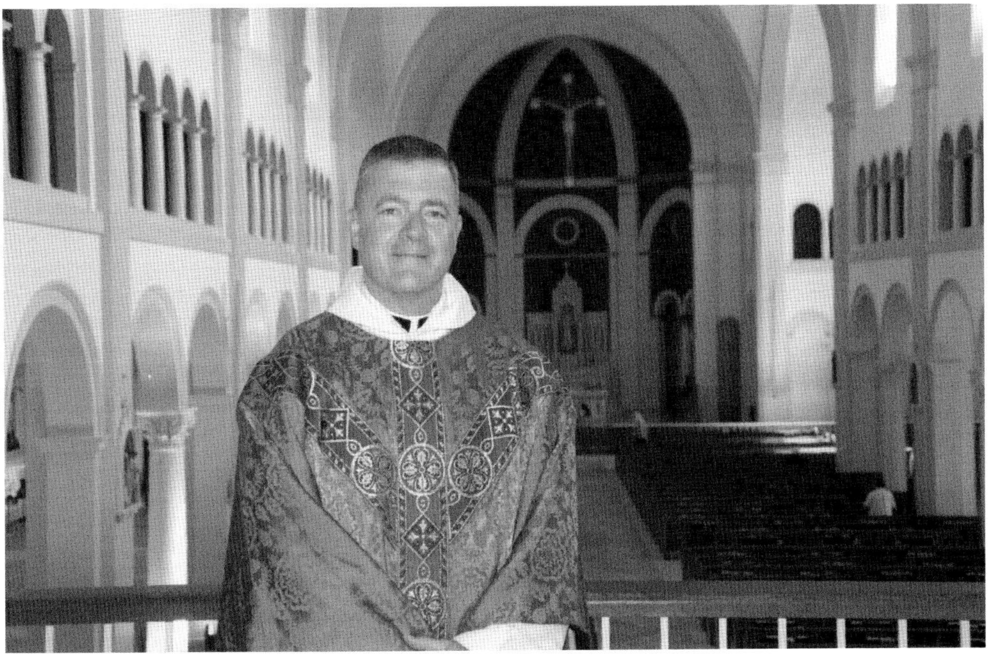

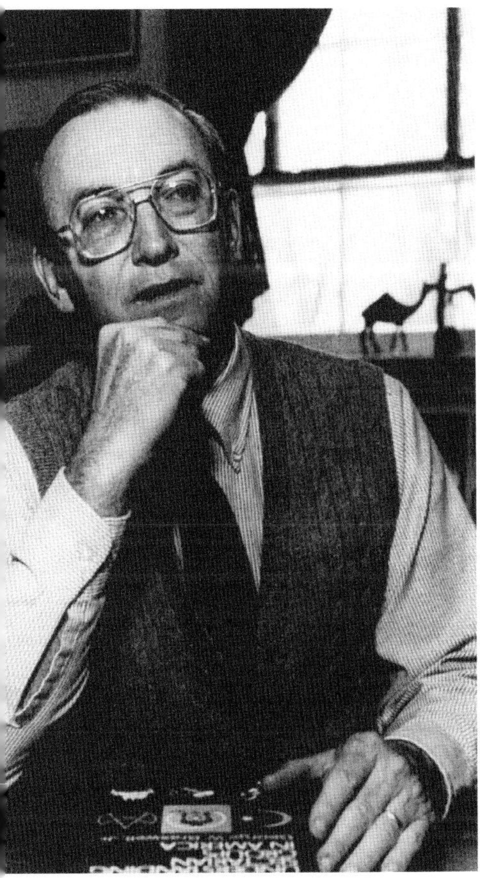

Philip Tighe

Under the leadership of Fr. Philip Tighe, Wake Forest's Catholic community has grown from 300 families in 1997 to approximately 3,000. To accommodate this tenfold increase, the congregation of St. Catherine of Siena Catholic Church launched a capital campaign and in 2013 unveiled a new cathedral that can easily seat approximately 1,500 worshippers. Father Tighe says, "When people of faith come together, God can accomplish anything."

George Braswell Jr.

A graduate of Wake Forest College, George Braswell Jr. taught at the University of Tehran from 1968 to 1974. With the fall of the shah of Iran, he returned to the United States to become a professor at Southeastern Baptist Theological Seminary and Campbell University. The author of numerous books on world religions, Braswell specializes in the study of Islam and has become a popular author and lecturer.

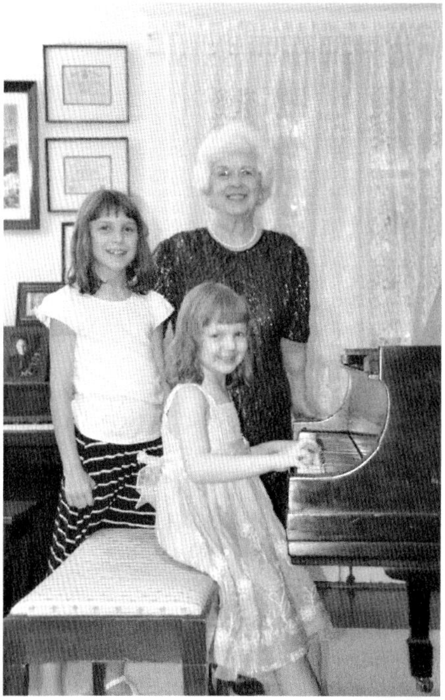

Kathaleen Chandley

Known by hundreds as the town's most prominent piano teacher, Kathaleen Chandley makes her home in the historic district. She is pictured with second-generation pupils Lauren (left) and Rachel Holding, whose parents, James and Heather Loftin Holding, were her students in the 1980s. Chandley is also known for having made North Main Street a bit more special with the sandwich and ice-cream shop she once operated across from the seminary campus, called The Corner. (Courtesy of Heather Loftin Holding.)

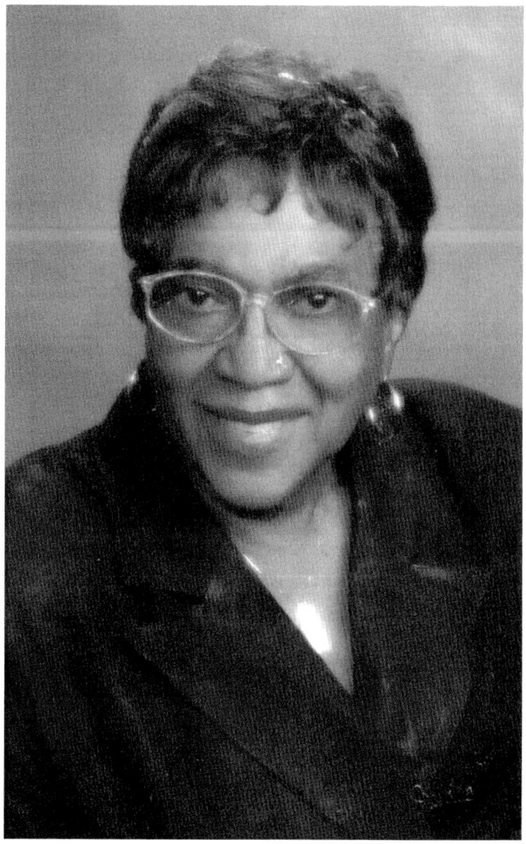

Doris Hill Adams

Doris Hill Adams moved to Wake Forest with her parents in 1931 and graduated from the DuBois School in 1944 before going on to earn degrees in English and French at Shaw University. She attended Teachers College of Columbia University and later earned a doctorate in education. Since settling in Georgia, Adams has headed the education department at Fort Valley State University and has also coordinated adult-education programs. (Courtesy of Doris Hill Adams.)

Rufus Forrest

Rufus Forrest arrived in Wake Forest in 1946 at age 33, becoming principal of Wake Forest Public Schools and later assistant superintendent in charge of business affairs for the Wake County School System. A World War II meteorological engineer who predicted the weather for B29 bombers in China, Forrest taught science and math at Wake Forest High School and Sunday school at Wake Forest Baptist Church.

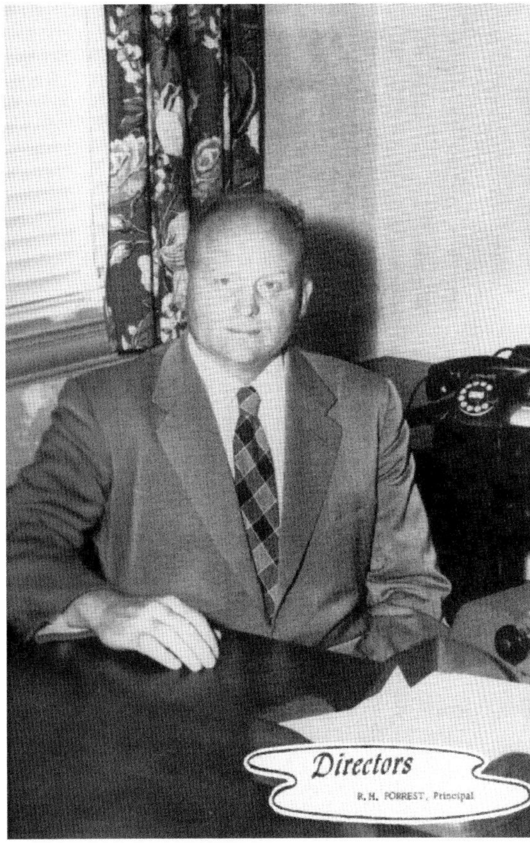

Catherine Lee

Pictured at a 1955 party, Catherine Lee taught biology and chemistry at Wake Forest High School. Feared and revered by her students, she covered her blackboard each day with impeccably written notes and then instructed the pupils to copy down every word. She wanted all facts memorized and believed that scrawling them out made them easier to remember. Lee taught throughout the 1940s to the 1960s and was adored by generations of students. (Courtesy of Durward Matheny.)

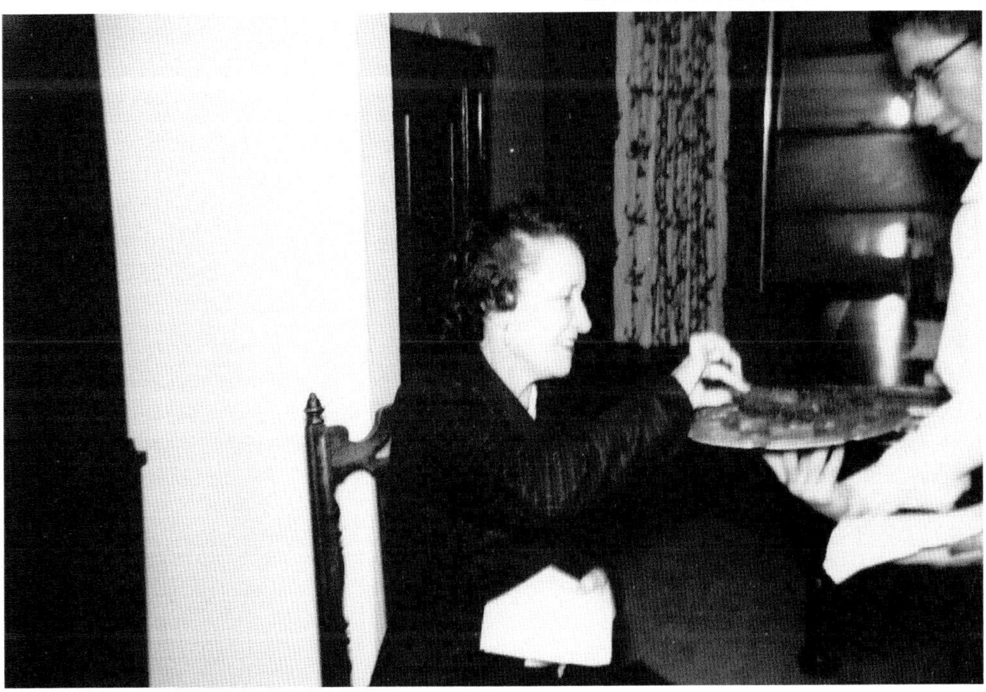

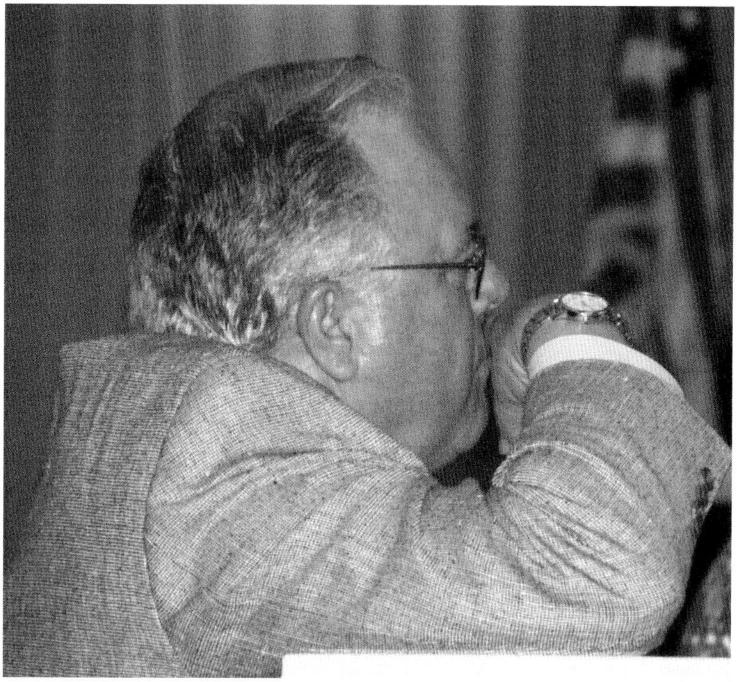

Bill Fisher

Having first served as principal of Wake Forest High School, Bill Fisher went on to a position with the Wake County Public Schools Department of Transportation before returning to town to serve as longtime principal of Wake Forest Elementary School. He helped shepherd the establishment of the magnet school program in Wake Forest and, after retiring, was elected to the Wake County Board of Education. (Courtesy of David Leone and the *Wake Weekly*.)

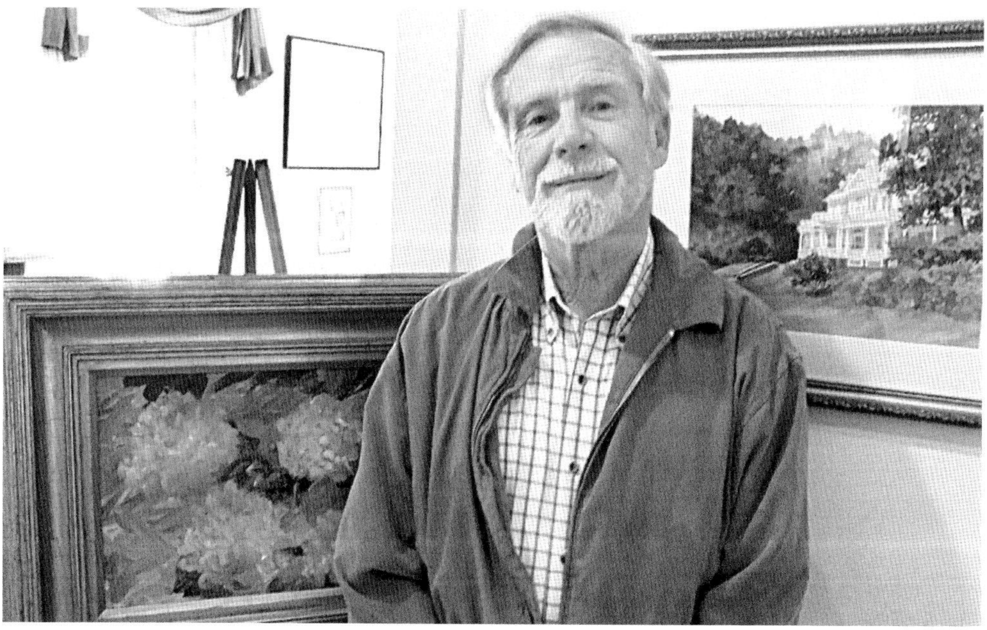

Billy Farmer

Arriving here in 1961, Billy Farmer made a name for himself by creating incredible works in everything from music, to dance, to painting. He twice taught music at Wake Forest Elementary School (first during the 1970s and again in the 1980s and 1990s), eventually staging student productions nearly as elaborate as Broadway musicals. Farmer also wrote an original musical about the history of Wake Forest called *Salute to Our Town*. Additionally, his collectible artwork is famous. (Courtesy of David Leone and the *Wake Weekly*.)

CHAPTER FIVE

Entrepreneurship and Innovation

Entrepreneurship and innovation are the twin engines behind the steady progress that has kept Wake Forest humming for nearly two centuries. Initially a center of religious education, the college and town grew along parallel paths. Beginning with the founding of the college in 1834, the wide swath of former farmland got its own railroad depot, textile plant, business district, streets, schools, and neighborhoods.

Early in the 20th century, the town's largest and most profitable business was the Royall Cotton Mill. Located at the north end of Faculty Avenue, it employed hundreds of workers who manufactured a variety of fabrics. Another major employer was W.W. Holding and Company. Based on South White Street, in the building now known as the Cotton Company, Holding purchased tons of raw cotton from local farmers, loaded it onto trains, and distributed it to factories across the Southeast.

Many other shops, eateries, and services flourished during the years when the college was here. Those days were easy. But when the school left for Winston-Salem in 1956—and the local economy suffered a near-fatal blow—Wake Forest had to start over. As the 1960s dawned, the town recruited factories to provide much-needed jobs. In the 1990s, developers began constructing planned communities. Today, more than 60 years after Wake Forest lost its college, the town's basic identity is clear; this is a place with the will, ingenuity, and determination to survive.

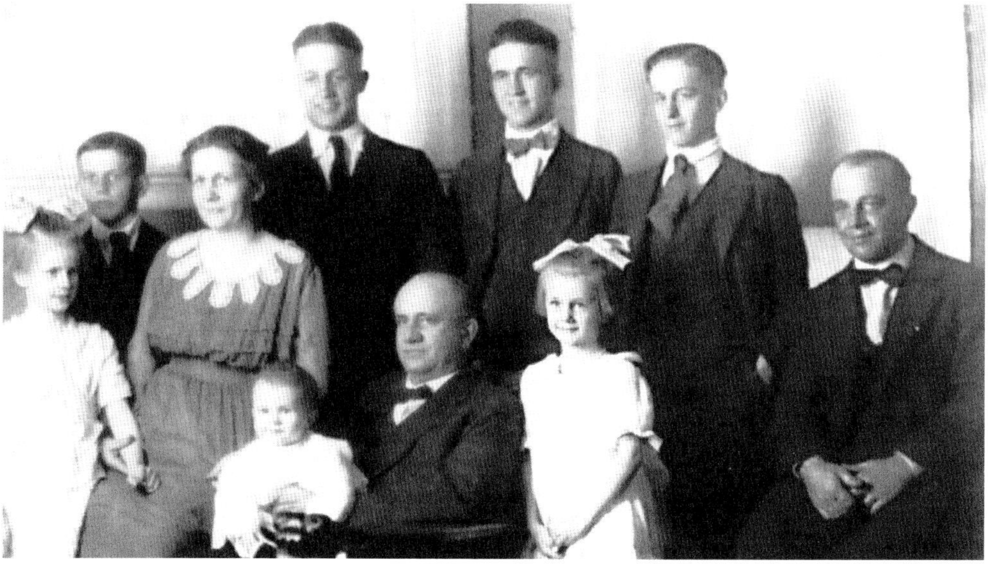

George Henry Greason

In 1899 Wake Forest College graduates Robert E. Royall, Thomas E. Holding, and William C. Powell built a cotton mill north of the town limits. For many years, George Henry Greason was superintendent of the Royall Mill and also served as mayor of the Mill Village. He is seen here surrounded by his family, including his son Murray (back row, center), who would later become a popular basketball coach at Wake Forest College (see page 62).

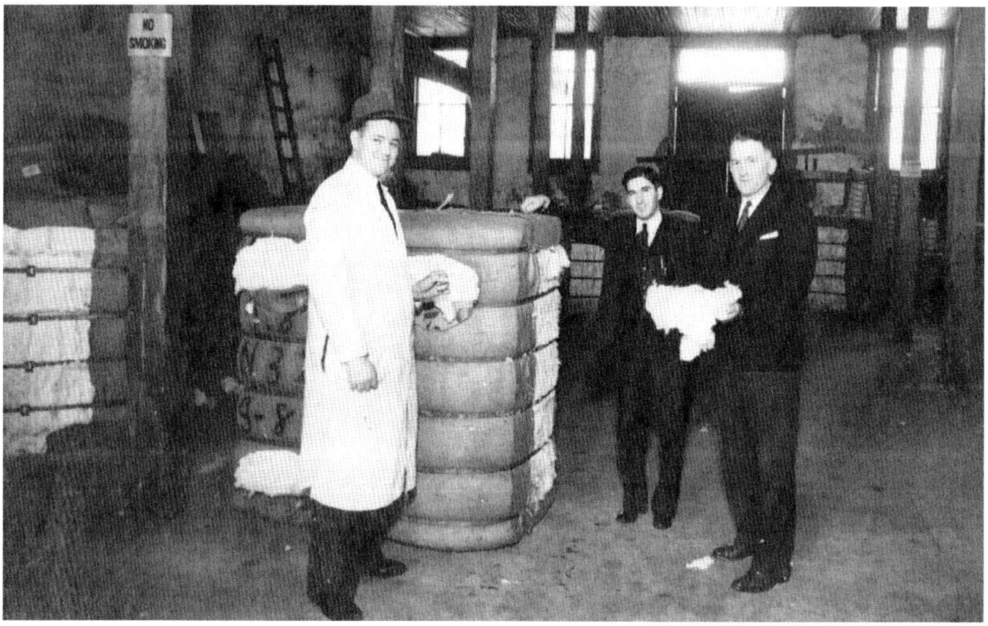

G.W. Hooks, Charlie Sabiston, and William Holding

This early-20th-century image was taken at the business owned by W.W. Holding, who used the loading dock behind his South White Street warehouse to move bundles of raw cotton onto railroad cars for delivery to textile factories far and wide. This location is the present-day Cotton Company.

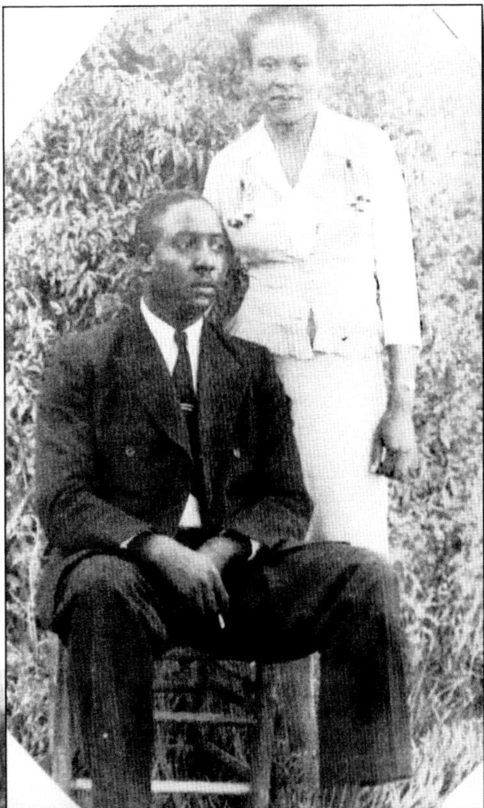

Oscar C. Smith

Oscar C. Smith's shoe shop was a local landmark that catered to both black and white customers, its owner respected by everyone in town. Smith (pictured with his wife, Bettie Massenburg Smith) found great joy in teaching, mentoring, and training young people. His goal was to help them build successful lives. In a 1971 interview with Bob Allen of the *Wake Weekly*, Smith said, "It is a joy to me to train them in business. I get more out of that than anything else in life." Smith served 10 terms as president of the North Carolina Volunteer Firemen's Association, was an active member of Friendship Chapel Baptist Church, and helped guide the Wake Forest School Advisory Council.

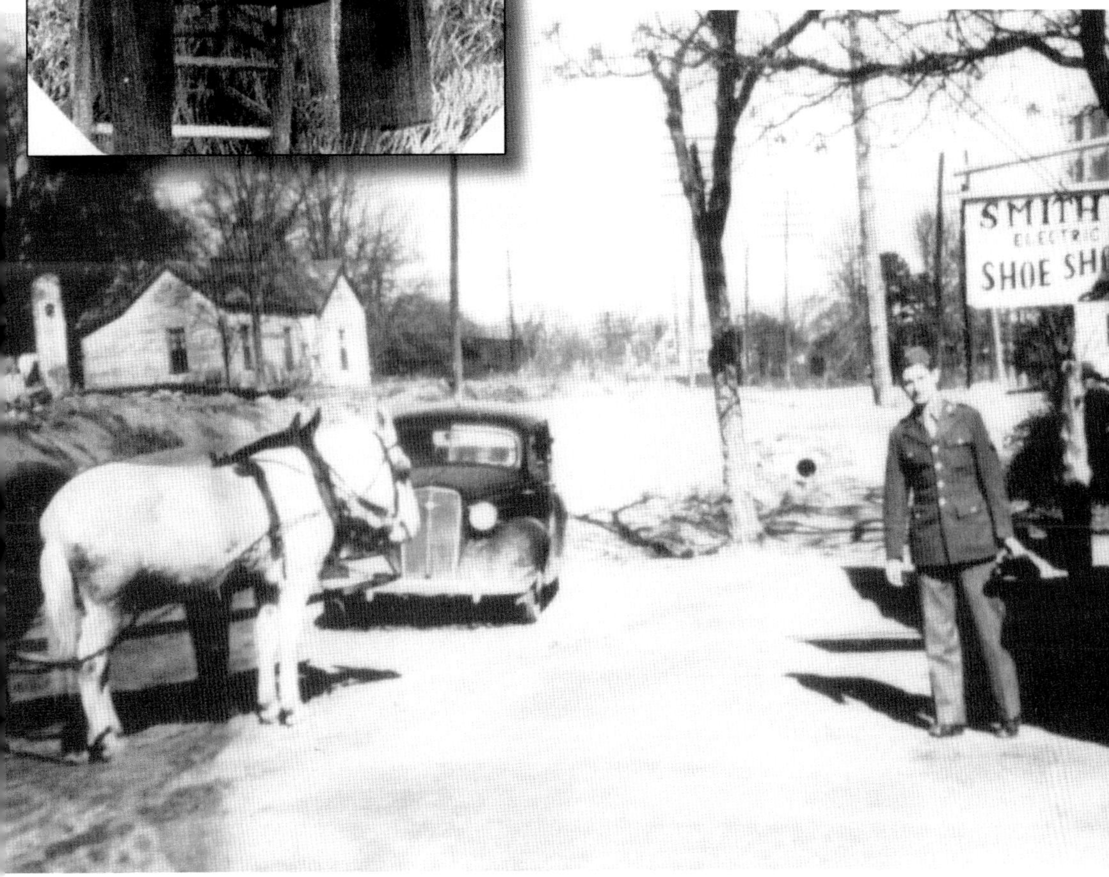

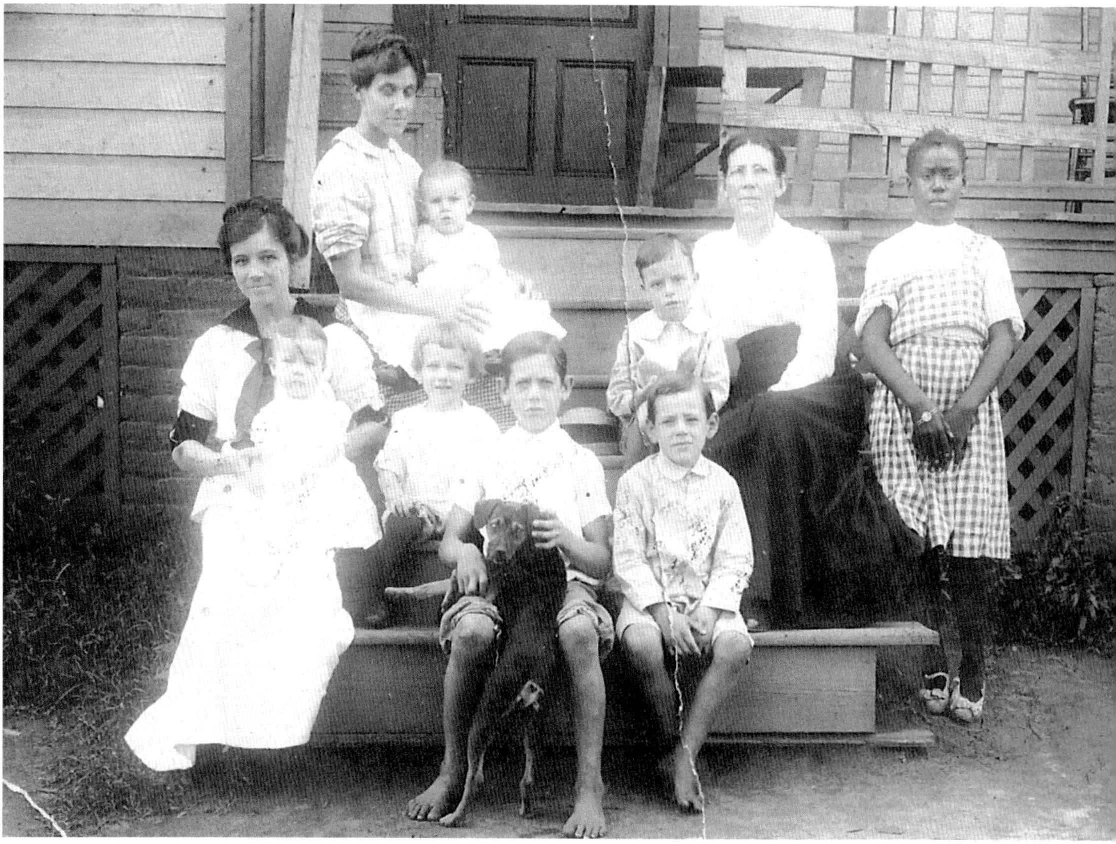

Ruby Reid

Ruby Reid (second from right) started out as the community's telephone operator and went on to become an astute businesswoman and founder of an insurance agency on South White Street. In the mid-1930s, she sold the business to Harvey Holding. Her will left an endowment that founded the Ruby Reid Daycare Center and provided childcare for generations of local families.

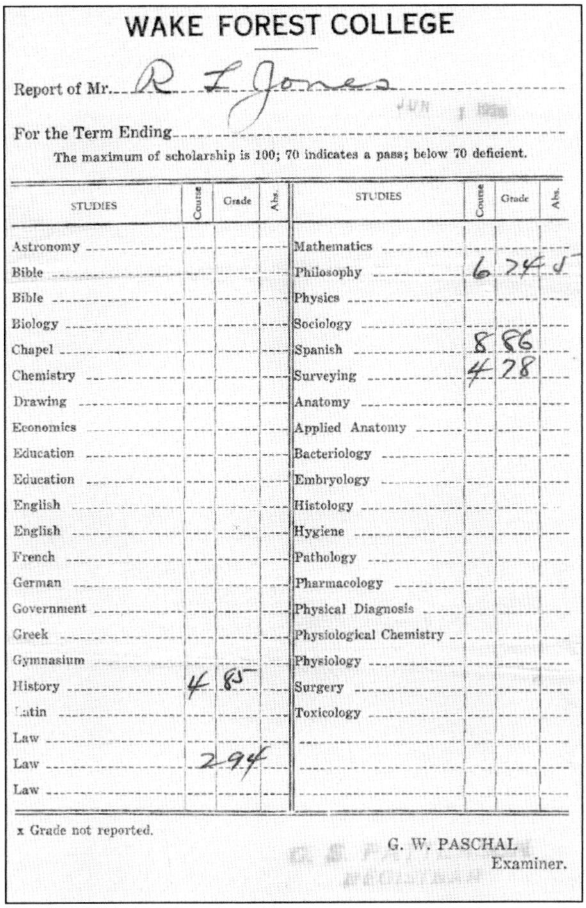

WAKE FOREST COLLEGE

Report of Mr. R L Jones

For the Term Ending

The maximum of scholarship is 100; 70 indicates a pass; below 70 deficient.

STUDIES	Course	Grade	Abs.	STUDIES	Course	Grade	Abs.
Astronomy				Mathematics			
Bible				Philosophy	6	74	5
Bible				Physics			
Biology				Sociology			
Chapel				Spanish	8	86	
Chemistry				Surveying	4	78	
Drawing				Anatomy			
Economics				Applied Anatomy			
Education				Bacteriology			
Education				Embryology			
English				Histology			
English				Hygiene			
French				Pathology			
German				Pharmacology			
Government				Physical Diagnosis			
Greek				Physiological Chemistry			
Gymnasium				Physiology			
History	4	85		Surgery			
Latin				Toxicology			
Law							
Law	2	94					
Law							

x Grade not reported.

G. W. PASCHAL
Examiner.

Robert Leland Jones

In June 1928, Robert Leland Jones's Wake Forest College grades were mailed to his father, I.O. Jones, founder of the Wake Forest Supply Company. The town and college enjoyed a close relationship, with faculty, staff, and students always welcome at popular local establishments. This store, later renamed Jones Hardware, stayed in business for nearly a century.

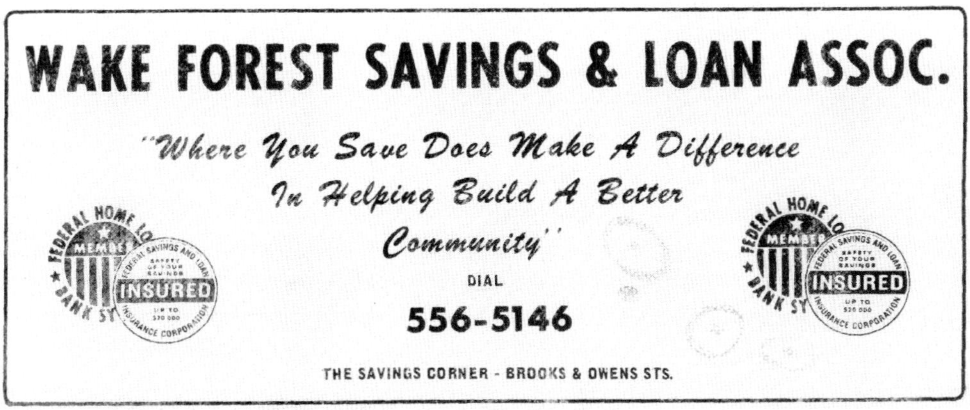

Wake Forest Federal Savings & Loan

The Wake Forest Federal Savings & Loan, started by a group of local men in 1922, was the only financial institution in town to survive the Great Depression, staying afloat as both banks failed. It remains in business today.

George Bolus

A native of Lebanon, George Bolus came to town with a pushcart of merchandise that he guided along White Street. He did well enough to eventually purchase a piece of property and open his own department store. Bolus is pictured in this c. 1920 photograph with daughter Elizabeth. As the first Catholic family in Wake Forest, the Boluses also helped establish the church and congregation of St. Catherine of Siena.

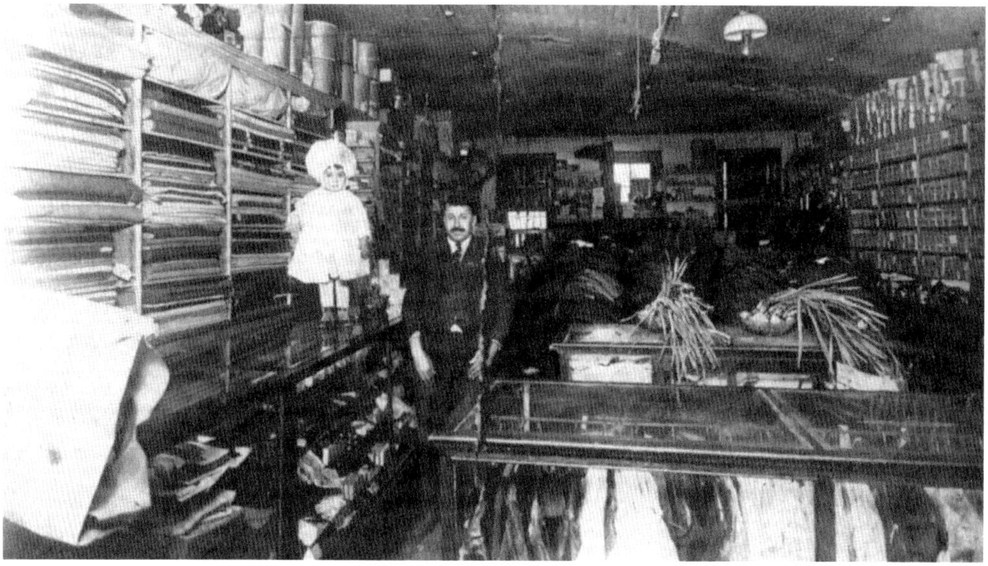

The Sidenberg Family

Sam and Reba Sidenberg were the first Jewish family in Wake Forest. They owned B&S Department Store, a mainstay of Wake Forest shopping and fashion from the 1940s to the 1970s. Reba would go to New York on buying trips, then call her local customers about the new styles she had found. Residents remember the store as a beautiful place to shop, as polished and sophisticated as any department store in Raleigh.

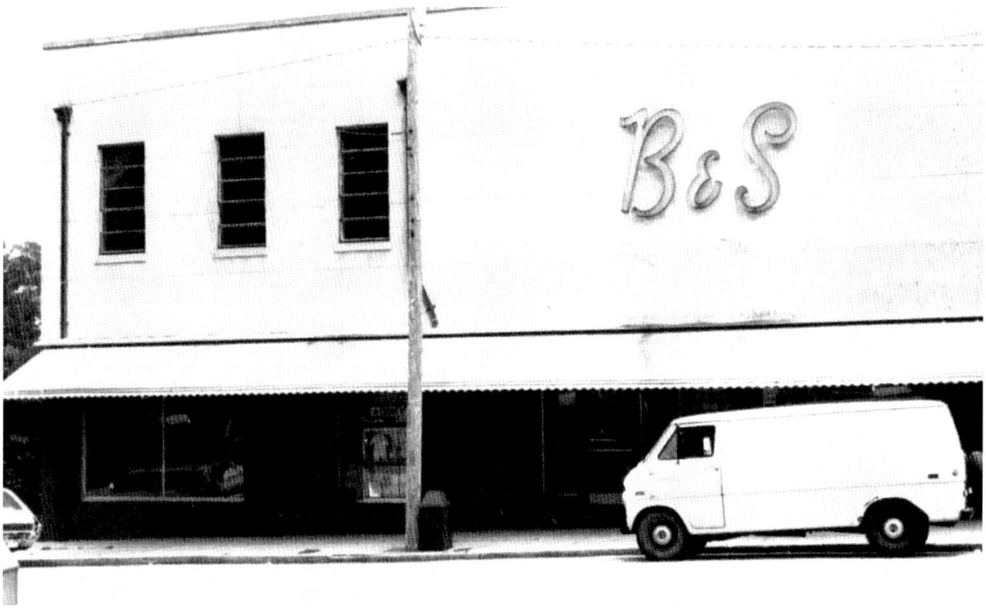

Jesse Hollowell and Barbara Hollowell Lyon

Jesse Hollowell, pictured in this c. 1937 photograph with daughter Barbara, came to Wake Forest in 1930 as the manager of the local grocery and, four years later, founded Hollowell's, a store focused on high quality, low prices, and customer service. Loved by town and college alike, Hollowell was badly burned in an accident in 1954, and the Wake Forest College football coach arrived at the hospital with members of the team to donate blood in his honor.

Barbara Hollowell Lyon and husband, John Lyon (see page 18), carried on the family business and together established Lyon's Grocery Store, which was the first business within town limits to sell alcoholic beverages. It remained open many years. As it used a lion as its logo, Food Lion was later required to purchase local rights to the name and image before entering the Wake Forest market. Barbara and John Lyon are longtime community leaders, Citizens of the Year, active members of Wake Forest Methodist Church, and supporters of the Wake Forest Historical Museum. (Photograph courtesy of Barbara Hollowell Lyon; receipt courtesy of the Wake Forest Historical Museum.)

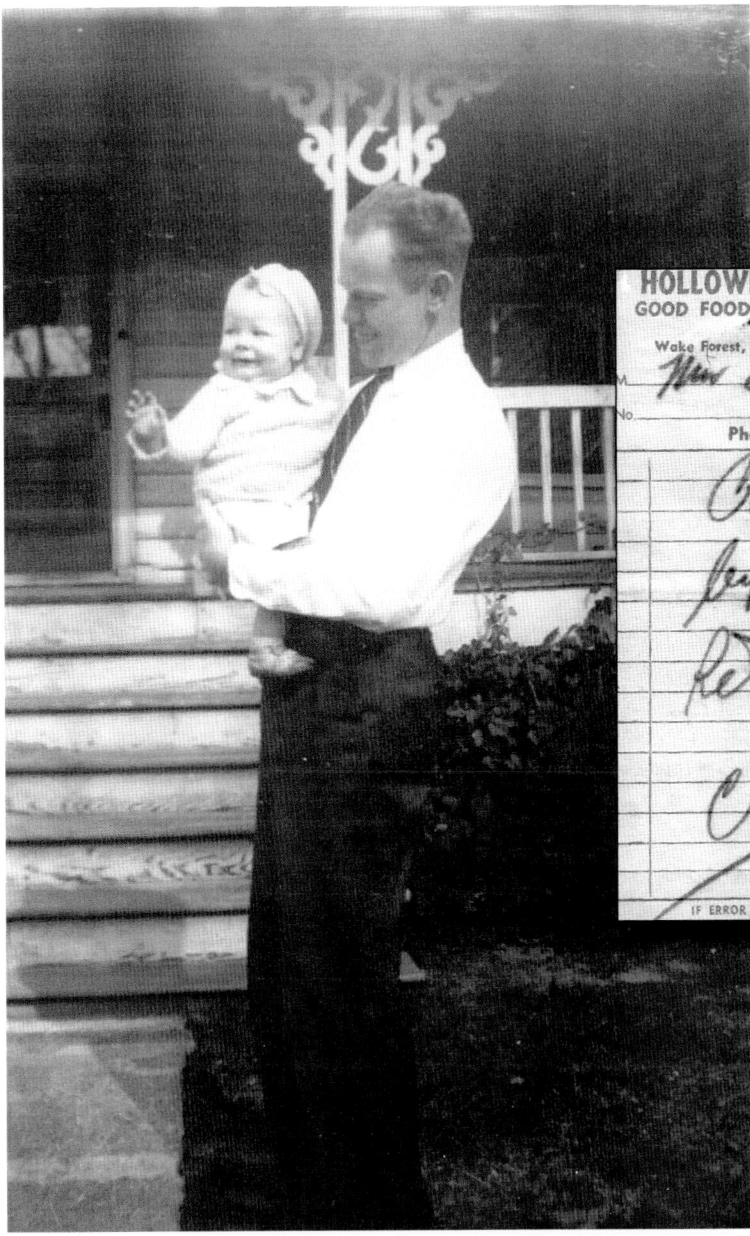

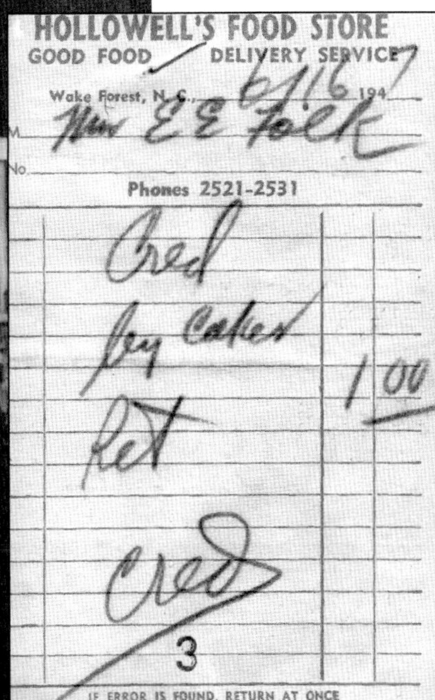

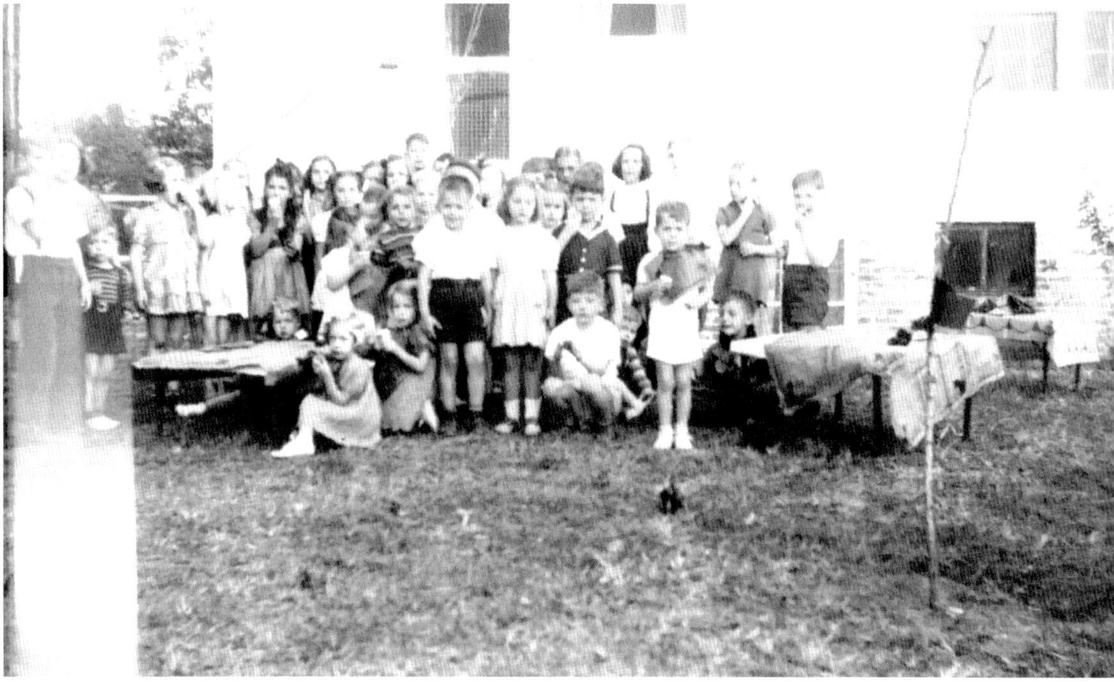

The Faculty Avenue Kindergarten

In the days when North Carolina public schools started at first grade, Ethel Mills opened a local kindergarten in the basement of her home in the 200 block of Faculty Avenue. A large number of local parents enrolled their children in her classes, which included instructional lessons, outdoor play, and snack time. The unofficial school was so popular, it was featured in a Wake Forest movie produced by itinerant filmmaker H. Lee Waters, who traveled the Depression-era South to film people on the streets of towns, at schools, and outside factories. He would return a few weeks later and charge a nickel admission for citizens to see themselves on the silver screen in the local movie house. Waters visited Wake Forest in October 1939; a copy of his film is held in the Wake Forest Historical Museum collection. (Courtesy of John Mills.)

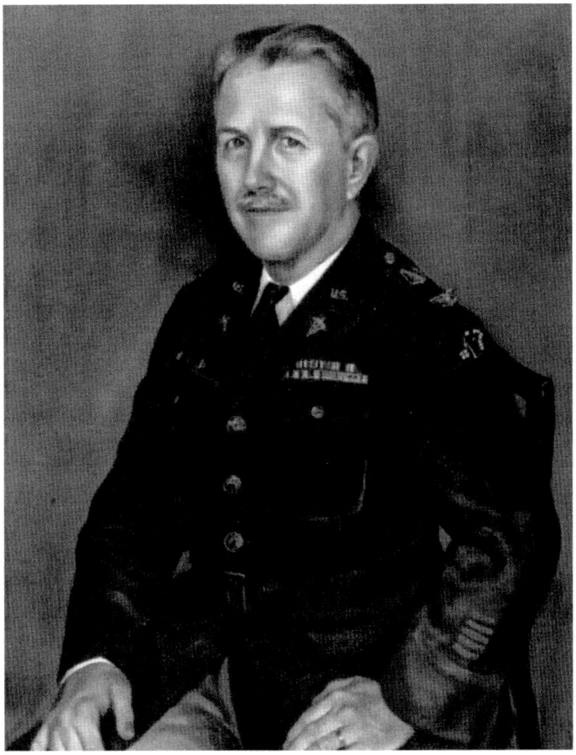

The Wilkinson Brothers
C.T. Wilkinson, pictured here, and his brother R.W. Wilkinson were the sons of the founder of Wilkinson Department Store, which was located on South White Street. They both became doctors, and they built side-by-side, identical homes (brick with white trim) on South Main Street. As they were not affiliated with the college, they specialized in treating patients from the mill village, East End, and rural communities.

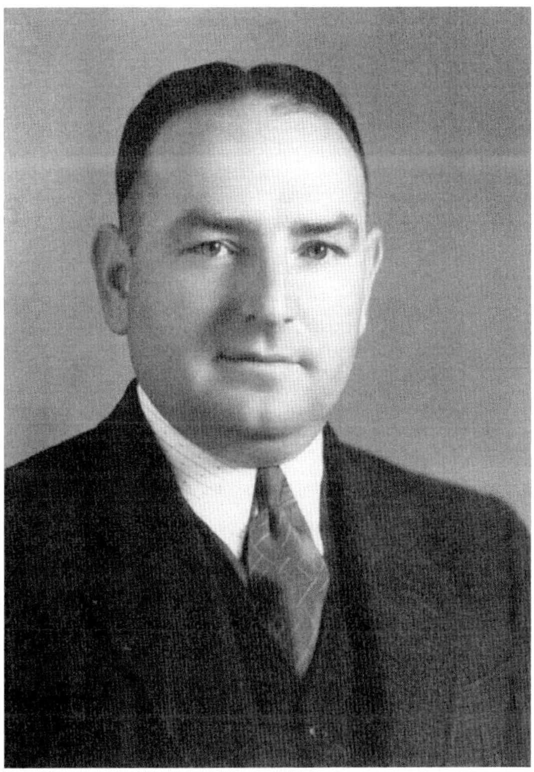

C.D. Matheny
Clarence Dickson Matheny, a 1931 graduate of Wake Forest College, served as principal of Rolesville High School and then became the town's Chevrolet dealer when he bought Service Chevrolet on South White Street from its original owner in the early 1940s. Matheny ran the business until the mid-1960s. A strong supporter of local entrepreneurs, he was a founding member of the Wake Forest Chamber of Commerce.

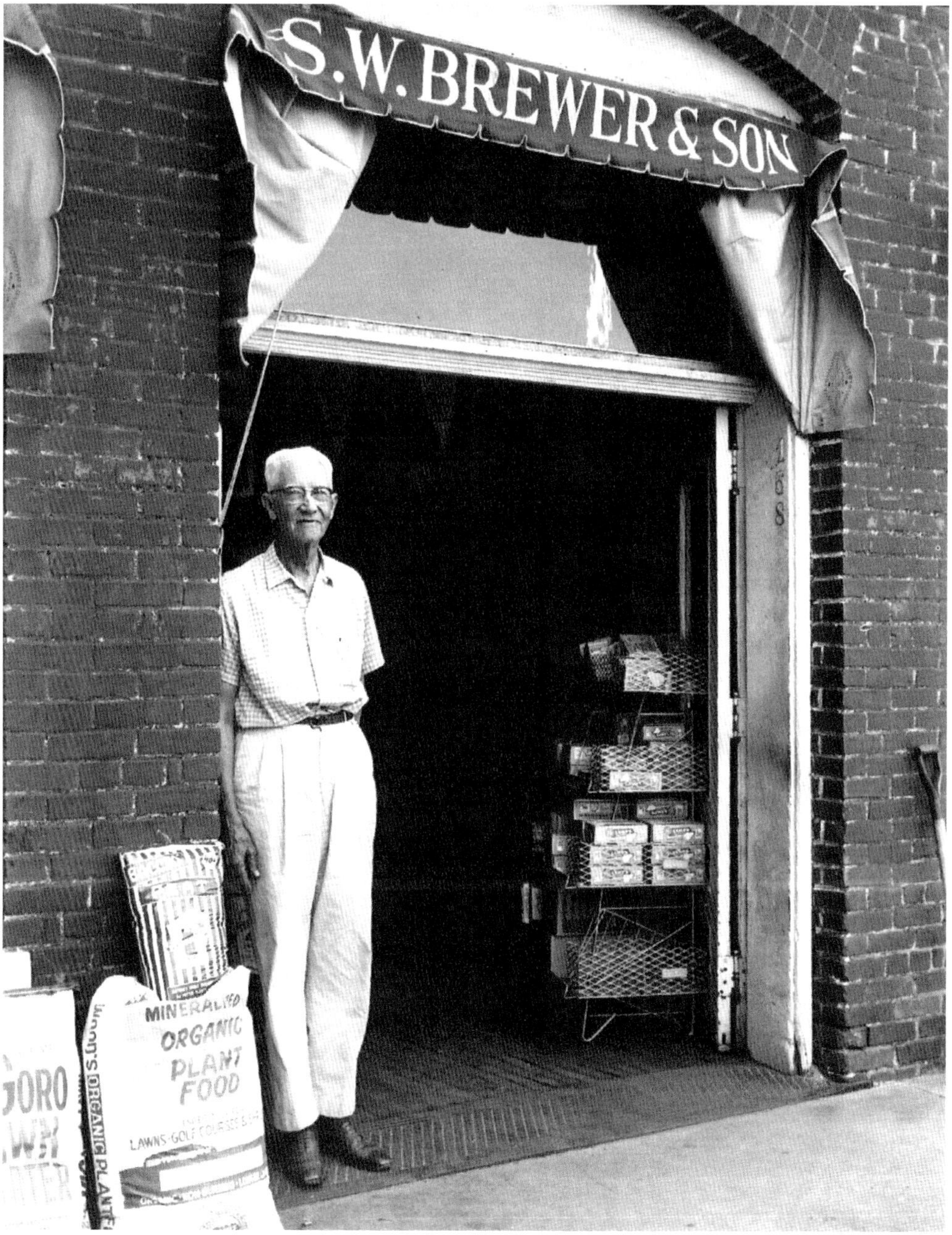

Samuel Wait Brewer

A direct descendant of the first president of Wake Forest College, Samuel Wait Brewer was highly regarded and very well connected. He founded a seed-and-fertilizer store downtown, selling seed, mulch, and other planting supplies to local gardeners and area farmers. His son, Wait Brewer, went on to become mayor of Wake Forest and was the husband of Jenny Brewer (see page 31).

Everette Snyder

Everette Snyder, manager of the College Book Store from 1930 to 1960, was famous for always knowing the names of the approximately 1,500 members of the student body and faculty. As the biggest single advertiser in student publications and on the college radio station, he sold drinks and sandwiches, T-shirts, pencils, notebook paper, and textbooks. When asked what he liked best about Wake Forest, Snyder responded, "Everything!"

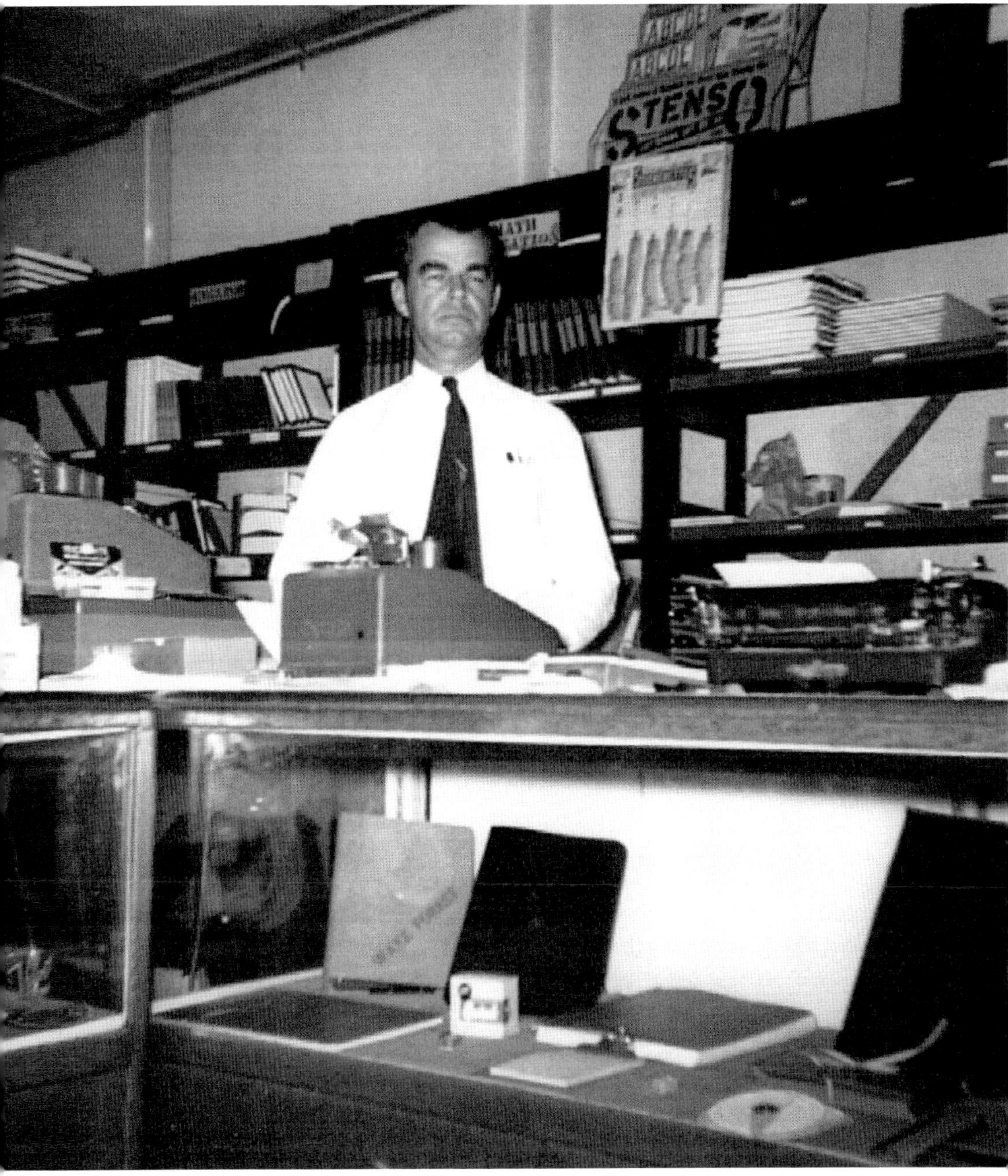

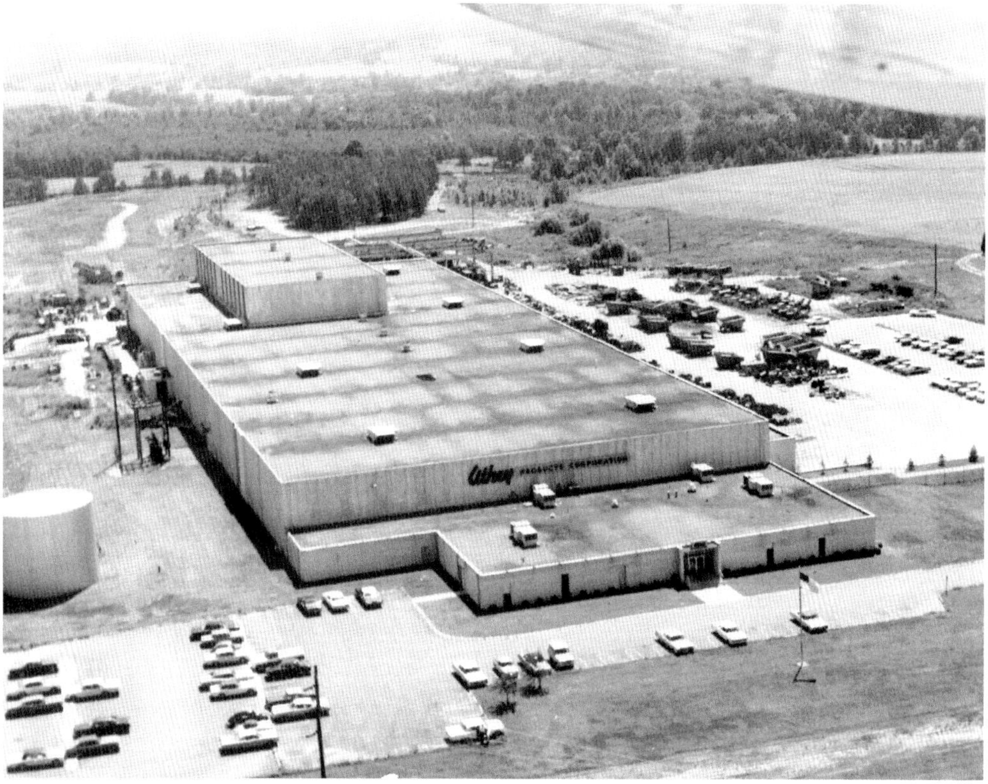

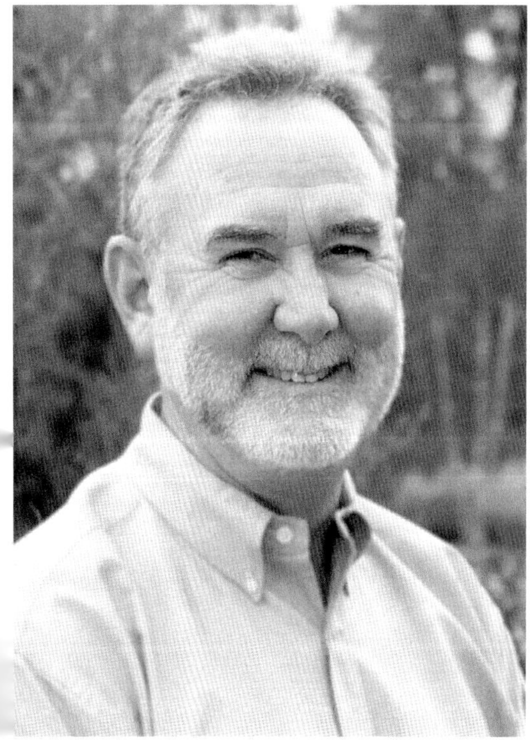

Wake Forest Industrial Development Corporation, 1964

With the town floundering after the college's departure, and Burlington Industries the only factory around in the 1950s, the Wake Forest Industrial Development Corporation was created to attract industry and help Schrader Brothers move into its new plant, which would manufacture cylinders and valves. This kicked off a period of prosperity. Athey Products arrived next, shown here in its heyday, followed by the Neuse Plastic Company, Mallinckrodt, and others. (Courtesy of Southeastern Baptist Theological Seminary.)

Andy Ammons

The Athey plant later became the Factory, developed by the Ammons Group. Heritage Wake Forest owes its existence to the entrepreneurial vision of land developer Andy Ammons. A Raleigh native, Ammons grew up visiting Wake Forest and was determined to preserve its special atmosphere. To create an attractive family community, he sold land at a reduced price to Wake County Public Schools, provided nearly $8 million in road improvements, and added buffers to protect valuable wetlands. (Courtesy of the Ammons Group.)

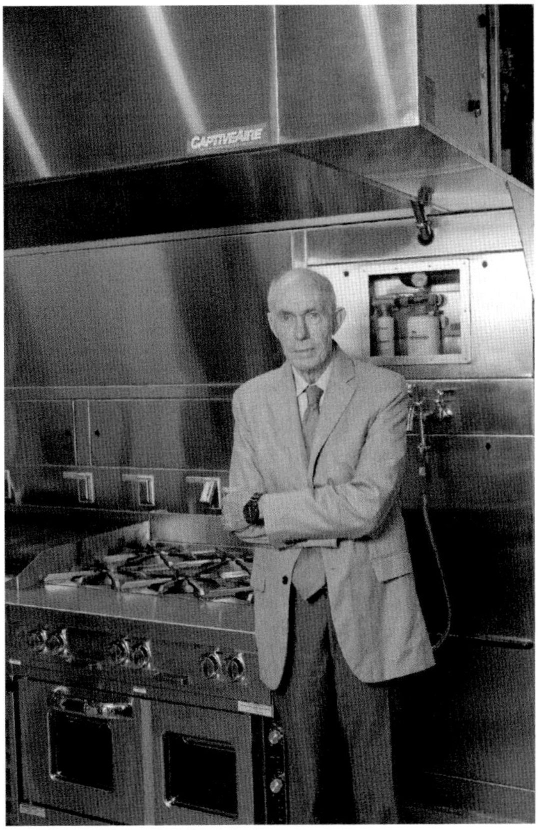

Bob Luddy
An innovator and entrepreneur, Bob Luddy brought development, school choice, and jobs to Wake Forest and Franklin County. The company he founded in 1976, CaptiveAire Systems, has grown into the largest producer of commercial kitchen ventilation equipment in the United States with sales topping $300 million a year. Luddy also went on to found the Franklin Academy charter school and the Thales Academy chain of private schools. (Courtesy of CaptiveAire.)

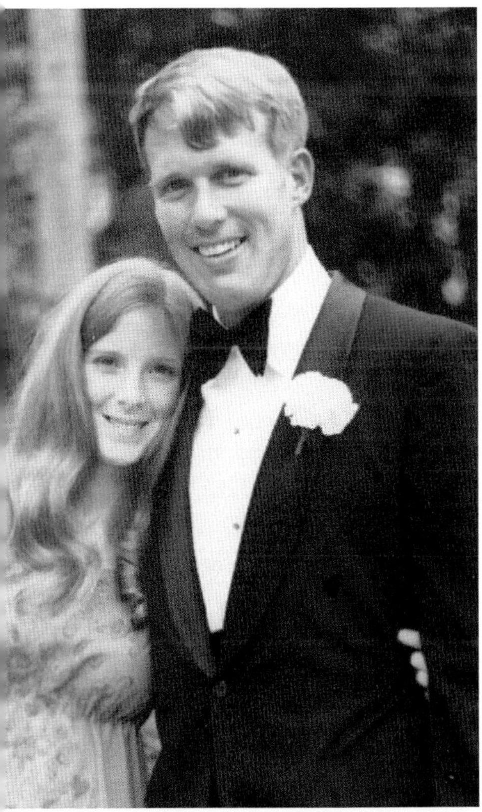

David and Pinky Cooke
After serving as a Marine pilot in Vietnam, David Cooke brought his wife Pinky to Wake Forest, and together they purchased and restored the Heartsfield House on Ligon Mill Road. In 1978, they founded the Utility Service Agency, a manufacturer's representative agency for electrical utility products. To serve as an office, they first restored the Medlin Store at 501 North Main Street and later the Gulley-Mackie House at 340 North Main Street, where their business is now located. (Courtesy of the Cooke family.)

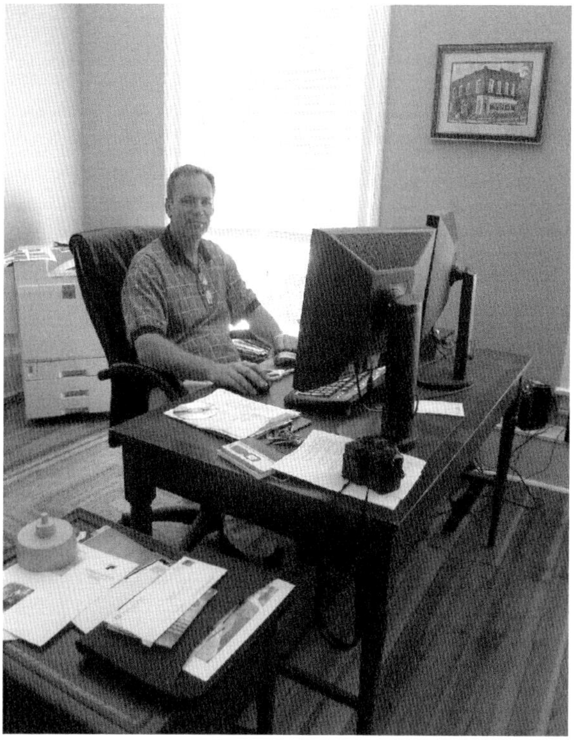

Marty Ludas
Marty Ludas is a fingerprint and footwear expert who retired after 30 years of consecutive service working as a forensic examiner with three different law enforcement agencies. Now a resident of Wake Forest's Historic District, he runs a multimedia fingerprint-training channel on YouTube. Tutorials provide distance learning for students enrolled at Wake Technical Community College and utilize widescreen, high-definition video content. (Courtesy of David Leone and the *Wake Weekly*.)

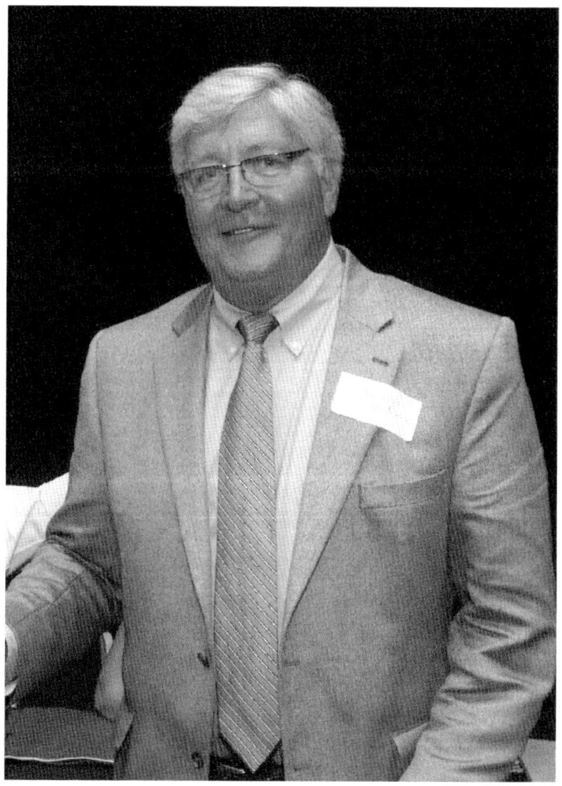

Buddy Willis
A native of Wake Forest, Buddy Willis is the owner and operator of B&W Hardware on South White Street. Entrepreneurship is in his blood; his father founded one of the town's older funeral homes, Willis Funeral Service. A graduate of Wake Forest High School, Willis is a strong supporter of the buy-local movement. (Courtesy of David Leone and the *Wake Weekly*.)

CHAPTER SIX

Citizens and Civic Organizations

Baptist and collegiate in an era when men were leaders and women were frequently limited to tasks such as household chores, child-rearing, community support, and entertaining, Wake Forest historically had two groups of achievers: the men in the spotlight, and the women behind the throne. The women's tradition began with Sarah Merriam Wait—wife of Samuel Wait, the first president of Wake Forest College—who supported her husband as he took a leadership role at the newly established manual-labor institute. Together, they worked to shape what eventually would become one of the world's leading universities.

As years passed, women proceeded to fill many of the town's most vital civic roles. Annie Gill Harris and the Wake Forest Garden Club spearheaded the effort to save the historic Calvin Jones House. In 1970, Geraldine Hall-Taylor served as the African American copresident of the Wake Forest High School PTA, a job she held alongside a white counterpart during the first years of integration. Kathleen Mackie Lake spent decades driving her doctor husband on nightly house calls.

With changing times came dedicated power couples such as Sherrill and Susan Brinkley, Bill and Louise Howard, and Bob and Elizabeth Johnson. All have put a contemporary twist on the citizenship model pioneered by the Waits nearly two centuries ago.

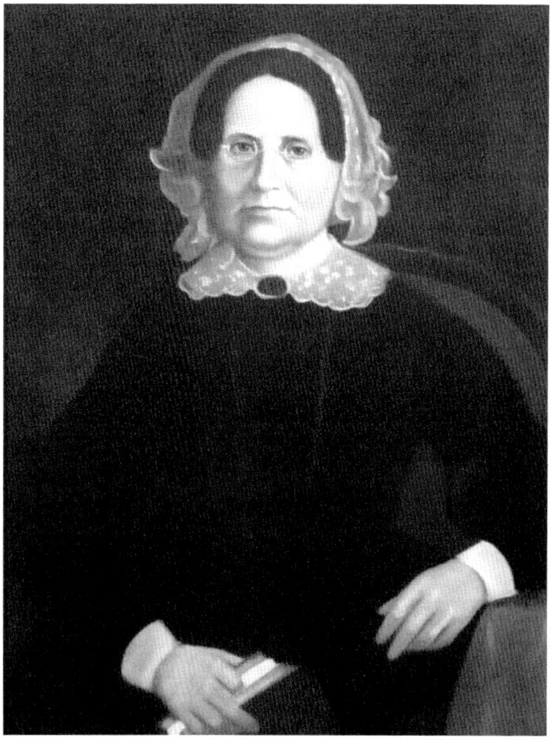

Sarah Merriam Wait

Wife of first Wake Forest College president Samuel Wait, Sarah Merriam Wait encouraged her husband to enter the ministry. When he became a Baptist preacher concerned about the quality of religious education, she supported him in his endeavors and willingly accompanied him from New York to their new home in North Carolina.

Irene Mangum, Lib Greason, Irene Holding, Isabella Gill, and Nancy Harris

Listed from left to right, these friends made a lasting mark on the mid-20th-century college town. As society doyennes, sports fans, church members, and civic-group volunteers, they were a fun-loving bunch who used their special brand of energy and enthusiasm to help Wake Forest develop into a more sophisticated place to live, learn, and enjoy life.

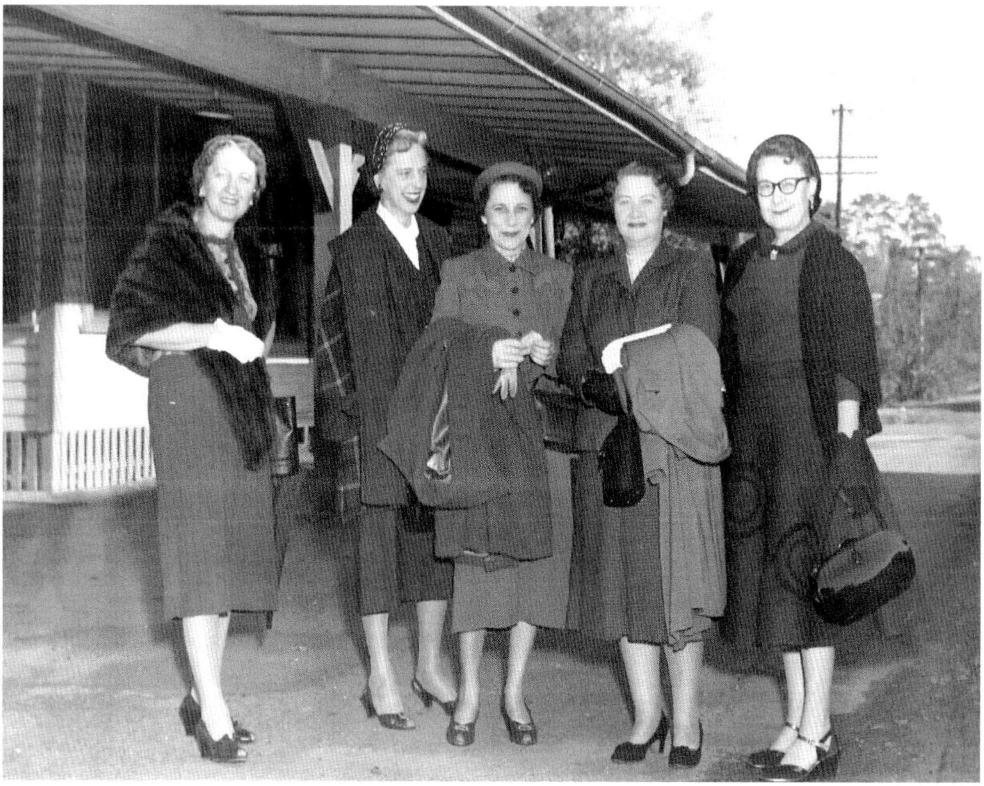

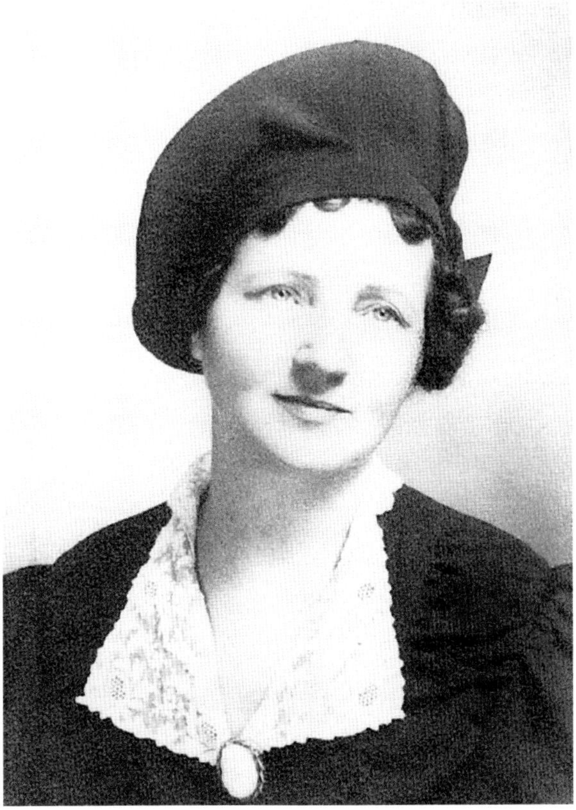

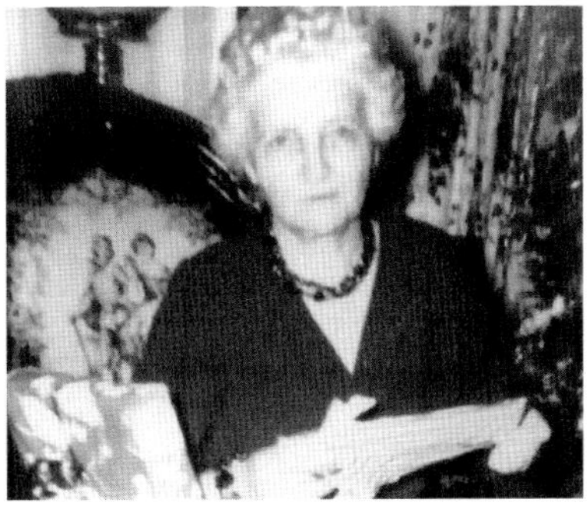

Annie Gill Harris
A native of Franklin County, Annie Gill Harris spent much of her adult life bettering the Wake Forest community. Involved in numerous civic organizations, she is perhaps most noted for leading the effort to save the Calvin Jones House after the departure of Wake Forest College in 1956. The historic home, now a regional museum, was preserved and restored largely due to her concern, leadership, and perseverance.

Large gardens, small gardens, a child's
minute plot,
A porch box,a fern in a red flower-pot:
Or just a heart-garden which never does
show -
Its owner too weary to make flowers grow.
My Wake Forest gardens, I cherish you -
all -
Through summer's delight and the gold of
the fall;
Chrusanthemums; then for a time the
Frost King;
And slowly the blessed resurgence of
spring.
I stand for security, balance and hope
So, Children, who oft through bewilder-
ment grope
- Dear Children, whose fingers are stain-
ed with the sod -
Look upward tome. And beyond me, to
God.

Edith Earnshaw

Wake Forest Garden Club
As a longtime member of the Wake Forest Garden Club, Edith Earnshaw composed this poem that originally appeared in 1948 as part of a Garden Club event program. As the group of stalwart volunteers who first rallied behind Annie Gill Harris to save the Calvin Jones House, the Garden Club members are still among the museum's strongest supporters.

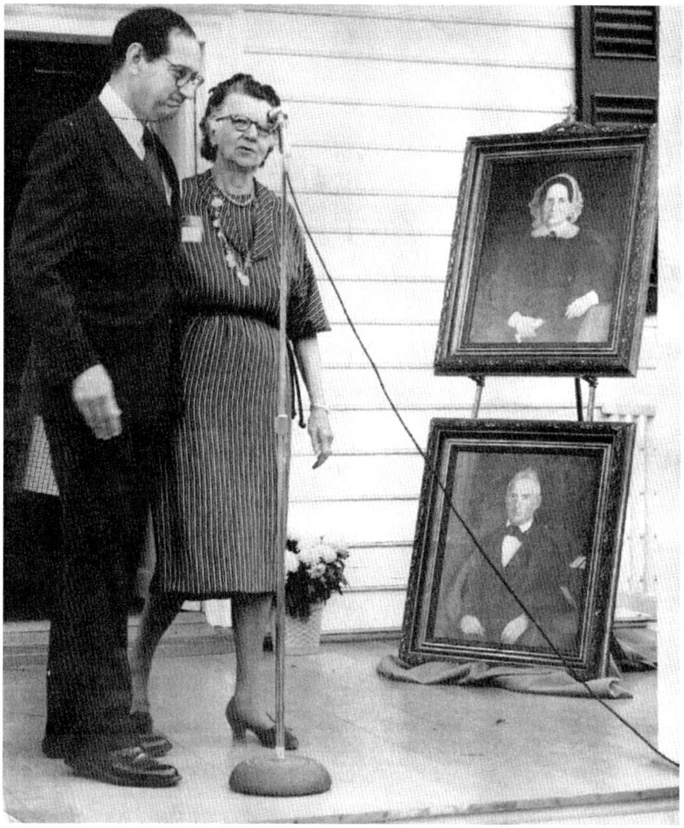

Kathleen Mackie Lake

Born in 1911 to an affluent family on Philadelphia's aristocratic Main Line, Kathleen Mackie Lake made enormous contributions as the wife of town and college physician Dr. George Mackie. She spent many nights driving her exhausted husband on house calls. Also a founding member of the Wake Forest College Birthplace Society, she is pictured here on the house steps at the college's sesquicentennial celebration in 1984. After her first husband's death, she married family friend and former gubernatorial candidate I. Beverly Lake Sr. (see page 110).

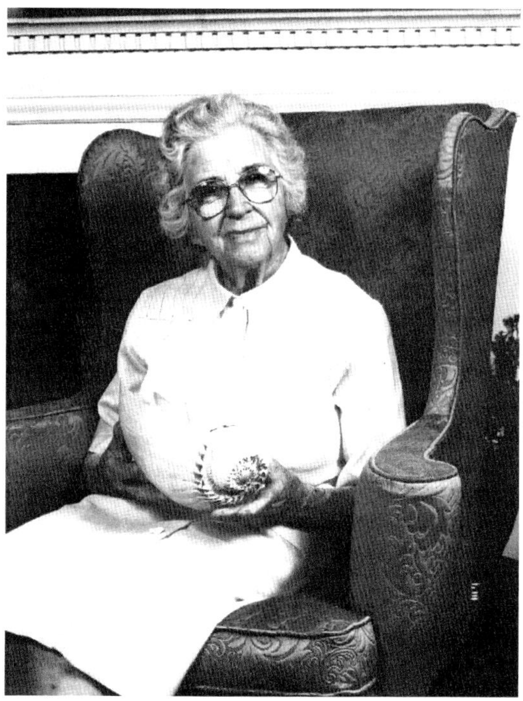

Ruth Snyder

Ruth Snyder and her husband, Everette (see page 81), operated the college bookstore for 30 years, first in Wake Forest and then Winston-Salem. Remaining active in the community, Snyder helped save the Calvin Jones House before retiring to Wake Forest in 1960. In 1980, Snyder received the town's Citizen of the Year Award in recognition of her lifetime of community service.

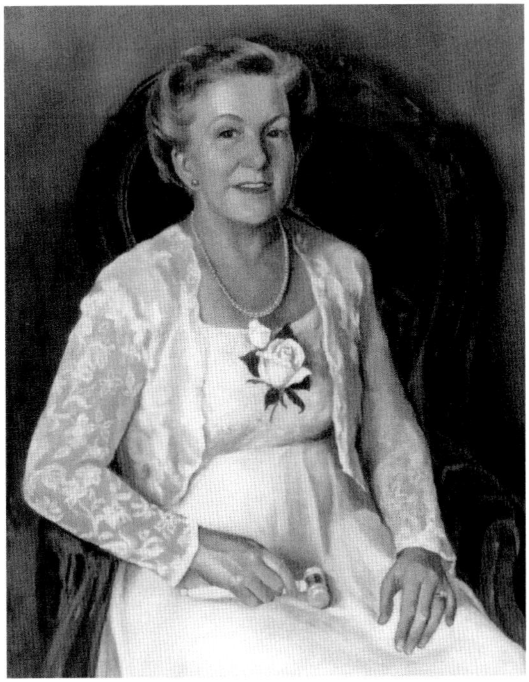

Ursula Bernstein Wilkinson
Known for her boundless energy, Ursula Wilkinson worked to make the world a better place. She held numerous leadership positions at her church, the Wake Forest Garden Club, the North Carolina Medical Society Auxiliary, and more than 10 additional organizations. Wilkinson ultimately received the town's Citizen of the Year Award for her many contributions to town life.

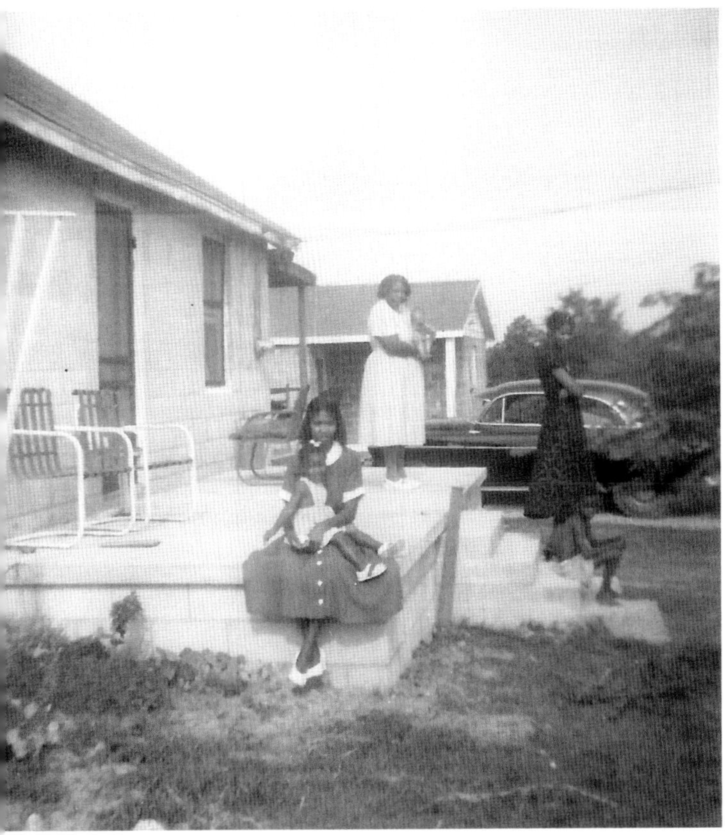

Annie Bullock and Geraldine Hall-Taylor
Daughter of community activist Annie Bullock (center), Geraldine Hall-Taylor (left, holding her baby daughter) remembers going up the fire escape behind the Forest Theater as a child so she could watch movies from the balcony reserved for "colored" audiences. As an adult, Hall-Taylor served as the "black PTA president" alongside a white counterpart during Wake Forest's first years of integration in the early 1970s. She later helped Bullock lobby for water and sewer improvements in the East End. (Courtesy of Geraldine Hall-Taylor.)

Robert R. East

In the 1950s, North Carolina State Highway Patrolman and Wake Forest resident Robert R. East posed with this sign as part of a public service campaign encouraging motorists to slow down and drive safely. Tragically, East died in 1972 from injuries sustained in a wreck while in pursuit of a suspect. The Neuse River Bridge on Capital Boulevard was named in his memory, to honor his years of service and sacrifice. The specific location was chosen because East was well known for patrolling the roads between Wake Forest and Raleigh. The Trooper Robert R. East Bridge remains a familiar span of highway for the thousands of commuters who drive Capital Boulevard each and every day. (Courtesy of Shirley Matheny.)

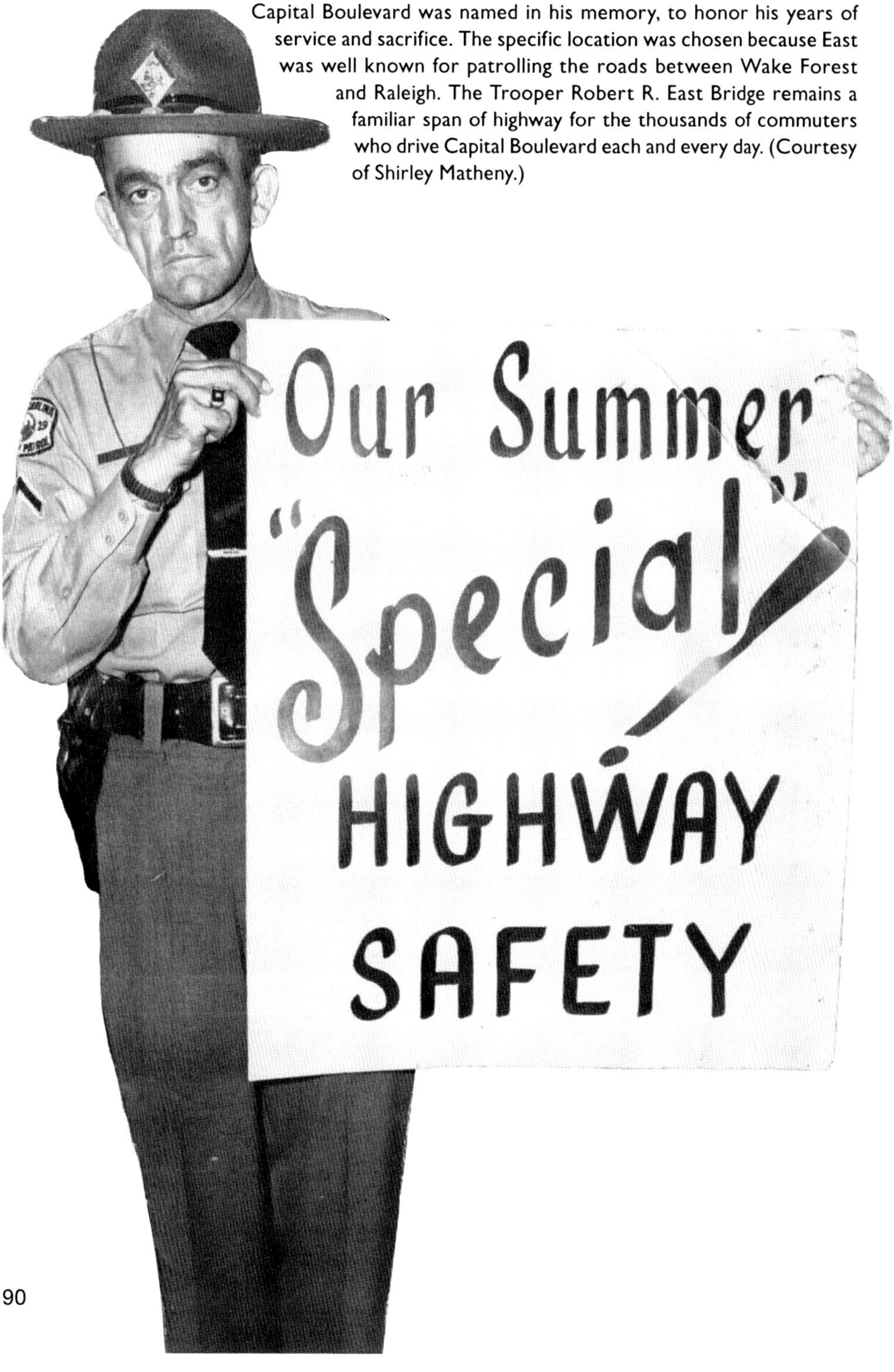

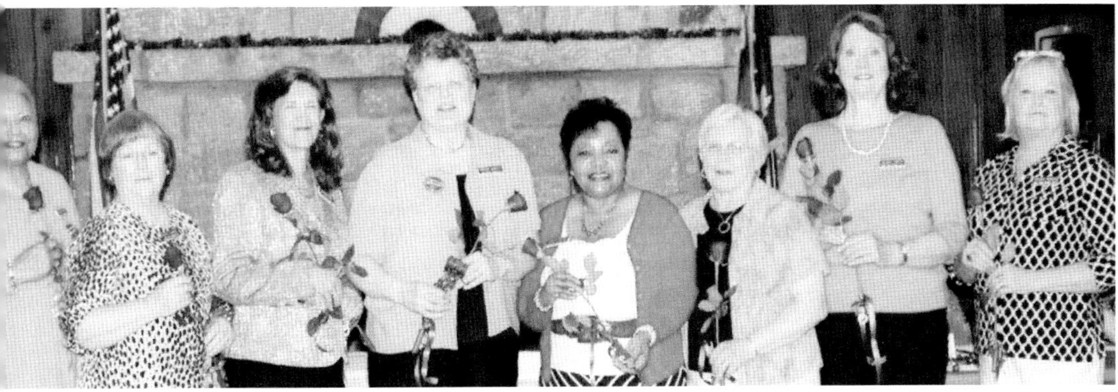

Wake Forest Woman's Club
The Wake Forest Woman's Club began in 1961 and continues to support the community through Backpack Buddies, Meals on Wheels, Habitat for Humanity, and more. Members have also placed free books in Laundromats, made toys for shelter dogs, and provided art supplies to local teachers. From left to right are Salina Gary, Kathy Norris, Sue Meehan, Marilyn Bonnett, Hilda Parler, Martha Loftin, Susan Smith, and Gorland McBride. (Courtesy of the Wake Forest Woman's Club.)

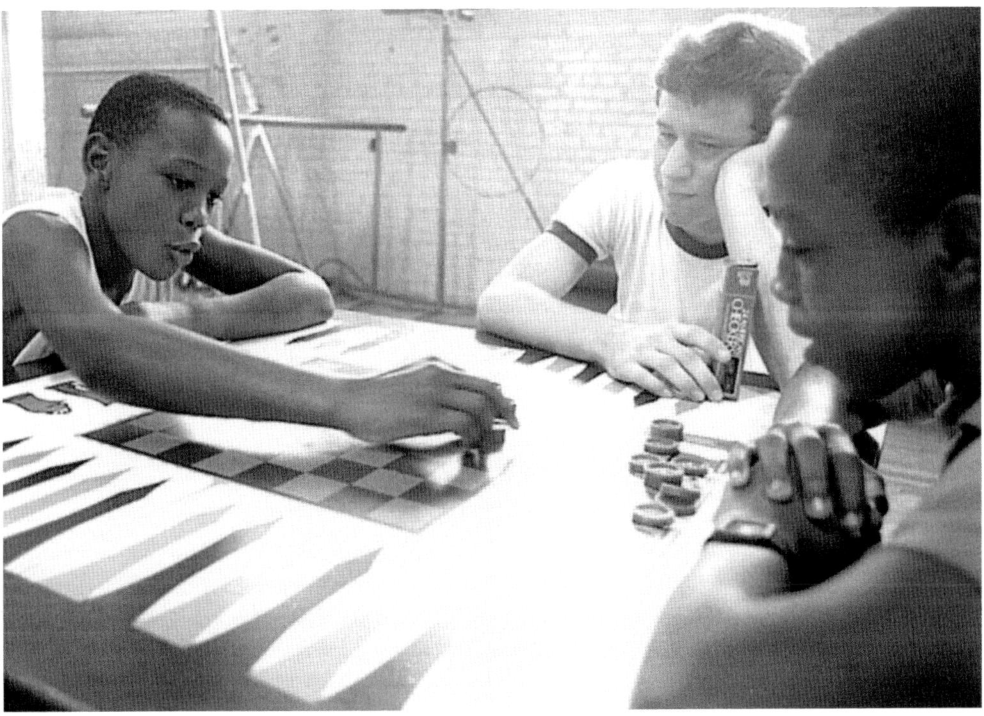

Wake Forest Boys and Girls Club
When they began meeting in the Wake Forest Elementary School gym, this group was known as just the Boys Club. The name soon changed, and in 1998 the Boys and Girls Club moved to its current home on South Wingate Street. The club contributes to the community by reaching all types of families with programs focused on healthy lifestyles, academics, good citizenship, and sports and fitness. The photograph shows Tomek McFadden, left, enjoying a game of checkers with Mike Rouse and George Bynum on the club's opening day in 1986. (Courtesy of the *Wake Weekly*.)

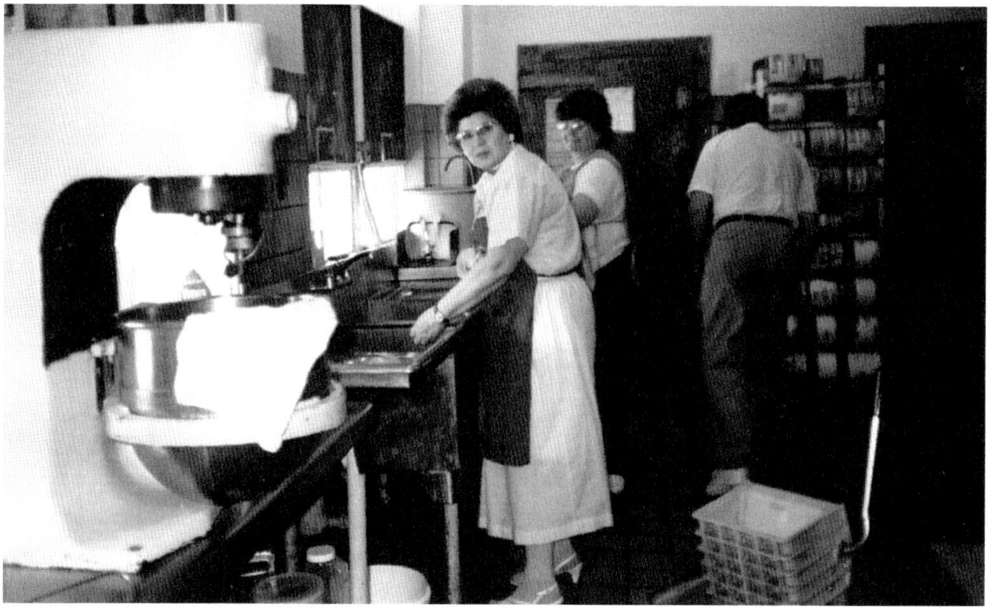

Wake Forest Kiwanis Club

The first male-dominated civic club in Wake Forest to admit women, the Kiwanis Club was formally organized 1987 with charter officers Thomas Dimmock, James Reason, Penny Parrish, and C. Bickett Aycock Jr. It contributes to high school scholarships, playgrounds, and the Wake County Terrific Kids program, which is aimed at rewarding all students for doing their best. This 1988 photograph shows charter member Peggy Allen working with kitchen staff at the seminary cafeteria to prepare a meal for up to 500 people on Mother's Day.

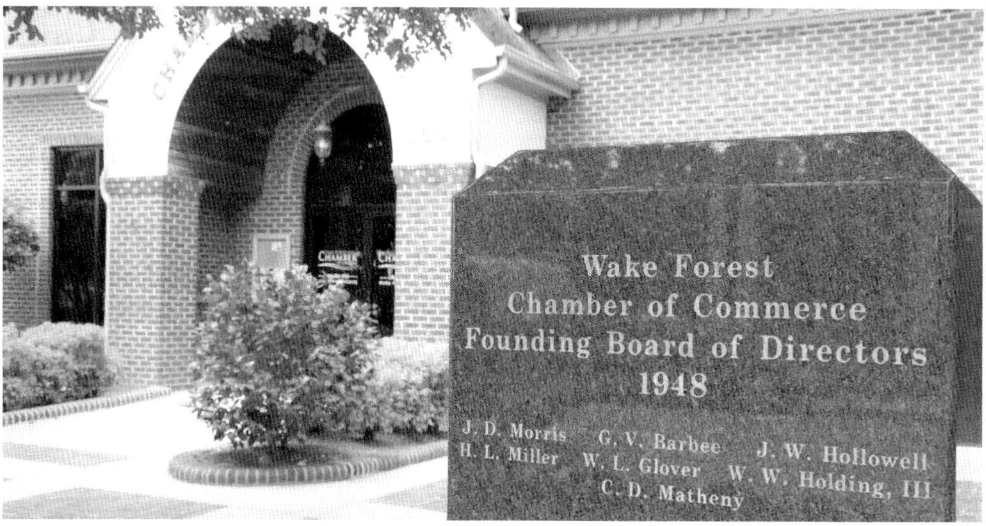

Wake Forest Chamber of Commerce

Organized in February 1948, the Wake Forest Area Chamber of Commerce had its first meeting at the home of John Wooten. The town's leading businessmen all attended. In those early days, the chamber had approximately 30 members. Now in its seventh decade and serving a membership of more than 700, the chamber is considered the "voice of business" in Northern Wake County.

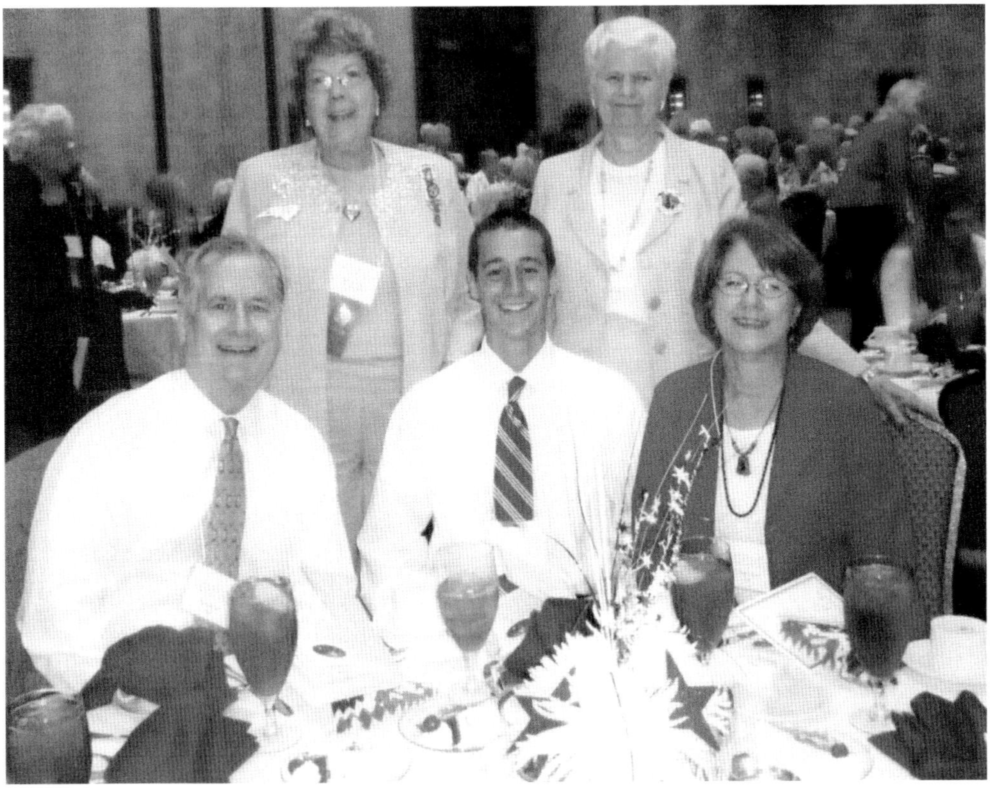

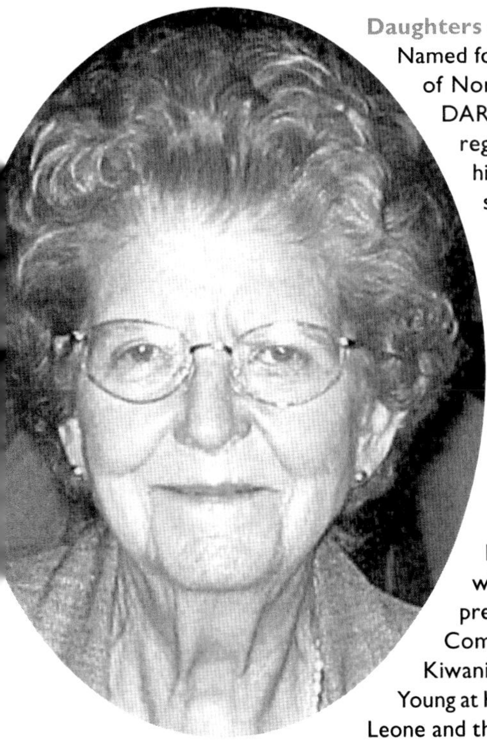

Daughters of the American Revolution

Named for the first brigadier general of the Continental Forces of North Carolina, the Gen. James Moore Chapter of the DAR was formed in 1933 at the home of the organizing regent, Loula Briggs Brewer. Its mission is to promote historic preservation, education, and patriotism. Members sponsor students at local high schools, visit hospitalized veterans, participate in Memorial Day and Veterans Day ceremonies, and annually donate more than 5,000 volunteer hours. In 2013, the DAR presented Ethan Porter with a $1,000 college scholarship. From left to right are (first row) Michael Porter, Ethan Porter, and Tamara Porter; (second row) Donna Lynam and Carolyn Coordes. (Courtesy of Carolyn Coordes.)

Thelma Fuller Wright

Born in the mill village, Thelma Fuller Wright married Electric Motor Shop founder Thomas Wright. She worked with the NC Department of Vital Records, served as president of the Woman's Club, chaired the Wake Forest Community Christmas Dinner, and volunteered with the Kiwanis Club, the Garden Club, the Homemakers Club, the Young at Heart Club, and Community Council. (Courtesy of David Leone and the *Wake Weekly.*)

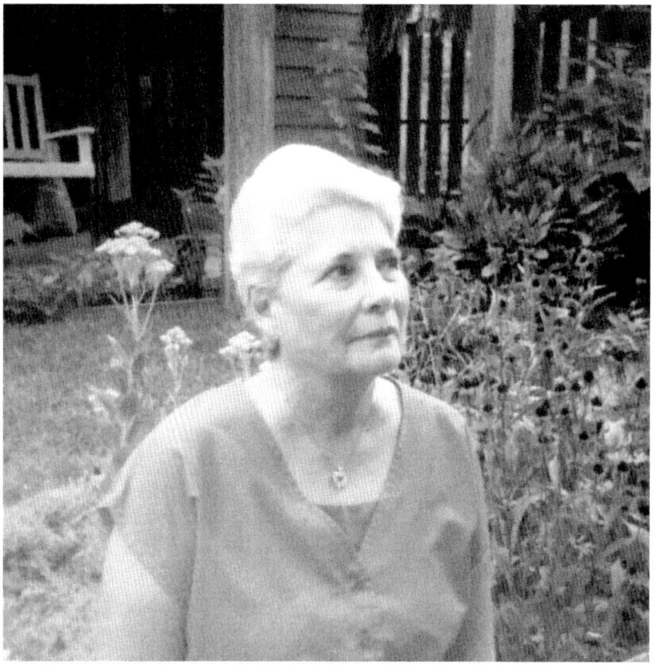

Margaret Johnston Wineinger
One of the pillars of the Wake Forest Garden Club and the Wake Forest College Birthplace Society, Margaret Johnston Wineinger was the sister of Johnny Johnston (see page 112), the college's 1950s-era golf coach. A longtime volunteer at the Wake Forest Historical Museum, Wineinger was largely responsible for creating the Calvin Jones House gardens, bringing her own plants, weeding, and growing much of the landscape still on the property today.

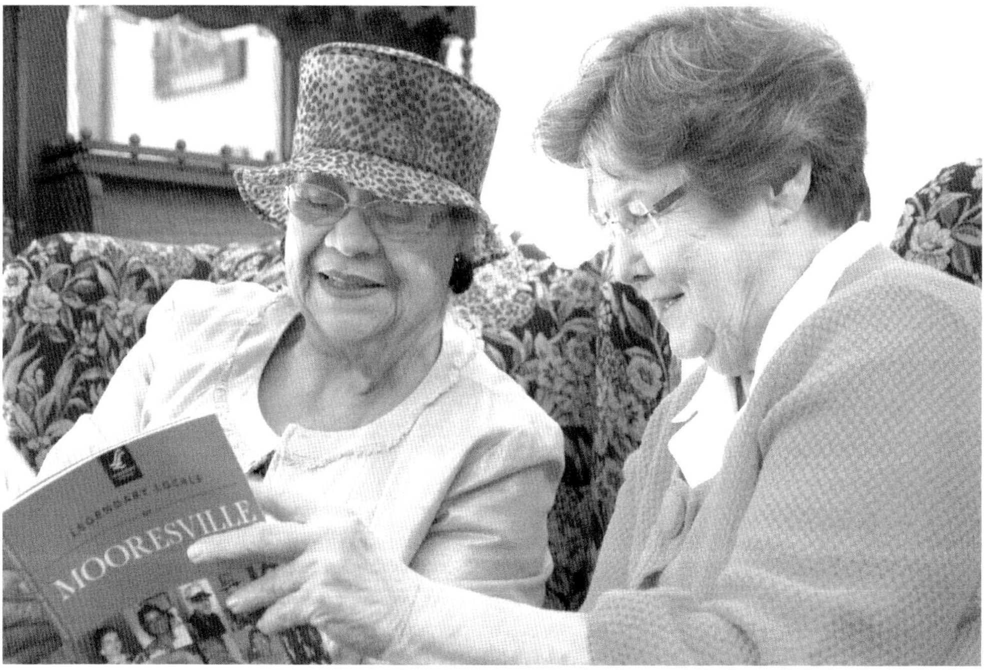

Eunice Haywood and Beverly Whisnant
When Eunice Haywood (left) and Beverly Whisnant met in the 1970s, both were teaching assistants at Wake Forest Elementary School. Each has a special area of expertise. Haywood is a gifted quilter whose works focus on color, art, and African American heritage. Whisnant is a historian who has volunteered with local civic organizations and leads the docent program at the Wake Forest Historical Museum. She was the town's 2002 Citizen of the Year.

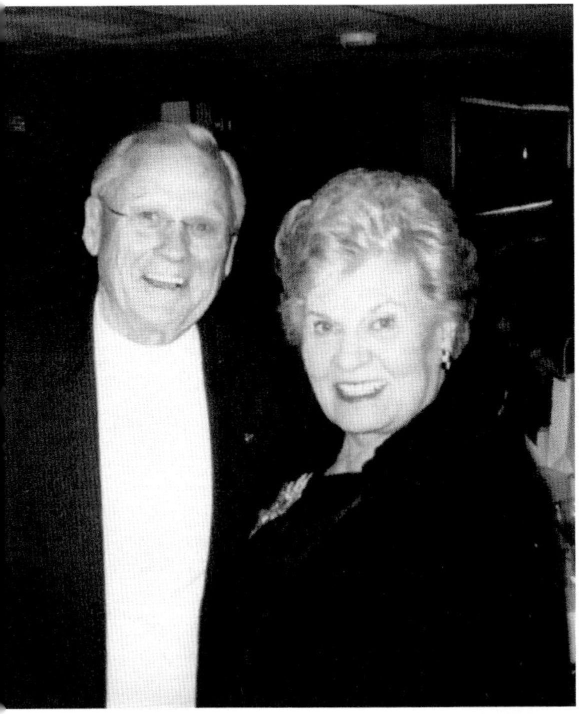

Bill and Louise Howard
Bill and Louise Howard breathed new life into North Main Street when they bought the historic J.L. Reid House and turned it into the town's first bed-and-breakfast. The dilapidated 9,000-square-foot mansion was essentially dismantled and reconstructed as the Lions Gate Inn, which opened in late 2007. In the years since, the Howards worked to beautify the North Main Street historic district with grass, flowers, and trees. Sadly, Bill passed away on July 5, 2014.

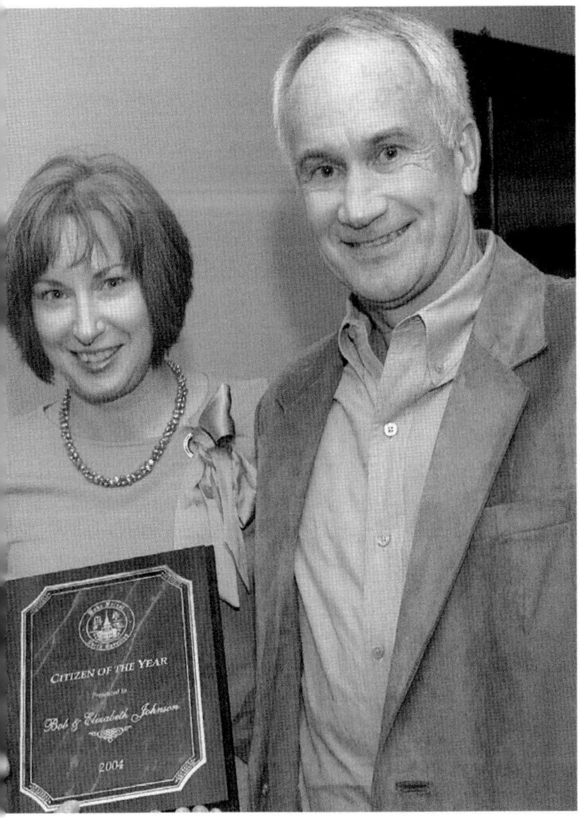

Bob and Elizabeth Johnson
The 2004 Wake Forest Citizens of the Year, Bob and Elizabeth Johnson turned an old warehouse on South White Street into the regional shopping destination known as the Cotton Company. The family also established the Graham Johnson Cultural Arts Foundation in memory of the teenage son they lost in 2006. Dedicated to the arts, the foundation promotes Graham's love of music, cooking, poems, and plants. (Courtesy of David Leone and the *Wake Weekly*.)

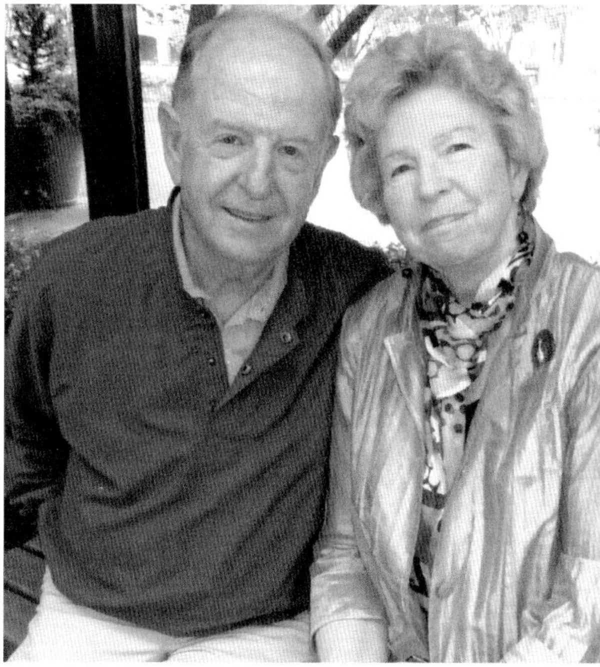

Susan and Sherrill Brinkley

When North Carolina held the Special Olympics World Summer Games in 1999, Susan and Sherrill Brinkley headed the Wake Forest committee responsible for hosting a group of athletes from the Bahamas. They have served for decades at Wake Forest Baptist Church, and Susan was the 20-year president of the Wake Forest College Birthplace Society. Her vision for a world-class facility was realized when the new museum opened in 2010.

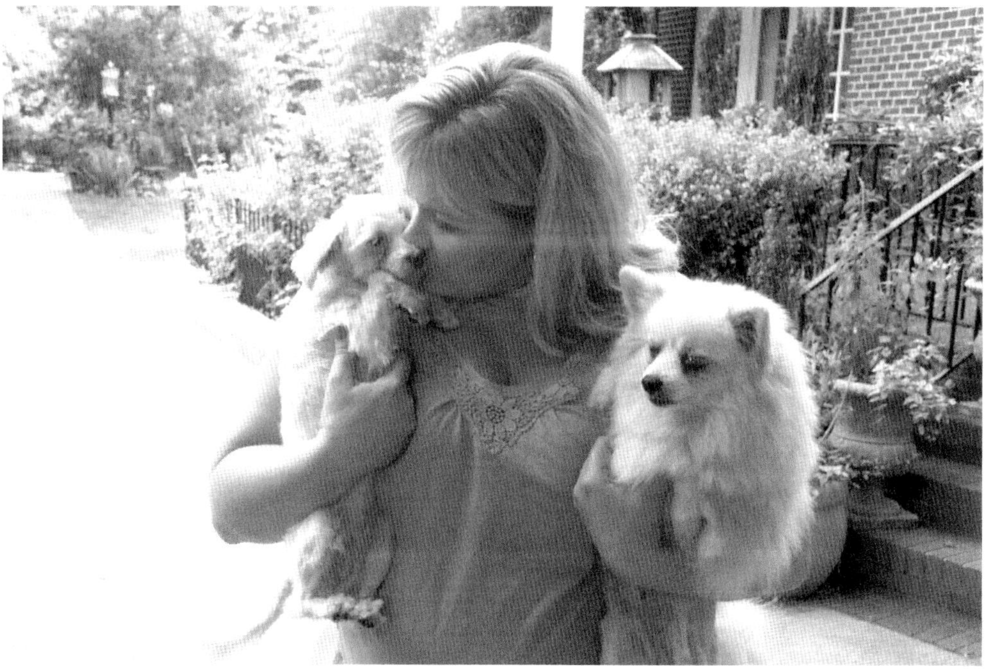

Molly Goldston

Transforming her family's century-old, 10-acre farm into a puppy playground, Molly Goldston founded an animal-rescue operation that handles nearly 1,000 dogs a year. Goldston evaluates each animal individually and then works to find the perfect family. The operation, which opened in 2004, is called Saving Grace Animals for Adoption and specializes in rescuing dogs from kill shelters and puppy mills across North Carolina. (Courtesy of David Leone and the *Wake Weekly*.)

CHAPTER SEVEN

Larger than Life

To the outside world, the heroes, leaders, and overachievers often represent the character of a community. For Wake Forest, this brings up an interesting question: Did these exceptional citizens shape the town, or did the town shape them? What is clearly evident is that, in the course of only a few decades, this place managed to cultivate many diverse talents, including a future Hollywood screenwriter, a groundbreaking educator born in Barbados, a Civil War soldier wounded five times in battle, and a man immortalized as the greatest golfer of his generation.

It is probably safe to say that Wake Forest produces interesting people because it is an interesting town. It is charming, wholesome, and soulful, but also striving, determined, and ambitious. The school that began with a strong religious and intellectual foundation evolved into a college with a fierce work ethic and a fighting spirit. However, it was the town that developed and sustained this environment. As 1950s basketball star and North Carolina Sports Hall of Fame member Jack Murdock once said, "This little school just seemed to make you play harder, try harder . . . You had plenty of reason to try hard here."

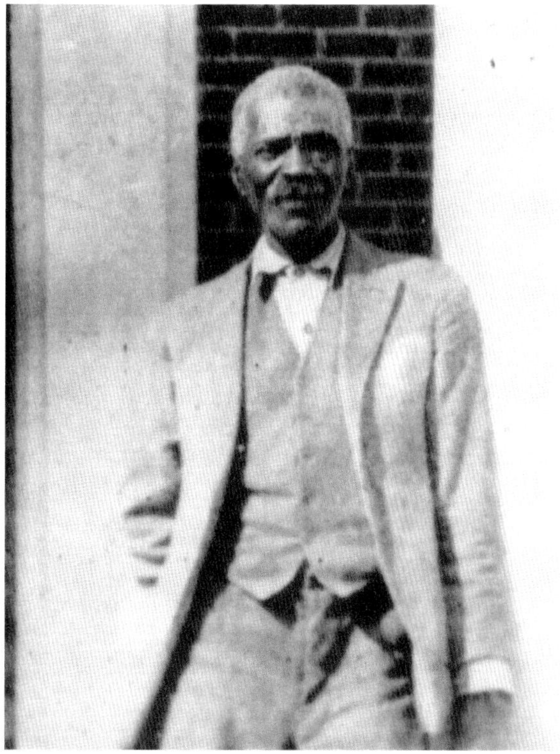

Tom Jeffries

Born a slave in Virginia, Tom Jeffries came to Wake Forest College in 1884 and is most famous for building the 3,000-foot stone wall that encircles the campus where he worked for 43 years. Jeffries was a sharp-witted philosopher, and students who sought his advice gave him the honorary title of "Doctor." When he died in 1927, his funeral was held in the college chapel with the faculty serving as pallbearers.

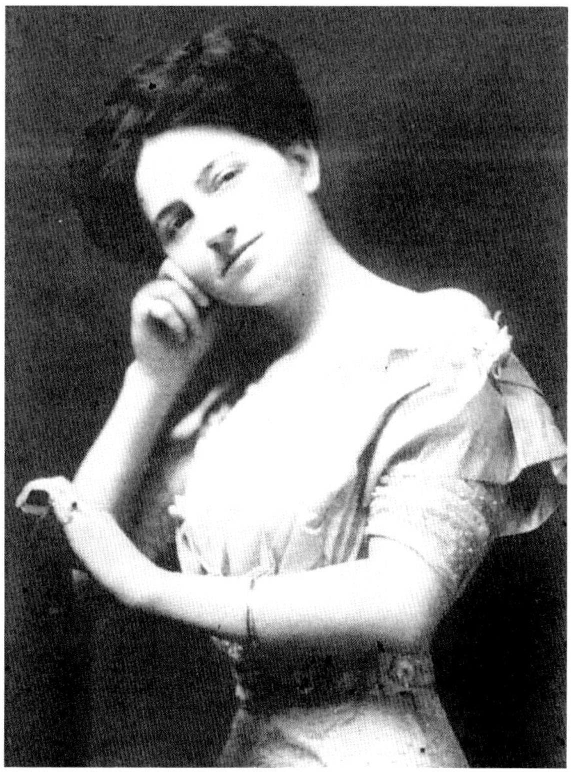

Hallie Powers Arrington

Hallie Powers Arrington, born in 1888, was the great-granddaughter of original Wake Forest College president Samuel Wait. Considered "the belle of Wake Forest," she was also among the first local suffragettes to register to vote when women were granted the right in 1921, and she frequently invited students to hold celebrations in her living room to get past the strict rules against dancing on the Baptist college campus.

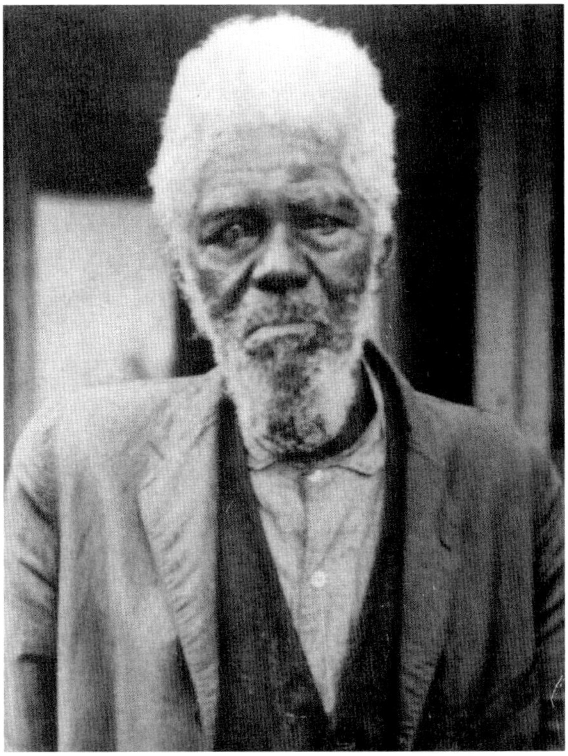

Nelson Ligon
Nelson Ligon was a spiritual man who had spent his life as a slave in the Wake Forest area. In 1866, while attending a worship service at Forestville Baptist Church, he was so moved by God's glory that he leapt from the colored balcony and fell into the pews reserved for the white congregation below. Surprised and somewhat unsettled by the level of his devotion, white church leaders decided to help establish a separate chapel for African American worshippers. Called Friendship Chapel Baptist Church, this church remains an active force in the Wake Forest community, and Nelson Ligon is revered as its founding member. (Courtesy of Friendship Chapel Baptist Church.)

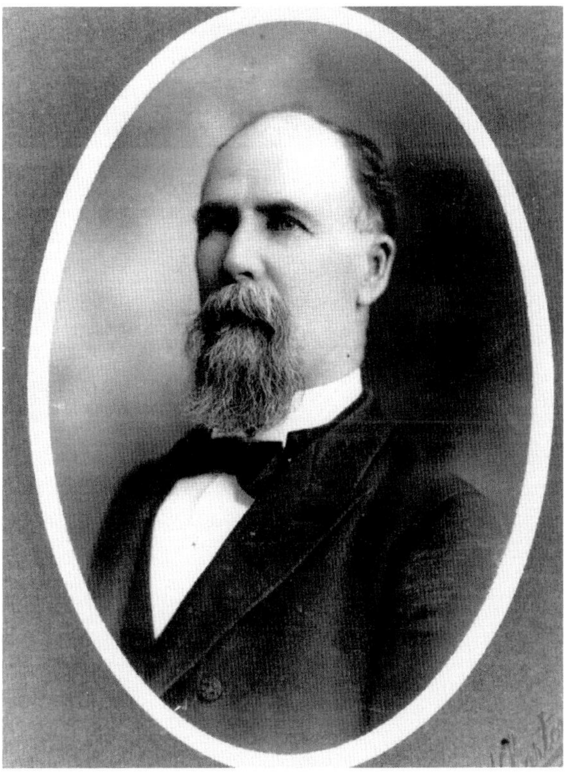

Thomas Toon
Thomas Toon graduated from Wake Forest College in the spring of 1861 and immediately joined the Confederate army. He was wounded five times in battle, had two horses shot out from under him, and attained the rank of brigadier general. Toon was later elected state senator from Columbus County and, in 1901, became state superintendent of public instruction. He died in office in 1902 and is buried in Raleigh's Oakwood Cemetery.

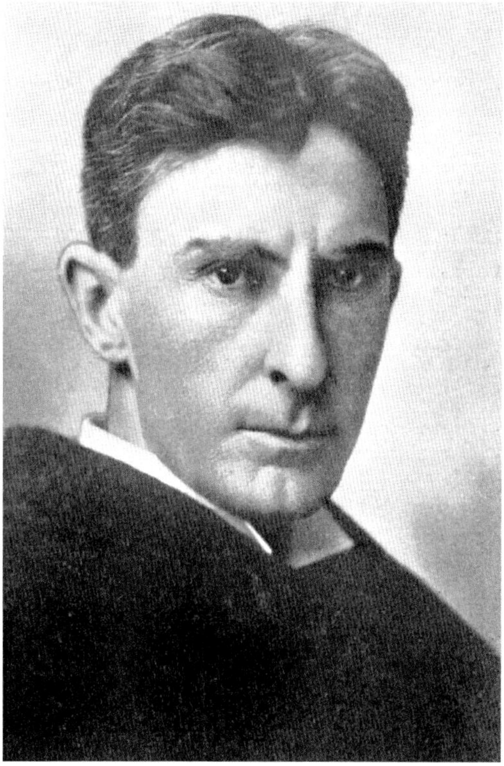

Thomas Dixon Jr.
Today, just as in his lifetime, controversy and notoriety are attached to the name of Thomas Dixon. A Wake Forest College graduate, Dixon worked as an actor, lawyer, minister, and lecturer before becoming a popular novelist. Books such as *The Clansman*, upon which early movie director D.W. Griffith based his silent epic *Birth of a Nation*, assured his place in history while unleashing a torrent of racism the author himself could never have imagined.

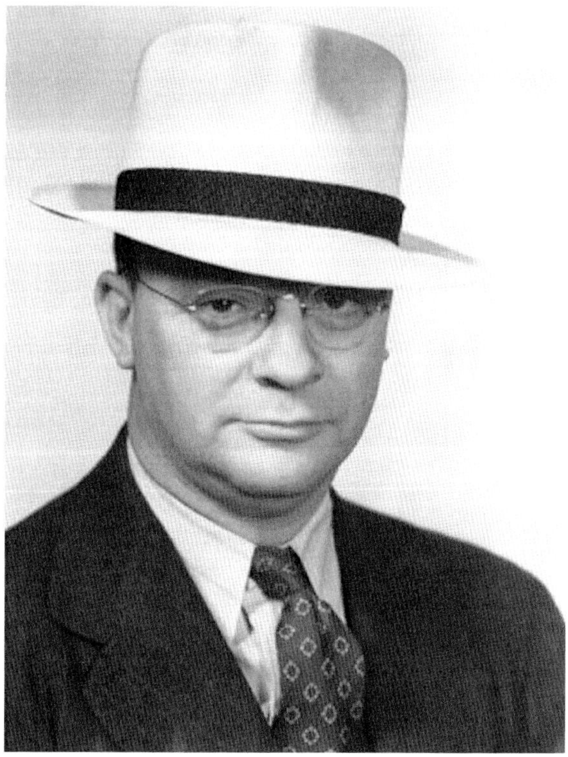

Wilbur Joseph Cash
A native Southerner, Cash graduated from Wake Forest College in 1922. His 1941 book, *The Mind of the South,* is still recognized as an intellectual masterpiece that illuminates regional history and remains in print even today. Cash died tragically young and under mysterious circumstances. He was found hanging in a Mexico City hotel room in 1941 less than a day after telling his wife that Nazi spies were following him.

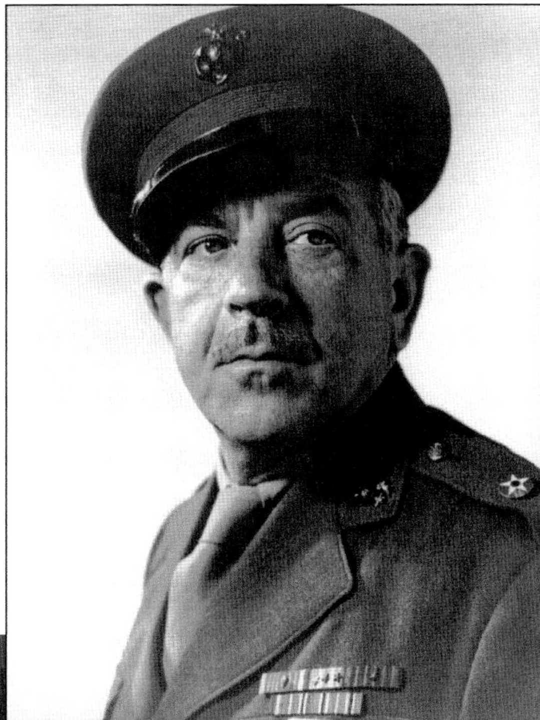

Laurence T. Stallings Jr.
A 1916 graduate of Wake Forest College, Stallings used his painful experiences in World War I as fodder for his many literary efforts. Two novels written 40 years apart, *Plumes* and *Doughboys*, convey some of the horrors of war. Stallings also had a career as a successful Hollywood screenwriter, working with some of the industry's leading directors throughout the mid-20th century.

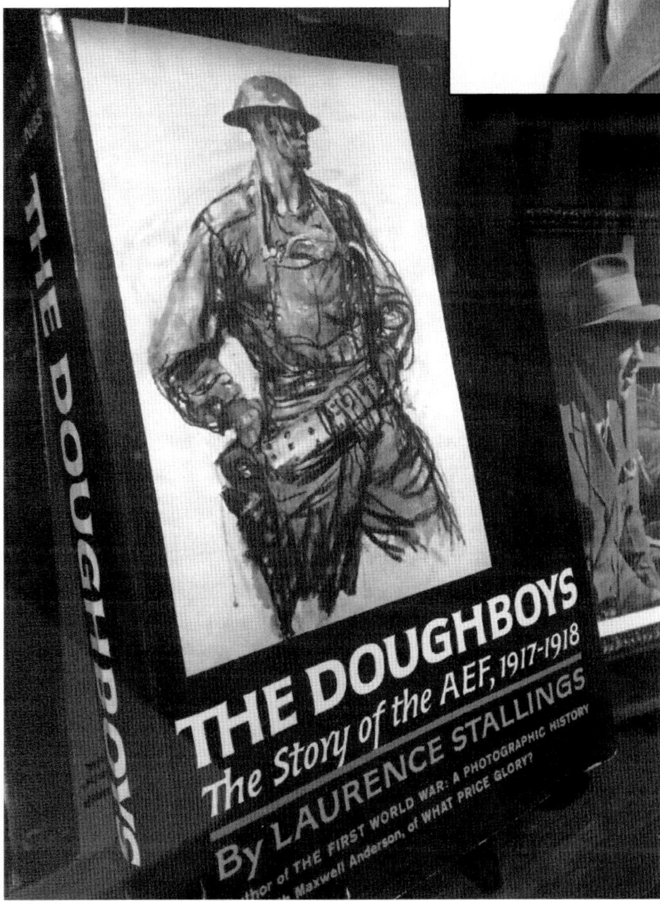

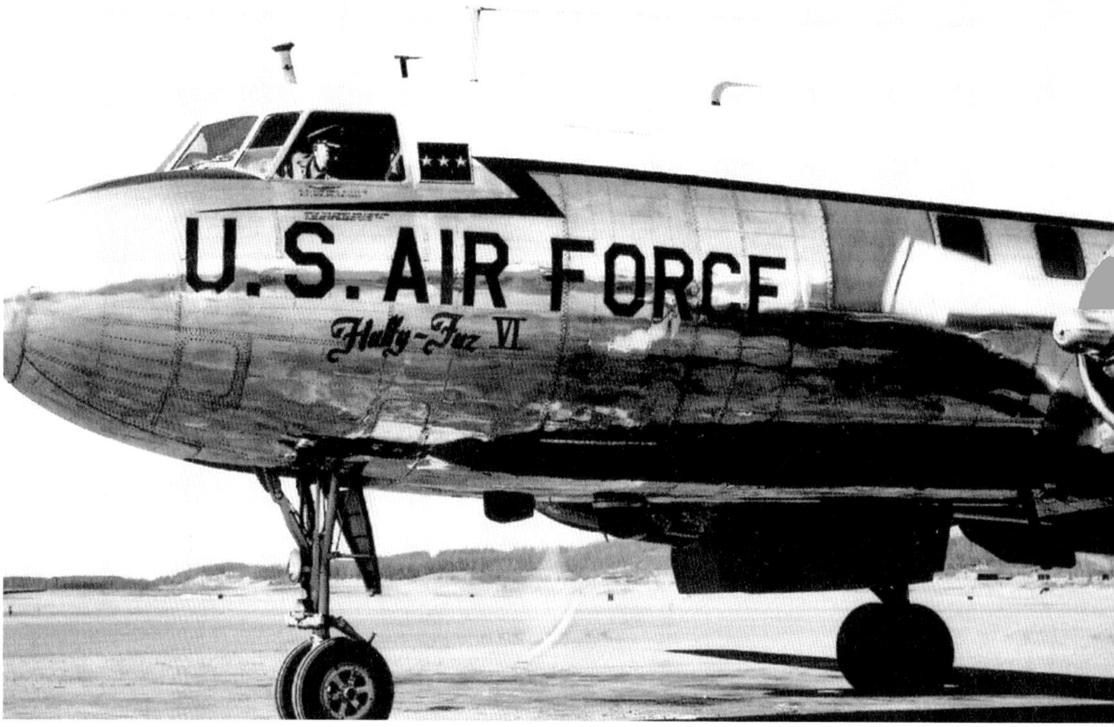

Frank Armstrong

Remembered as one of the best athletes Wake Forest College ever produced—a standout in baseball and football—Lt. Gen. Frank Armstrong went on to become one of the best pilots in the service. After graduating in 1925, he spent 14 years in the Army Air Corps before serving as chief of the American Bomber Command in England during World War II.

Among the most colorful characters of his era, Armstrong gained fame for leading heroic daylight bombing raids over occupied Europe at the height of the war. These daring attacks were later immortalized in the 1949 Academy Award–nominated film *Twelve O'Clock High*, starring Gregory Peck. Armstrong went on to receive the Distinguished Service Cross, the Distinguished Service Medal with oak leaf cluster, the Silver Star Medal, the Distinguished Flying Cross with four oak leaf clusters, the Air Medal with oak leaf cluster, and the British Distinguished Flying Cross. He once said of war, "I would advise you to go into it as a business; use your head—there's nothing to be afraid of."

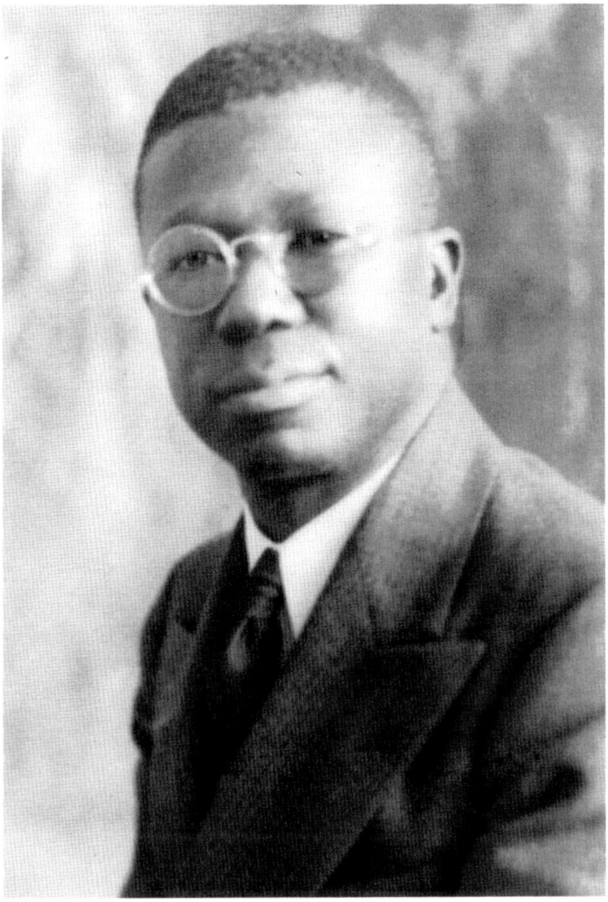

Lincoln Robert Best

He was a headmaster straight from Central Casting–a stern, bespectacled black man from Barbados with a clipped accent, perfect manners, and a passion for equal education that would change Wake Forest for the better. When Lincoln Robert Best arrived in 1936 to take a job as principal of the Wake Forest Colored School, one of his first acts was to change its name. Evelyn Alston Jones, who was a third grader that year and lived a block from the school, has said, "He had the parents come to the PTA and give a name. So everybody gave different names. I had never heard of W.E.B. DuBois. Nobody had. And everybody sent in Booker T. Washington, George Washington Carver and all of those different names, because that was who we had heard. And so, he said, 'No, I have a name.' And that's the name he gave us." Best chose that name to make a statement. DuBois had been the first African American to receive a doctorate from Harvard University and was an outspoken proponent of civil rights. He believed it was essential for blacks to defy racial stereotypes by exhibiting superior talent, intelligence, and hard work.

Deeply committed to this philosophy, Best developed a new curriculum. At the DuBois School, students memorized the poetry of Byron, Shakespeare, and Longfellow and recited passages in front of the class. Best lectured them on the value of good citizenship and gave instructions on etiquette. If he heard improper grammar, he would make the student repeat the statement correctly several times. In this way, he worked to shatter the complacent traditions of the Jim Crow South. Best was invited to debate the merits of higher education for blacks before an audience at Wake Forest College. He advised black children to set their aims high and to disregard the references to black inferiority they saw in their schoolbooks. "This is not who you are," he would tell them. "Nor your parents or grandparents. Don't you believe this." (Courtesy of Eric Best.)

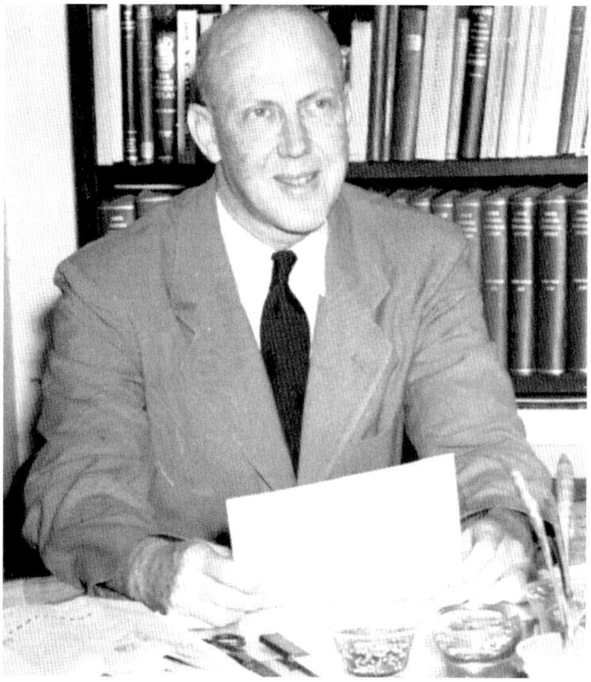

Christopher Crittenden

Born in 1902, Christopher Crittenden was a grandson of Wake Forest College president Charles Taylor. As executive head of the North Carolina Historical Commission, forerunner to the Department of Archives and History, Crittenden was responsible for creating the program that places markers at locations important to North Carolina history. (Courtesy of the State Archives of North Carolina.)

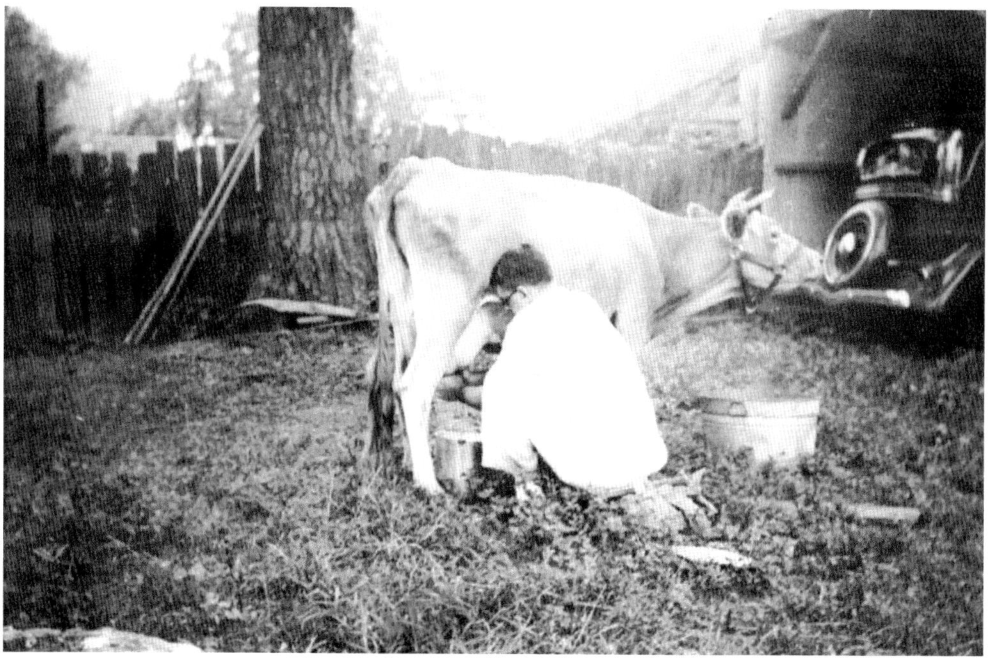

Mae West

In the days when Wake Forest allowed families to keep livestock within town limits, Mae West the cow was a familiar figure happily chewing her cud in an empty lot on the east side of Faculty Avenue. Owned by the Mills family, she was responsible for providing a daily supply of milk during the hard days of the Great Depression. Mae West entered local folklore and became a legend in her own right. (Courtesy of Suzanne Mills Erskine.)

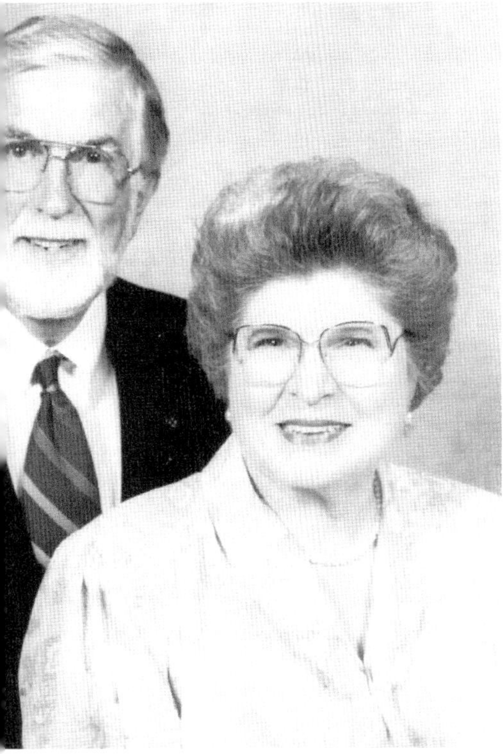

Bob and Peggy Allen
A graduate of Wake Forest College, Peggy was serving as youth director at Wake Forest Baptist Church when she met Bob Allen, a newspaperman whose family published the *Wake Weekly*. Their shared ambition was to produce a small, local paper of outstanding quality, and as a married couple they made their Wake Forest publication a continuing success. Peggy died in 2005; the next year, she and Bob were inducted into the North Carolina Journalism Hall of Fame. The Allen family still owns the *Wake Weekly*.

Tom Arrington
Pictured with daughter Hallie Arrington Hearn and Wake Forest University president Thomas Hearn (no relation) at the school's sesquicentennial celebration in 1984, Tom Arrington (left) was a direct descendant of the first president of Wake Forest College, Samuel Wait. Known for his devotion to community and a wide-ranging brilliance that stretched from mathematics to plumbing to electric train sets, the legendary Arrington was one of the town's most endearing characters.

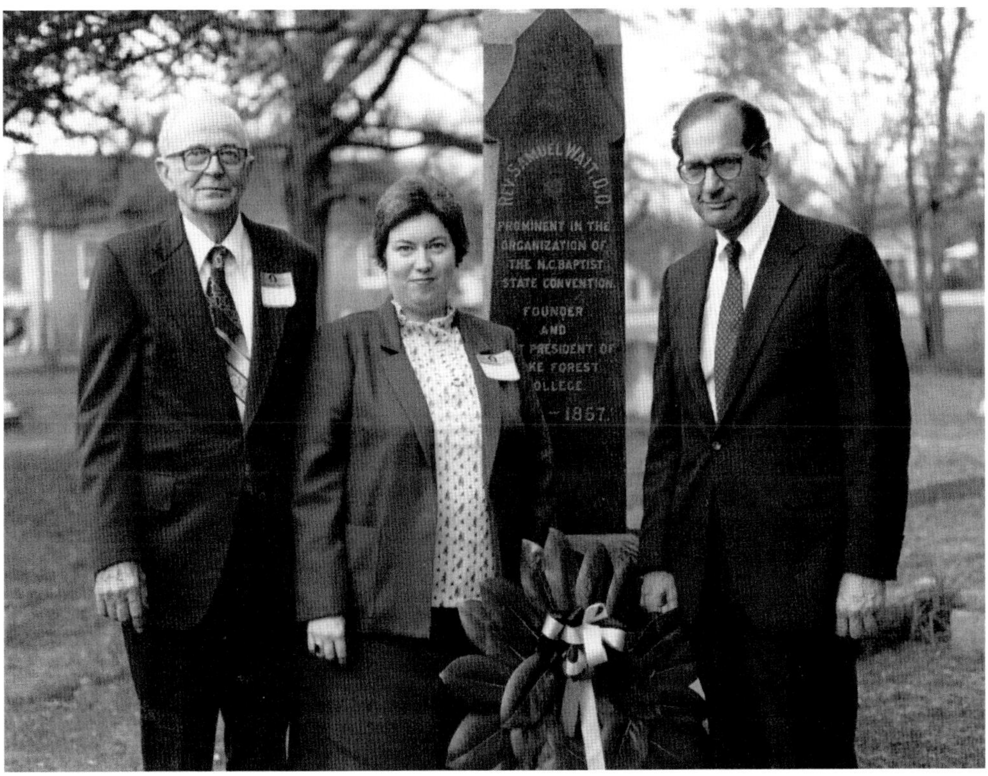

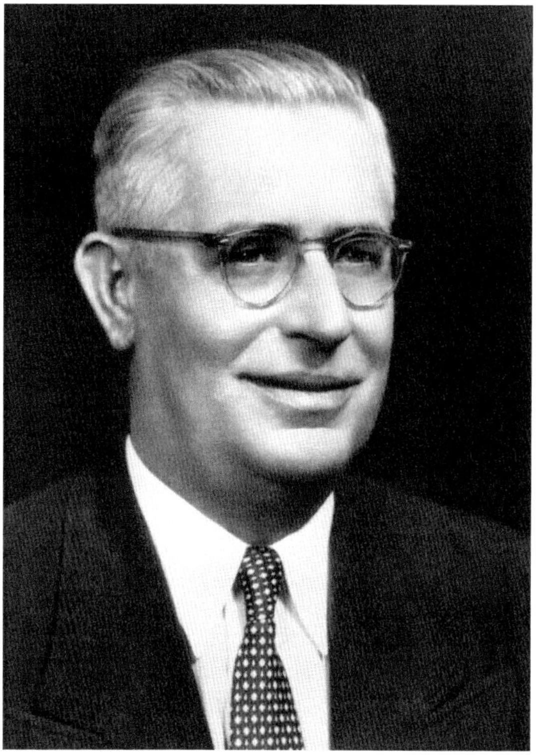

George Mackie

As a college student in the 1920s, George Mackie arrived for an education but stayed on as a faculty member at Wake Forest College. Serving as town and campus doctor, Mackie worked round the clock, maintaining a punishing schedule of clinic hours and house calls. Mackie is said to have "worked himself to death," succumbing to a fatal heart attack at his North Main Street office in 1969.

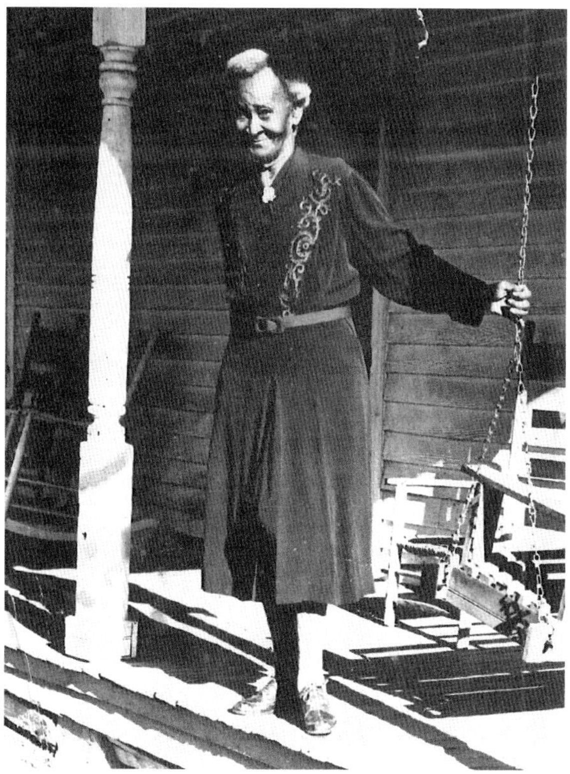

"Mama" Ellen Lewis

Ellen Lewis, later known as "Mama" Ellen or "Aunt" Ellen, was an enslaved teenager on a Wake Forest farm when the Civil War ended. As an adult, she became a famous nurse and midwife. In a newspaper article published shortly before her death in 1950 at age 101, a reporter wrote, "Aunt Ellen doesn't like to talk about mistreatment of the slaves . . . memories of those days make her feel bad, and she wants to be happy in the present."

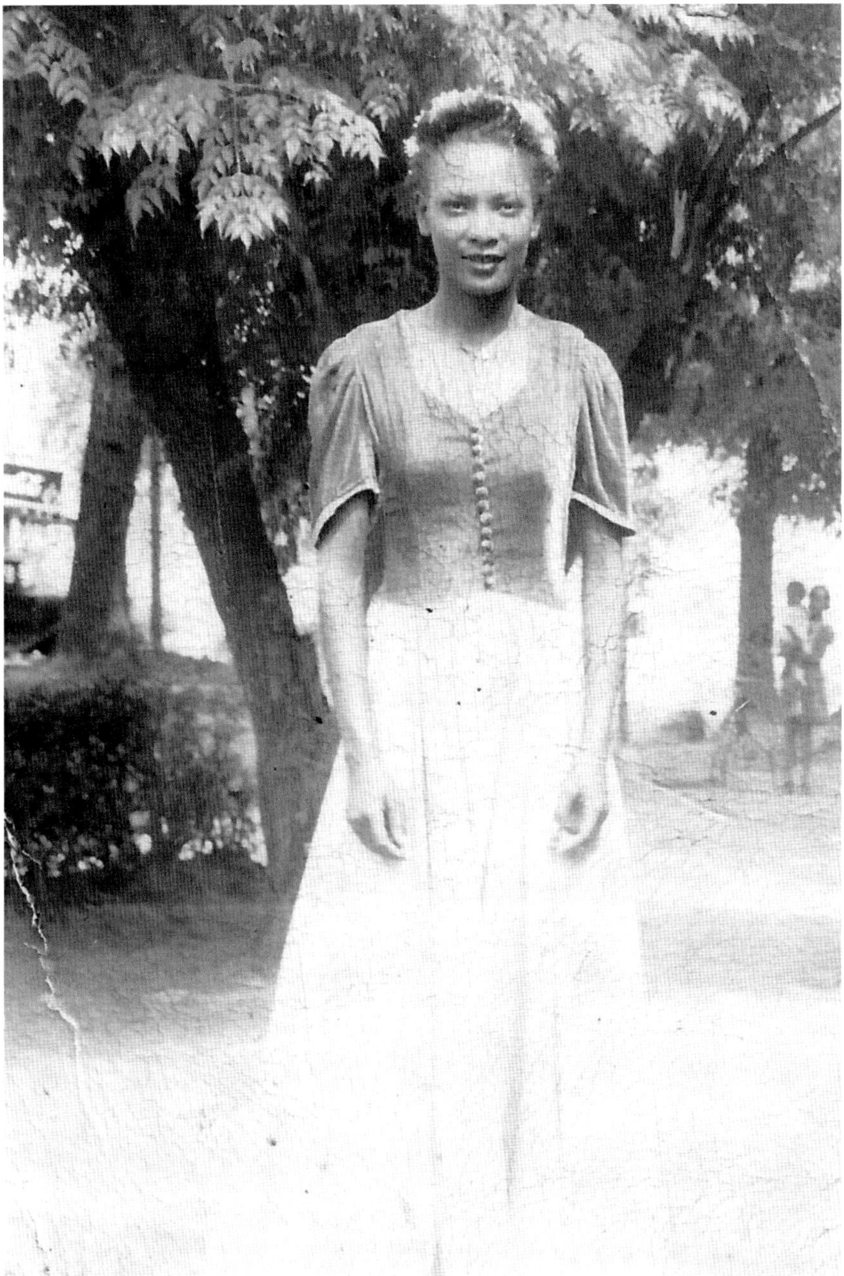

Evelyn Alston Jones

The great-granddaughter of "Mama" Ellen Lewis, Evelyn Alston Jones was born in 1928. She graduated from the DuBois School in the town's East End and went on to a career in education. In an oral history project funded by a grant from the North Carolina Humanities Council, Jones stressed the important lessons passed along by mothers and grandmothers in the African American community. Jones remembered her own mother's advice to hold her head high, show her intelligence, and never back away from a fight. "I don't take back. I don't get back. No further than I will knock back. And ain't nobody going to knock me back." This c. 1942 photograph shows Jones dressed for a neighborhood dance at about age 14.

Joyce Alford Davis

In the early part of the 20th century, Wake Forest was a town with muddy, unpaved streets, no public schools, and not a single stretch of sidewalk. But it did have Wake Forest College and, along South White Street, a thriving business district with groceries and department stores. And it had Glen Royall Cotton Mill, where Joyce Alford Davis was born in 1917. Both of her parents worked at the mill. Her father was a mechanic, and her mother also handled machinery. Davis recalls the mill village of her childhood—with its tidy, well-kept houses—as a happy, tight-knit community. As the child of a working-class couple, Davis took pride in outperforming the sons of Wake Forest College professors at her public school. And to underscore her dedication to education, she kept her grade school primer, a book issued by the state of North Carolina and filled with words and information young children in the 1920s were expected to read, repeat, and memorize. Davis eventually married and raised her family in Wake Forest. In the first of these photographs, taken around 1917, Davis appears with her father on the steps of their house in the mill village. In the second, taken in 2013, she sits for an oral history interview at the museum.

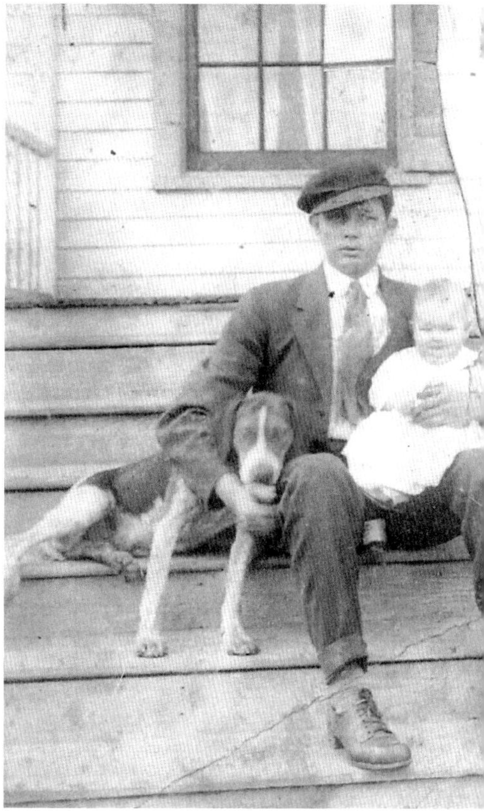

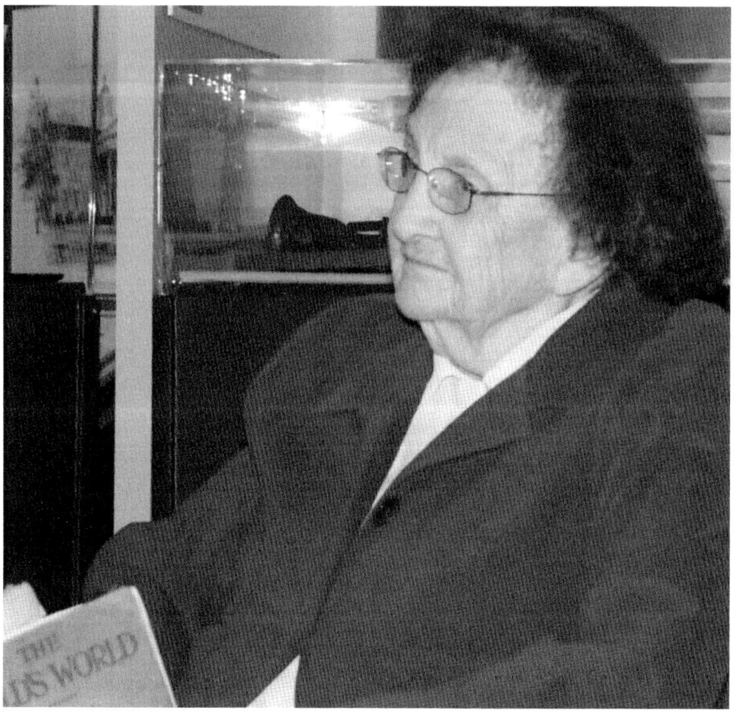

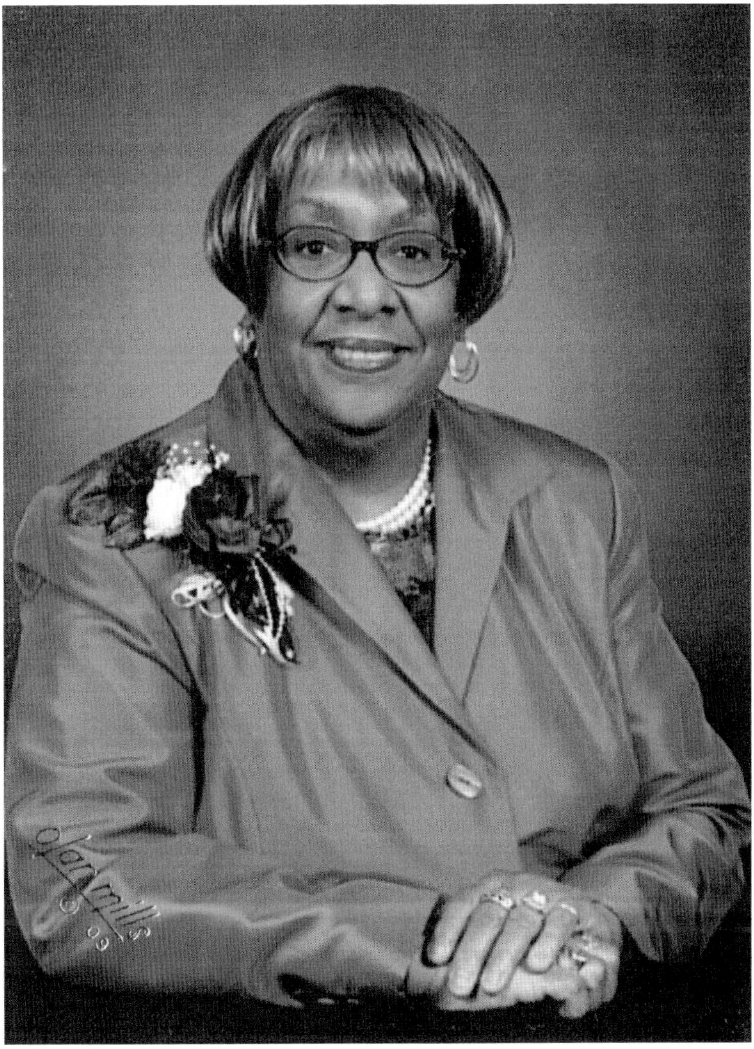

Theresa Watkins
After the Civil Rights Act passed in 1964, Theresa Watkins was faced with a decision. As a teenager at the segregated DuBois School, she could now enroll in the all-white Wake Forest High School. Four friends decided to join her: Evonne Peppers, Mittie Jeanette Massenburg, Pauline Battle, and Rhonda Hood. Though the establishment in Wake Forest was committed to allowing integration, the girls still faced some opposition when they reported to school for the fall term in 1966. Watkins says groups of boys routinely blocked them from coming up the steps to class, and she also recalls being pelted with black jellybeans and having someone break into her locker to slice the letters *KKK* into her books. But there was also support. John Byrne, son of baseball legend Tommy Byrne (see page 111), made it his job to escort the girls safely through the halls. Still, it was difficult. Three of the girls returned to DuBois, leaving only Watkins and Hood to become the first two African American students to graduate from Wake Forest High School. Watkins now says she never considered giving up. An ordained minister, she writes, "[We] endured much pain in order that other African-American children could receive an equal opportunity of education without the stress and pain of segregation and disenfranchisement. I pray that the struggle we endured has made a difference in the public school system of Wake County." (Courtesy of Theresa Watkins.)

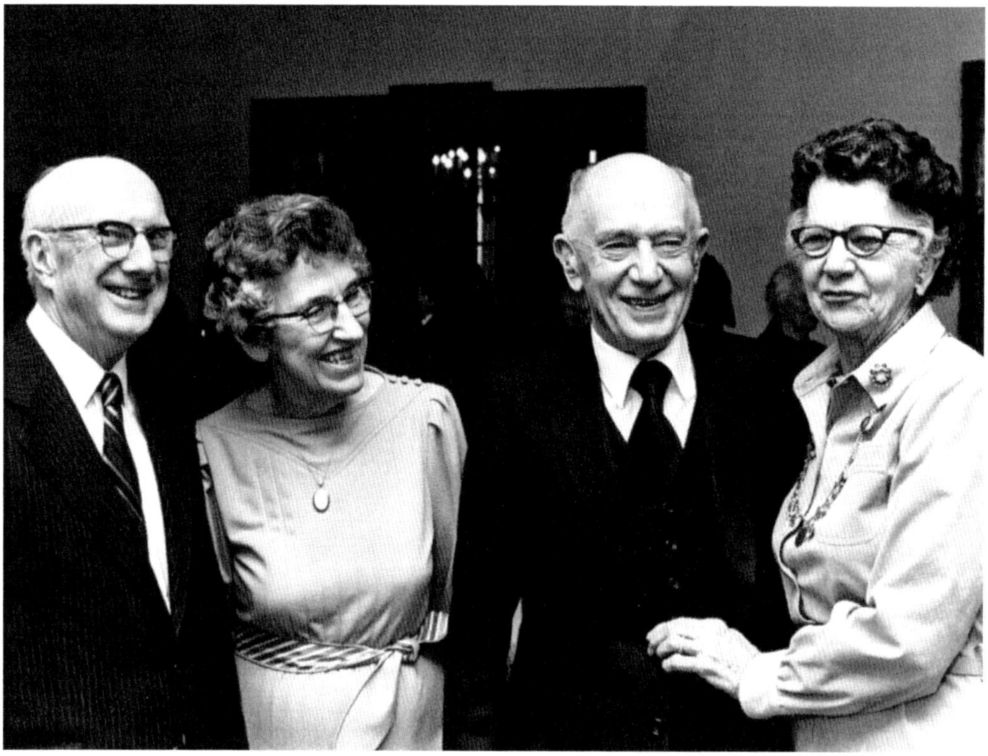

Olin T. Binkley, Pauline Binkley, I. Beverly Lake Sr., and Kathleen Mackie Lake
Two of the town's most prominent couples posed for this historic photograph taken during the Wake Forest College sesquicentennial celebration in 1984. Olin T. Binkley, a philosopher of religious thought in the mode of Albert Schweitzer, graduated from WFC in 1928 and became an ordained minister. He continued his training at Yale Divinity School before returning to Wake Forest, first as a professor at the college and later serving as president of Southeastern Baptist Theological Seminary. Pauline Binkley made her mark in local civic organizations, most significantly helping to save the historic Calvin Jones House as a founding member of the Wake Forest College Birthplace Society. Wake Forest native I. Beverly Lake Sr. was the son of a WFC physics professor. After graduating from Harvard Law School, Lake came back to teach as a law professor and later went into private practice before running for governor in the 1960 democratic primary. Lake stuck to a platform that strongly opposed public school integration, and he lost the nomination to future North Carolina governor Terry Sanford. He went on to serve on the North Carolina State Supreme Court. After the death of his first wife, Lake married close family friend Kathleen Mackie, a tireless champion of Wake Forest, its people, and its history (see page 88).

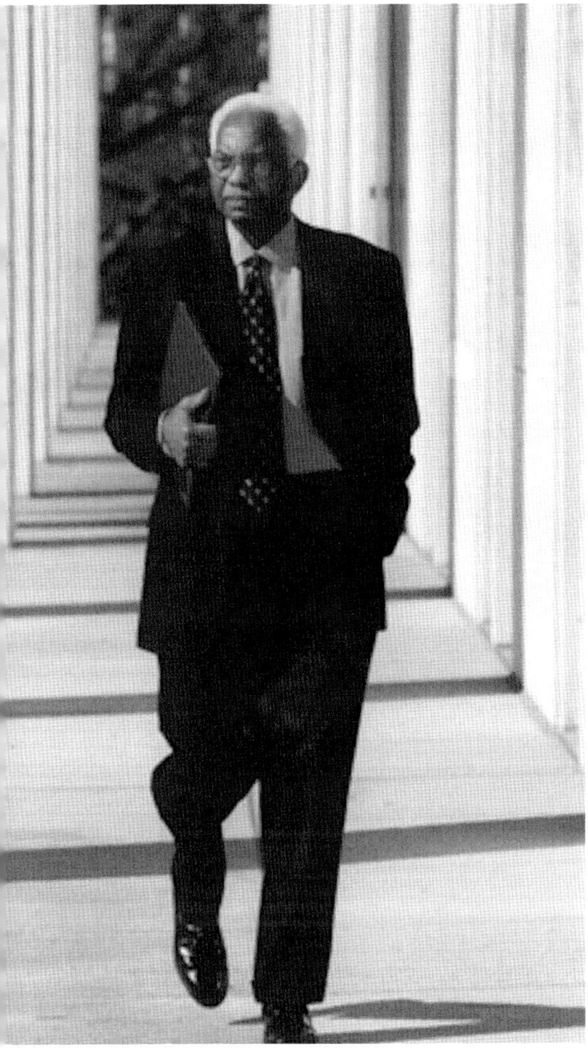

Vernon Malone

Born near Wake Forest in 1931, Vernon Malone graduated from the DuBois School and Shaw University. He worked as a teacher and educational administrator and guided the long process of public school integration in Raleigh and Wake County. Malone served as chairman of the Wake County Board of Commissioners and as a state senator in the North Carolina General Assembly. Upon his death in 2009, the lawmakers passed a joint resolution honoring his many contributions. (Courtesy of the Malone family.)

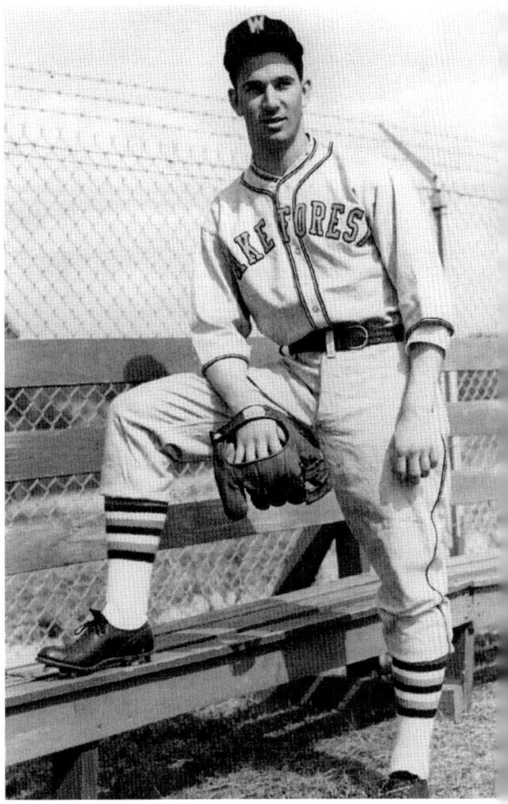

Tommy Byrne

A Wake Forest College graduate and star pitcher for the New York Yankees, Tommy Byrne has been inducted into the North Carolina, Maryland, and Wake Forest University Sports Halls of Fame. After his athletic career, he led the Wake Forest community as town mayor from the late 1970s to the early 1980s. Byrne also helped establish the Wake Forest Country Club.

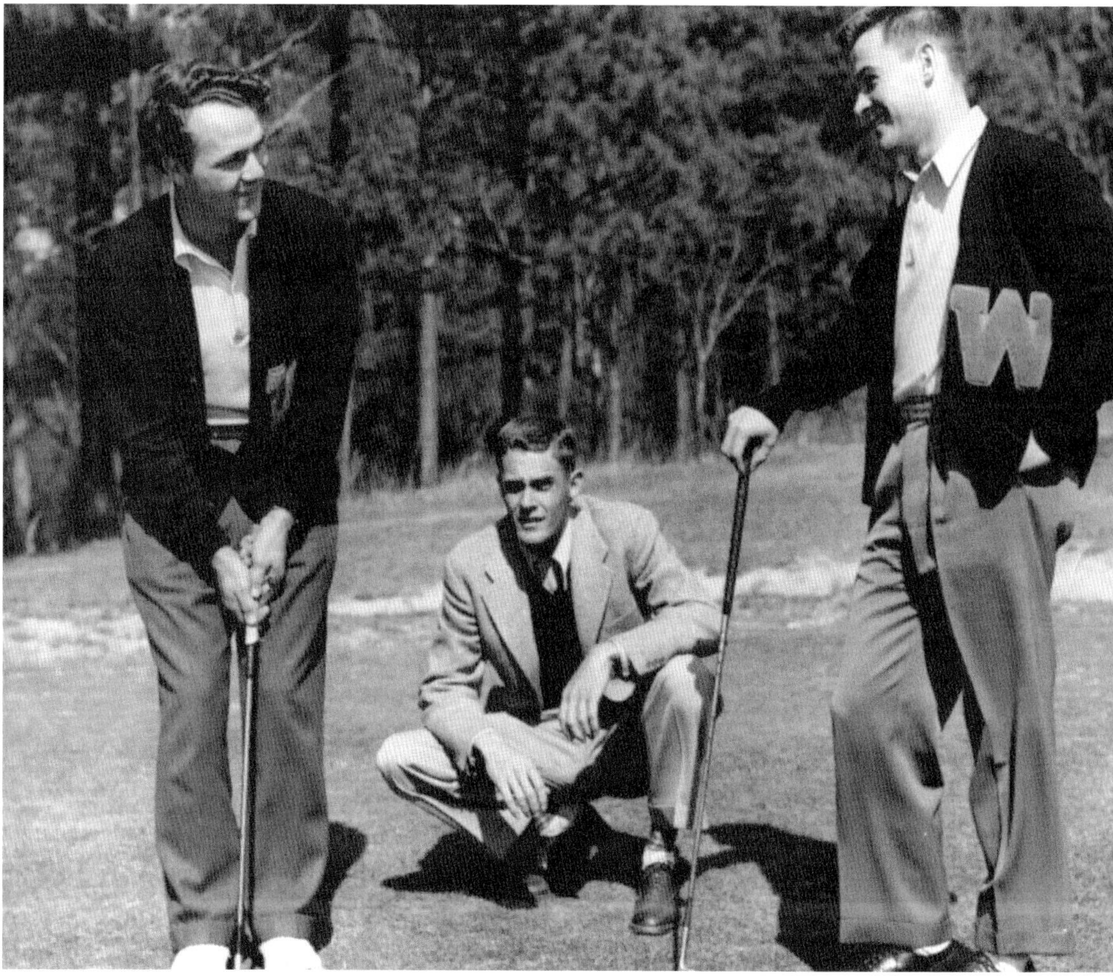

Arnold Palmer, Johnny Johnston, and Buddy Worsham

Legendary golfer Arnold Palmer is just one part of a mythic Wake Forest trio that represents the full spectrum of triumph and tragedy in sports and in life. Palmer was a high school student in Latrobe, Pennsylvania, when he learned about Wake Forest College secondhand. The college golf coach, Johnny Johnston, had telephoned Palmer's best friend, another great golfer named Buddy Worsham, to try and recruit him. After hearing the pitch, Worsham reportedly replied, "I've got this friend up here. He's my best buddy and we kinda wanted to go to school together. He's a pretty good golfer, and I'll come to Wake Forest if you'll give him a scholarship, too." Johnston conferred with his boss, athletic director Jim Weaver, and together they agreed to bring both Worsham and Palmer to WFC in the fall of 1947. But three years later, in October 1950, tragedy struck. Worsham was riding in a car on the way back from a homecoming dance in Durham when the driver lost control on Highway 98. Two students were killed—Worsham was one of them. Devastated, Palmer left Wake Forest. He would spend three years in the US Coast Guard before returning in 1954 to win the first-ever ACC golf championship. He later established the Buddy Worsham Memorial Scholarship Fund.

CHAPTER EIGHT

Eat, Drink, and Be Merry

Without beaches or a mountain view, Wake Forest is not among the many North Carolina towns that can sit back and rely on the beauty of nature to bring in a steady stream of tourists. Citizens hoping to boost the local economy by drawing visitors had to invent their own attractions, and over the course of the 20th century, the townsfolk became quite adept at tailoring their approach.

When Wake Forest was a college town, many of its businesses catered to the academic community. The Colonial Club started as a 19th-century hotel. It later became a dormitory for students on athletic scholarships. Eateries were also popular. A dining hall run by "Miss" Jo Williams became famous for serving hundreds of hot meals a day to students. For young men who liked a little entertainment with their food, there was Shorty's Famous Hot Dogs and its dimly lit backroom pool hall. This is the only college-era restaurant still operating in Wake Forest today.

After the construction of US Highway 1, which ran straight through town on its course from Maine to Florida, some Wake Forest homeowners turned their houses into motor lodges. A number of these establishments popped up on South Main Street and Faculty Avenue, their front yards decorated with signs declaring "free locked garage" or "comfort and service without extravagance." The most notable, Wooten's Hometel, had a large basement restaurant that hosted meals for local residents and civic groups. Other charming restaurants still have loyal fans—Jovi's was a place everyone loved in the 1990s, and La Foresta is among the eateries that brings customers into the historic downtown.

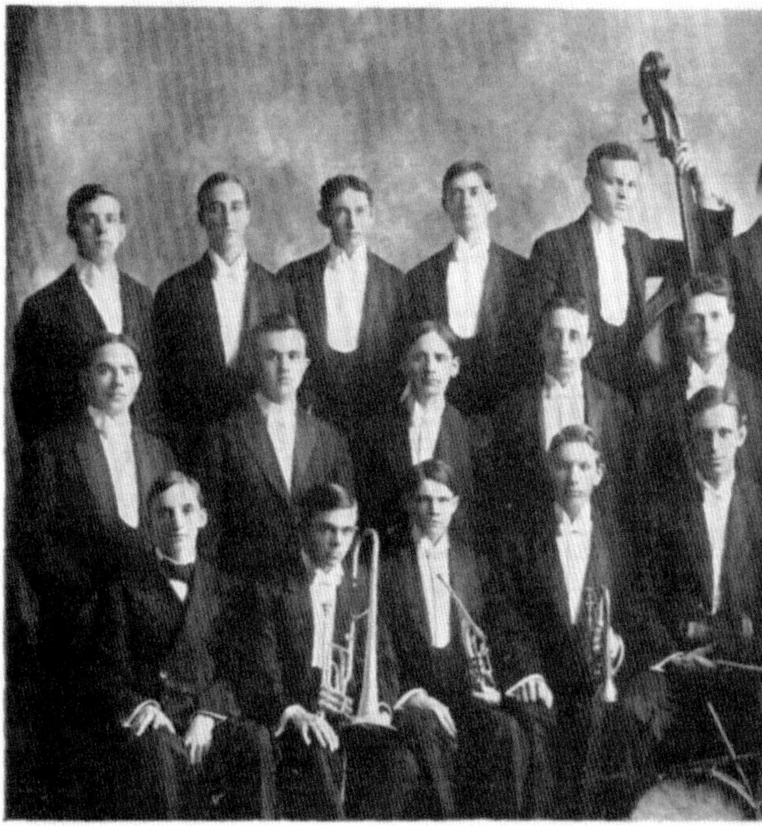

GLEE CLUB AND ORCHE

1908 **November** 1908

SUN.	MON.	TUE.	WED.	THU.	FRI.	SAT.
1	2	3	4	5	6	7
8	9	10	11	12	13	14
15	16	17	18	19	20	21
22	23	24	25	26	27	28
29	30		First Quar. 1st 30th	Full Moon 8th	Last Quar. 15th	New Moon 23d

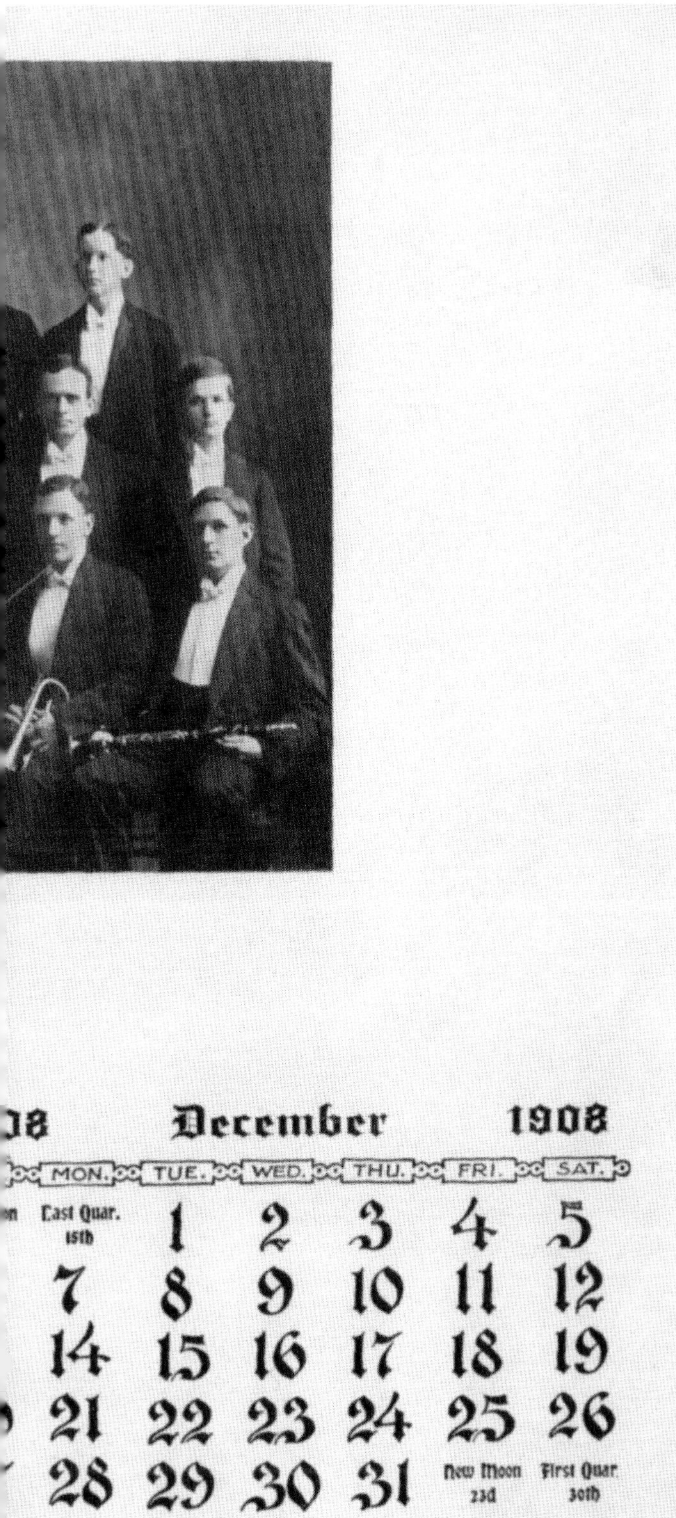

Wake Forest College Glee Club and Orchestra, 1908

On the pages of the school's decorative wall calendar for the year 1908, the Wake Forest College Glee Club and Orchestra share the months of November and December. The club was enjoying astonishing popularity following the 1903 arrival of Prof. Darius Eatman. Trained in music at Columbia University, Eatman managed to obtain for the campus a pipe organ from the Centenary Methodist Church of Richmond, Virginia. He also established a church choir that was soon considered among the best in the South. When Eatman left the college in 1907, the club looked to student Hubert Poteat (see page 118) for direction. Poteat, who had exhibited great musical talent and was the son of WFC president William Louis Poteat, moved into the leadership role while simultaneously handling the responsibilities of singing first bass with Charles Hardy, Lesley Hardy, Richard Pope, and Arthur Ray and also sitting first violin alongside Charles Oliver. The first song in the Glee Club Program that year was "O Here's to Wake Forest," with lyrics including this memorable line: "We'll ne'er forget our dear old College days."

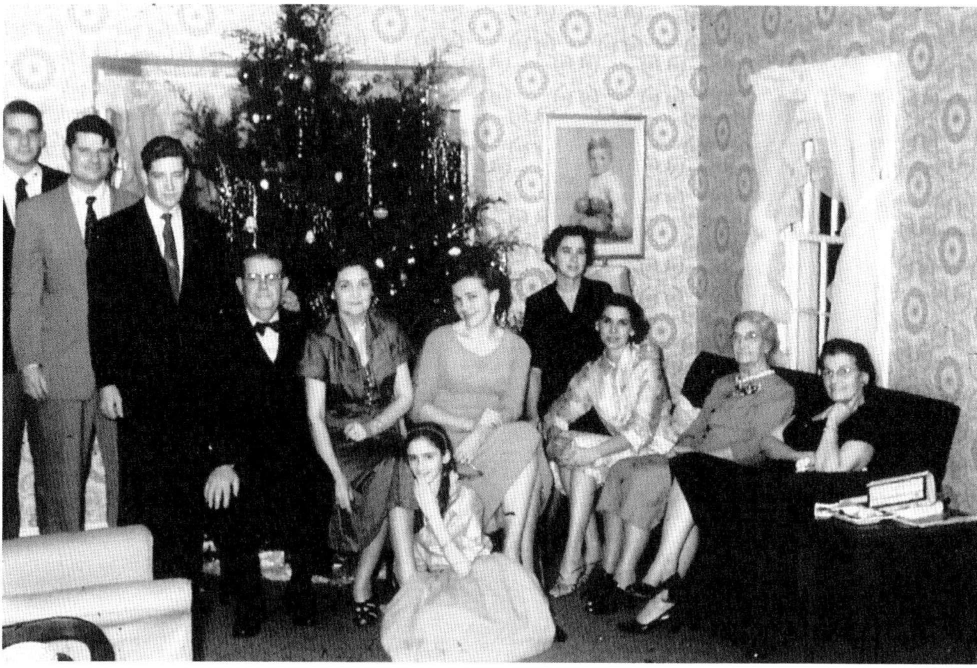

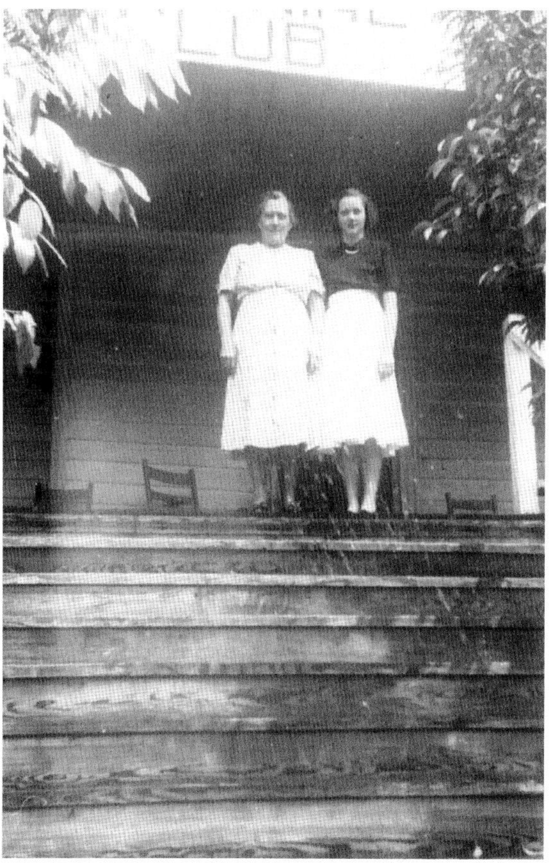

Christmas at the Mills Home

This c. 1958 photograph was taken at the home of John and Ethel Mills in the 200 block of North Main Street. The extended family included some of Wake Forest's best-known residents. From left to right are John Newton, Paul Newton Jr., John Garland Mills III, John Garland Mills Jr., Ethel Mills, Suzanne Mills Erskine, Edna Newton, Ruth Snyder, Sunny Snyder Newton, Annie Rose Turlington, and Minnie Newton. (Courtesy of John Garland Mills III.)

The Colonial Club

This two-story frame building near the Community House served as a dormitory and dining hall for Wake Forest College athletes, and "Ma" Stroud (left) was the resident dietician. Stroud planned meals, purchased the food, and supervised the kitchen staff from 1942 to 1956. At ease among the students, Stroud was quick to correct table manners, bake birthday cakes, and call her boarders "my boys." She did not tolerate profanity. In return, she was beloved by all.

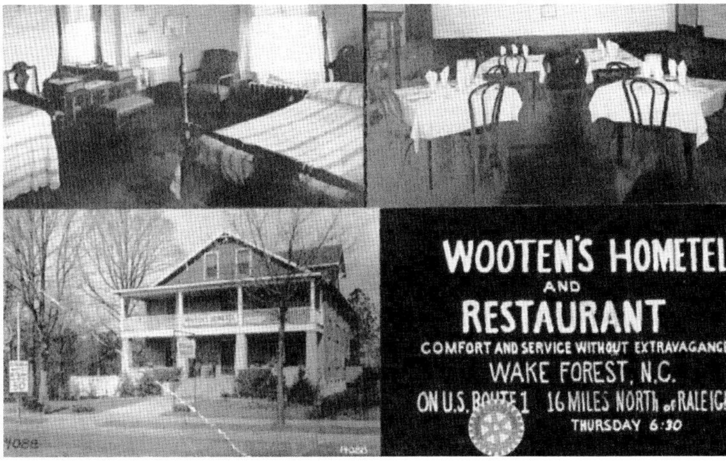

Wooten's Hometel

In the mid-20th century, Wooten's Hometel was extremely popular with students, town residents, and overnight travelers. Owned by John Ellis and Lillian James Wooten, who arrived from Alabama in 1935 and were the parents of noted Wake Forest leader John Wooten (see page 28), it was a cozy establishment where food was cooked and prepared in the downstairs basement restaurant; on many days, civic clubs held meetings around its tables. Considered one of the town's finest dining establishments in the 1940s and 1950s, Wooten's was famous for a breakfast menu that included waffles—it was virtually the only place they could be found in Wake Forest.

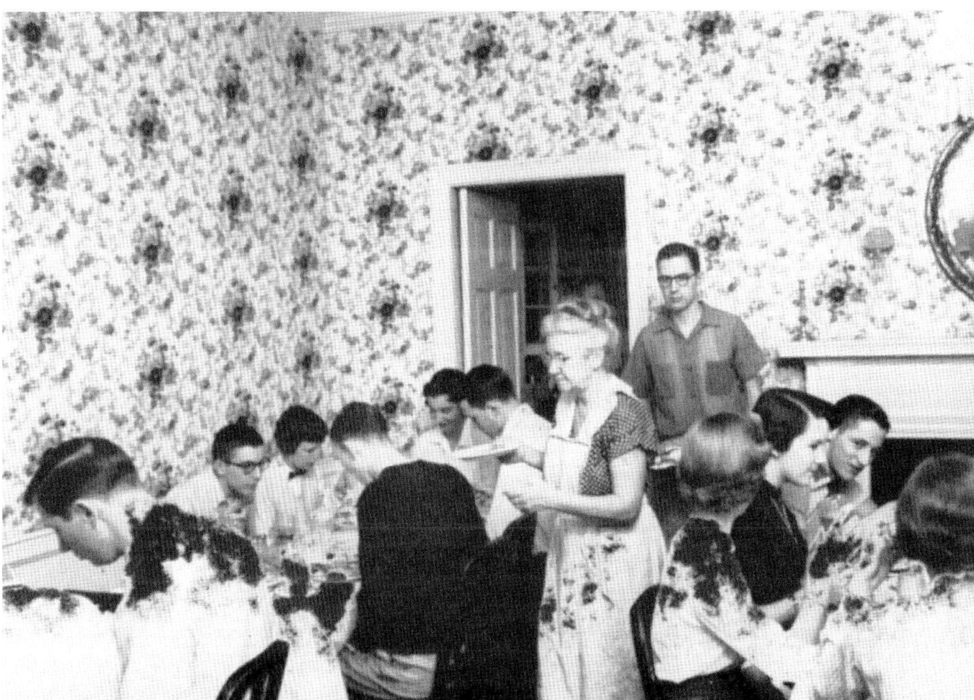

"Miss" Jo Williams

What Wake Forest residents called a "boarding house" was generally a place that served meals to students who paid a flat weekly rate. Jo Williams ran the most famous of these establishments, spending years preparing three hot meals a day for up to 100 diners at a time. The boarding houses began to disappear after World War II when the college started offering on-campus food service.

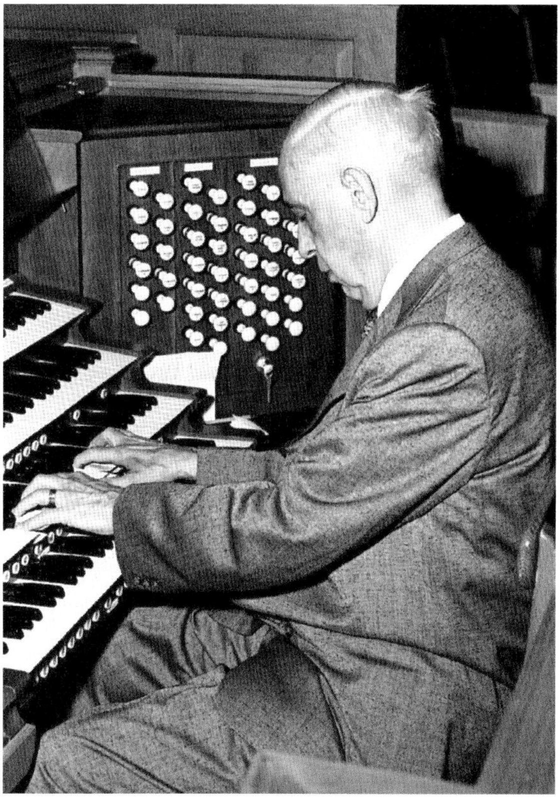

Hubert Poteat

Hubert Poteat, the son of Wake Forest College president William Louis Poteat (see page 58), joined the faculty in 1912 as professor of Latin language and literature. Ranked among the nation's leading Latin scholars, Poteat was a formidable character known by everyone on campus. He was a great orator and an accomplished organist who directed the Wake Forest Baptist Church choir for 40 years.

Cronje Earp

Classics professor Cronje Earp (left) was a fatherly figure, each summer sending handwritten letters inviting newly admitted Wake Forest College freshmen to sample his class. He opened his home to hundreds of students, sharing the family table and preserving a keepsake linen tablecloth on which the students signed their names for posterity. He also walked across campus once a week to the home of Hubert Poteat for a friendly chess match.

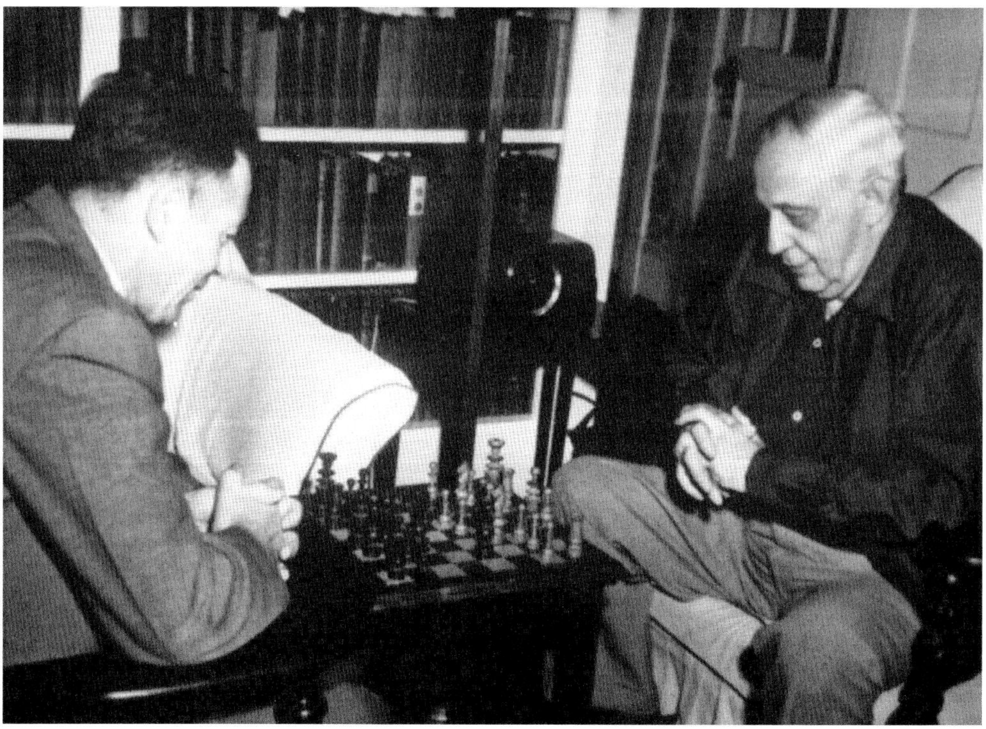

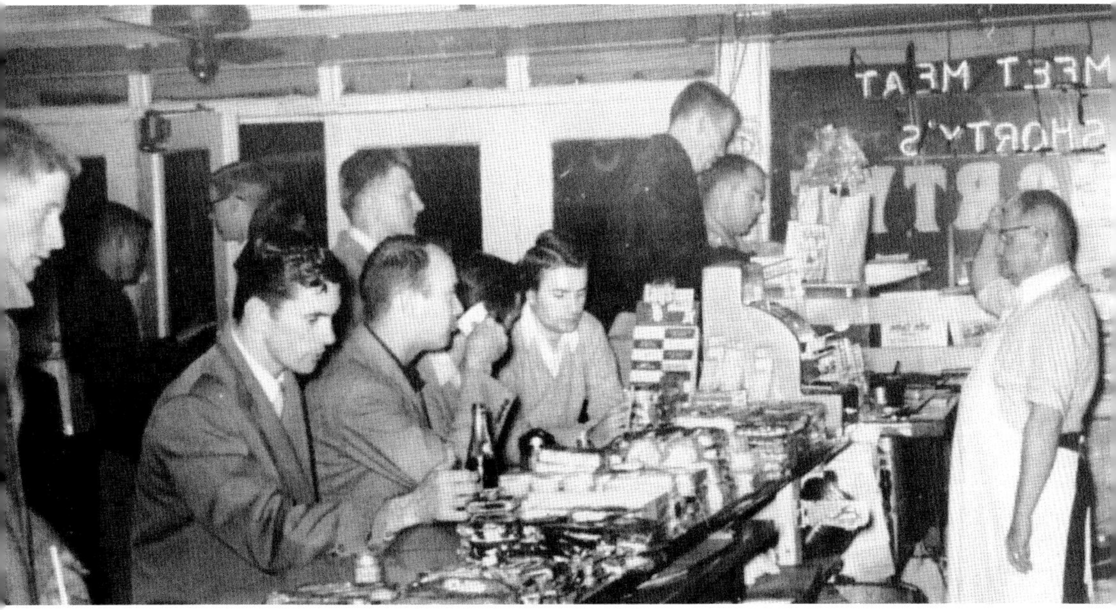

Millard "Shorty" Joyner

Serving customers since 1916, Shorty's Famous Hot Dogs is among the oldest hot dog shops in the country and was one of the few businesses to survive the departure of Wake Forest College. Its legendary proprietor, Millard Joyner, inherited the business from his father and uncle, who had originally owned a silent-movie theater and then decided to expand the property to include a hot dog restaurant. Occupying various storefronts along South White Street over its many years in business, Shorty's is still owned and run by the Joyner family.

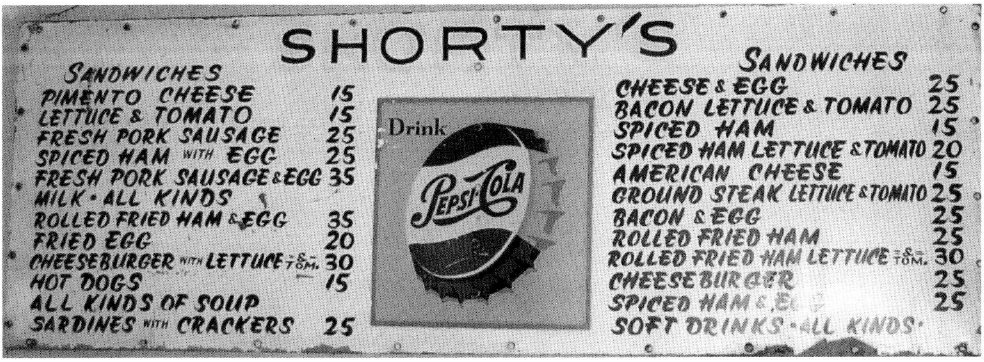

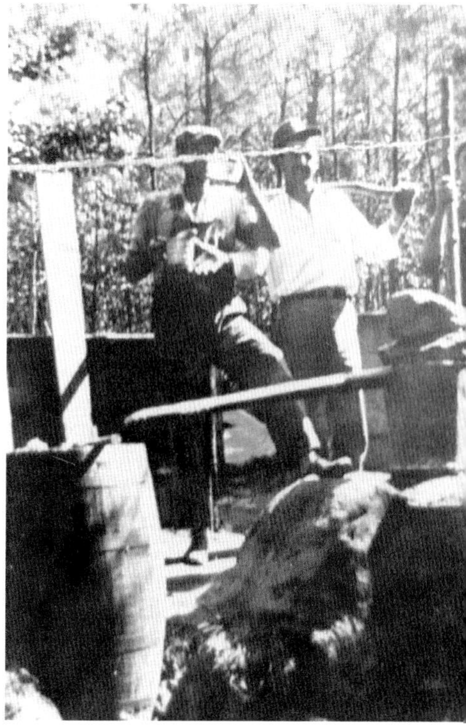

Harricane Moonshiners

Along the northwestern rim of Wake County runs the Harricane, named for a 19th-century storm that once ripped the area. Visitors asking directions were always told "the Harricane" was still "half a mile" down the road. The terrain was rocky, and farming difficult, and some chose to supplement their farming income by turning to whiskey stills. When a photographer captured this image in the 1970s, these men gave the impression of being lost in time.

The Southerners

Striking a more sophisticated pose, the Southerners were a local dance band that remarkably sprang into existence despite Wake Forest College's strict Baptist rule against dancing. Comprised of students, the band played for audiences in North Carolina, South Carolina, Virginia, and Georgia. Their theme songs, "Tenderly" and "Stardust," allowed members to earn up to $12 a night, helping cover tuition and other college expenses.

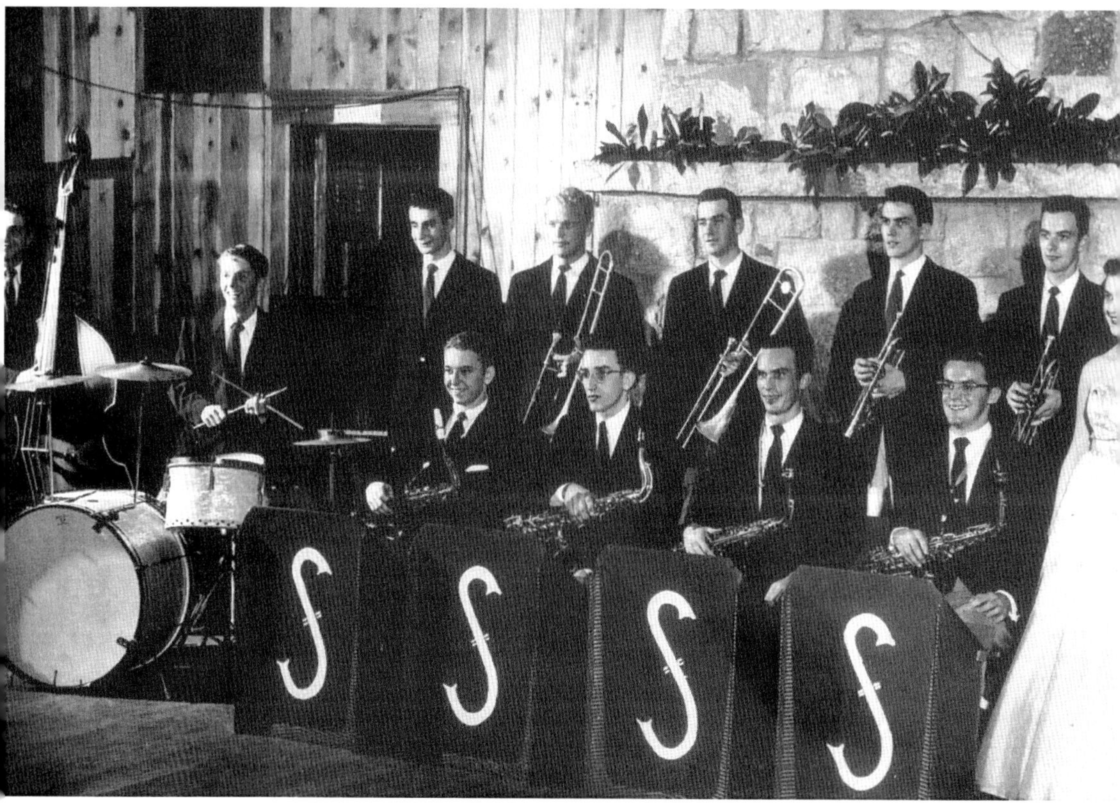

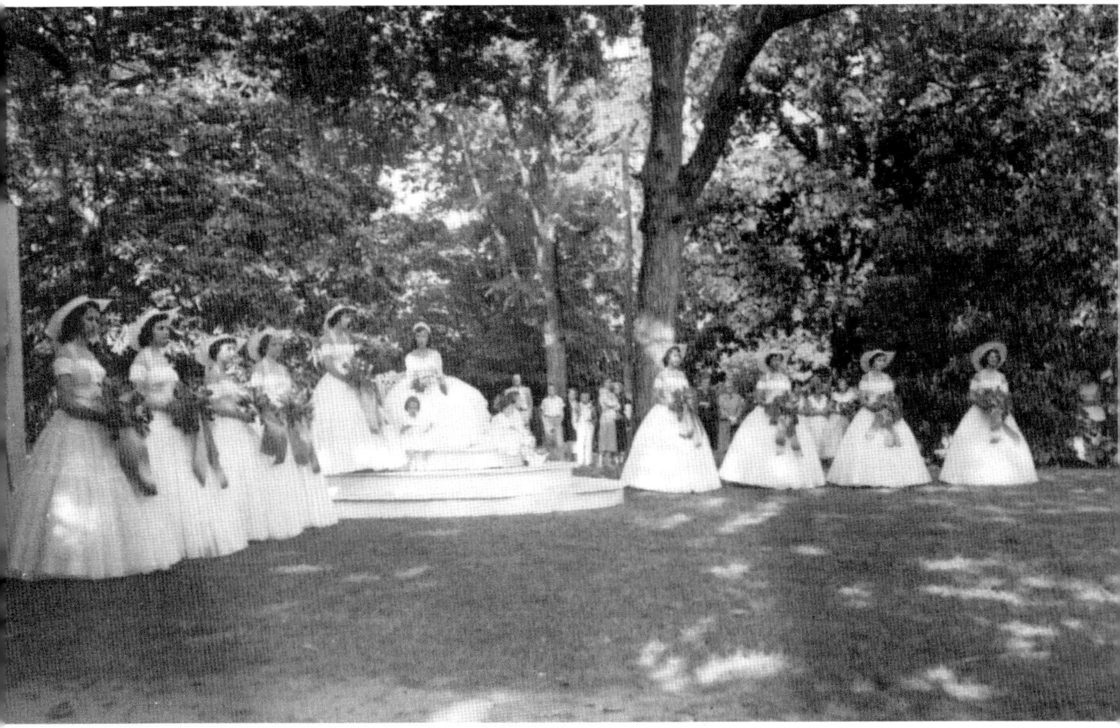

Magnolia Court

The women of the Magnolia Court were the glamorous stars of the Magnolia Festival, an annual event that began in 1948 and was staged each spring by the Physical Education Department of Wake Forest College. Pageants, dances, skits, and music were included in a program organized for town-and-gown audiences and performed primarily by college coeds. The highlight was the presentation of the festival queen. In 1956, the college's final year in Wake Forest, Queen Elizabeth Gouldman, maid of honor Dee Hughes, and the rest of the court were presented on the spotlighted patio of the Community House. The weeklong celebration also included a Glee Club concert, a folk-dancing exhibition, and an operatic performance of Mozart's *Così fan tutte.*

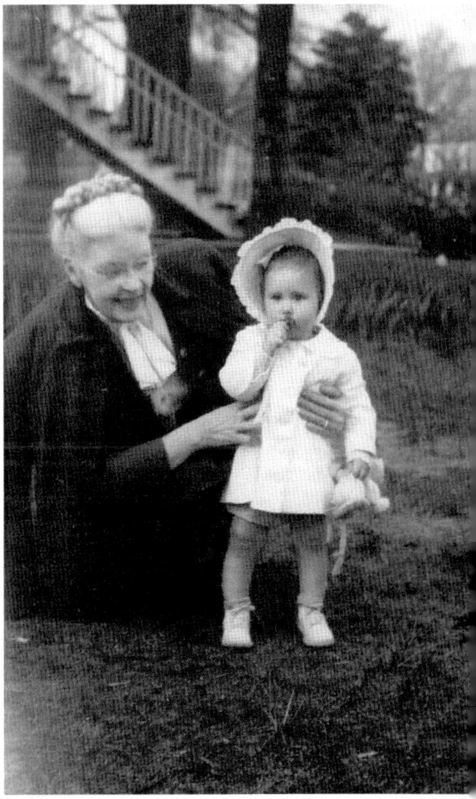

Ila Sanders

Once a fixture on Faculty Avenue, Ila Sanders lived in what was then known as the Brewer House, operating the downstairs as a boarding facility for Wake Forest College students while the upper level was inhabited by the fraternity brothers of Sigma Pi. In this c. 1946 photograph, she poses with Suzanne Mills Erskine, daughter of her next-door neighbors. (Courtesy of Suzanne Mills Erskine.)

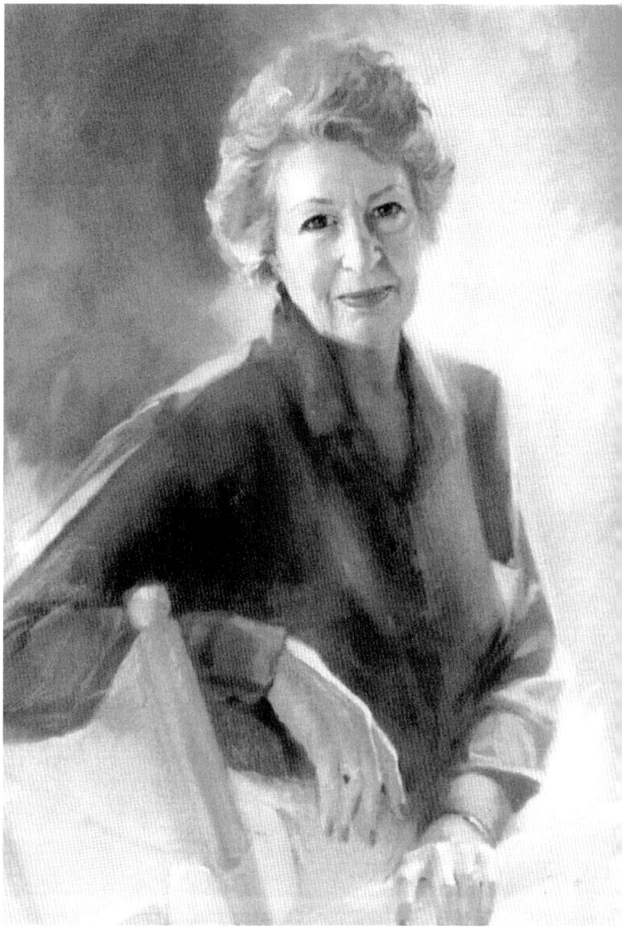

Elizabeth Hunt Holding

In 1942, a newly married Elizabeth Hunt Holding settled in Wake Forest after studying ballet under famous choreographer George Balanchine and performing with the Radio City Music Hall Rockettes. Holding opened a dance school where, for more than 30 years, she instilled a love of dance and classical music in the citizens of Wake Forest. From left to right in this recital photograph, taken at the Forest Theater on South White Street in 1958, are Myra Mathis Parker, Diane Holding, Alma Keith, Donna Rollins Pace, Lois Hollowell Chenault, Sally Osborne Whittaker, Rachel Nash Johnson, Suzanne Mills Erskine, Sarah Glover Bridges, Vicky Holding Nelson, Linda Joyner Whitley, Laura Jones Norris, and Vickie Andersen.

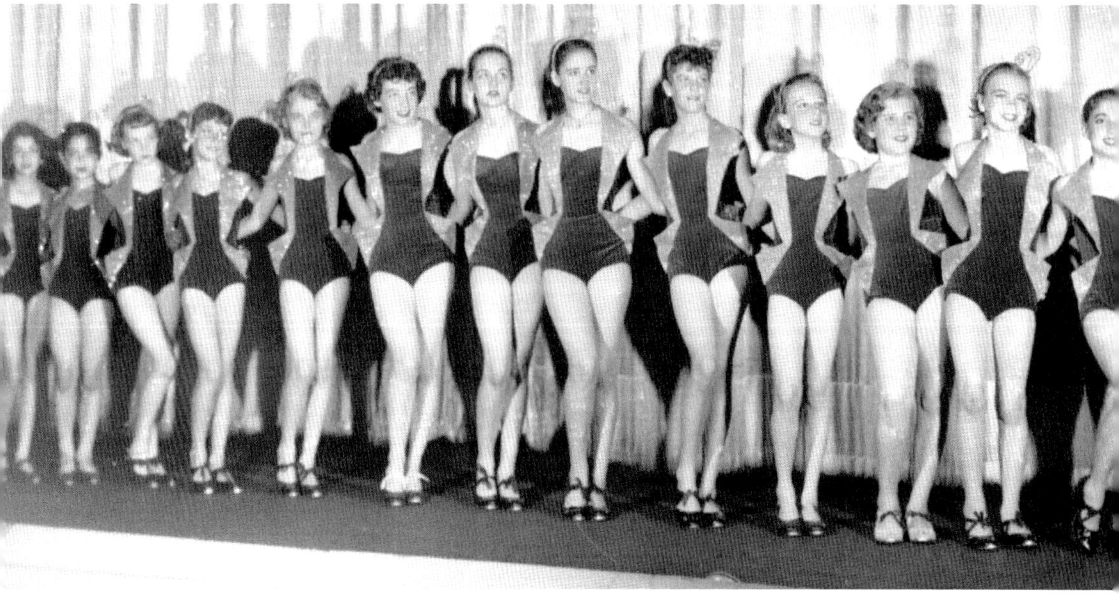

Jovi's Café

A 1990s landmark, Jovi's Café opened in the downtown historic district in 1991 as a joint venture between Jonnie Anderson and her sister Vivian Jones. Jones went on to become mayor of Wake Forest (see page 38). The restaurant, perhaps best known for its delectable miniature biscuits, lasted more than a decade before it closed.

jovi's
cafe & catering

221 east jones street • wake forest, NC • 27587
554-1243

Lunch Hours
Mon. - Fri. 11:00 - 2:00

Soups

Crab - creamy soup with lots of fresh crabmeat
Soup of the Day

Beverages

Iced tea, hot tea	1.00
Coffee	1.00
Soft drinks	1.00
Beer and Wine (please ask to see our wine list)	

Entree

Each day we prepare a special entree for your enjoyment. Ask your server about today's selection.

Salads

Garden Salad - a selection of the freshest garden vegetables we can find	4.25
Shrimp Salad - shrimp tossed with aillade sauce, served on a bed of crisp lettuces and garnished with black olives, tomatoes, and egg wedges	5.25
Caesar Salad - crisp romaine, Caesar dressing and freshly-made croutons	4.95
Chef's Salad - crisp garden vegetables topped with cheddar cheese, green olives, egg wedges, ham and turkey	5.25
House Salad - just like our garden salad, except smaller	1.95

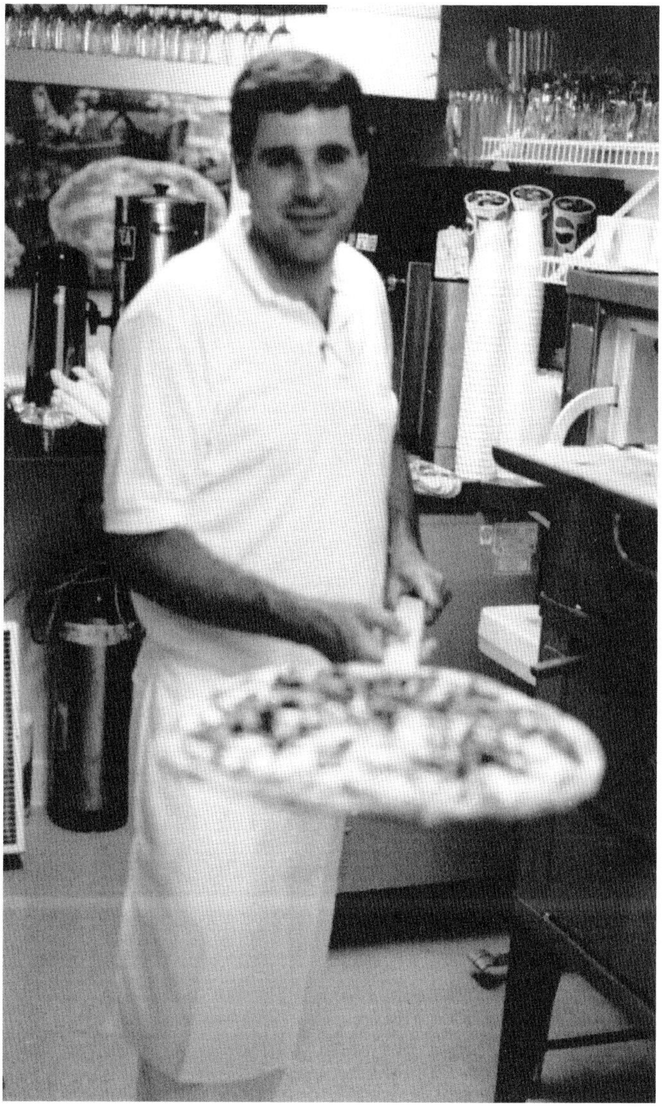

Steve Tarangelo
It was Steve Tarangelo's dream to own an Italian restaurant, and he did it with style. Moving from New York with his wife, Pam, in 1989, Tarangelo wanted to bring a neighborhood pizzeria to Wake Forest. Something of a renaissance man—with degrees in microbiology and environmental health, experience in real estate, training as a pilot, and a vast array of mechanical skills—Tarangelo opened La Foresta in a small downtown building along Highway 98 in 1992. He created a menu with spectacular old family recipes and filled the tables with friends and neighbors, eventually moving the operation to a larger facility on Brooks Street. The family-run establishment became a tremendous success, so when tragedy struck in 2012, the whole town held its breath. After suffering weeks of mysterious symptoms, the 59-year old Tarangelo was diagnosed with a brain tumor. When he died in September 2013, loyal customers turned out in droves to pay their respects. Tarangelo's wake at Bright Funeral Home had hundreds of visitors and lasted for hours, and there was hardly an empty pew during his funeral service at St. Catherine of Siena Catholic Church. Today, the restaurant continues. Tarangelo's wife, son, and loyal staff work to keep the dream alive as they honor Tarangelo's abiding belief that "food is love." (Courtesy of Pam Tarangelo.)

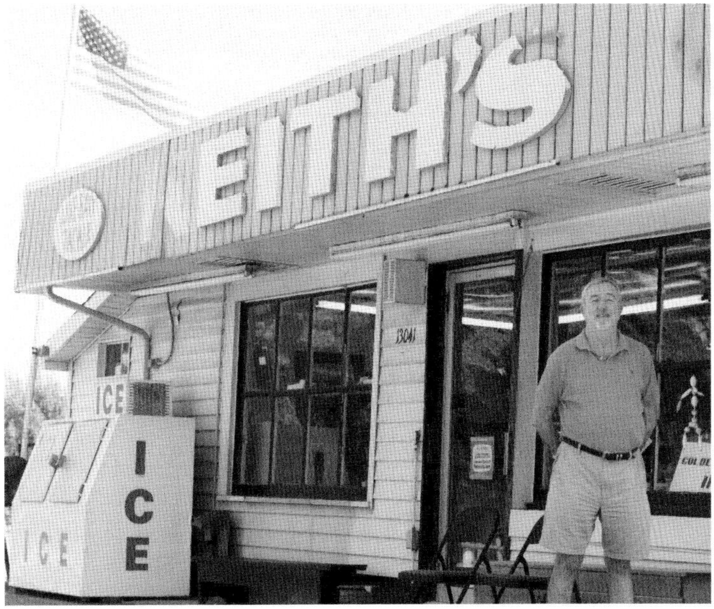

Keith's Store

In an area west of town known to locals as "Keith's Corner," Keith's Store has held onto a historic location between Wake Forest and the Falls Lake Dam. Run by members of the Keith family for generations, it has served as a gas station, convenience store, and restaurant. The once-rural area is now surrounded by the Wakefield community. Although in the midst of busy intersections, new houses, and roads, the store, run by current owner Jimmy Keith (pictured), remains a touchstone for old-timers.

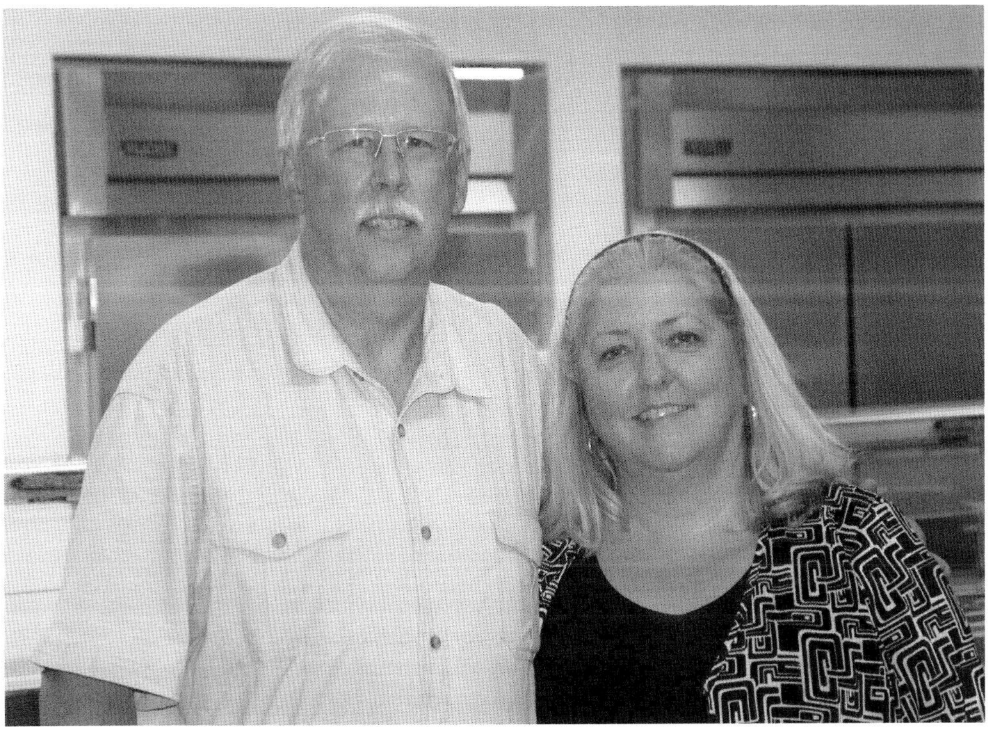

Karen and Don Winstead

Karen Keith Winstead continued the family business when she and her husband, Don, opened the Forks Cafeteria in downtown Wake Forest. Their establishment represents cherished traditions, offering free meeting space to civic groups, providing the location for the town's annual Christmas Dinner, and donating supplies to Hearts for Home, an organization benefiting families of deployed soldiers. As volunteer Beverly Whisnant said in the *Wake Weekly*, "They just don't bat an eye when asked."

INDEX

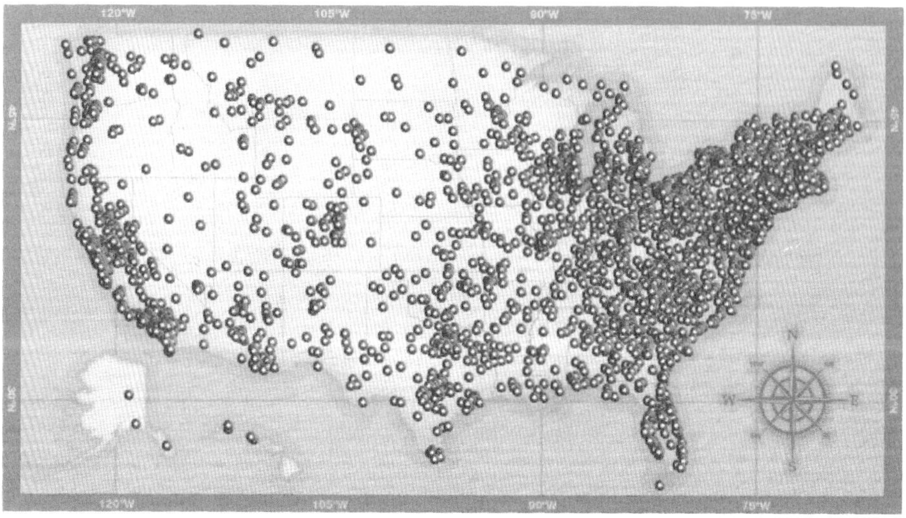

Consistent with our mission to preserve history on a local level, this book was printed in South Carolina on American-made paper and manufactured entirely in the United States. Products carrying the accredited Forest Stewardship Council (FSC) label are printed on 100 percent FSC-certified paper.

MADE IN THE USA